Burning to get the Vote

Burning to get the Vote

The Women's Suffrage Movement in Central Buckinghamshire 1904-1914

Colin Cartwright

Colin Cartwright

The University of Buckingham Press

First published in Great Britain in 2013 by

The University of Buckingham Press
Yeomanry House
Hunter Street
Buckingham MK18 1EG

A CIP catalogue record for this book is available at the British Library

ISBN 978-1-908684-09-7

Printed and bound in Great Britain by
Marston Book Services Limited, Oxfordshire

This book is dedicated to my Nan, Phylis, to my Mum, Miriam, to my wife, Chris, to my daughters, Bethanne and Emma, and to all the women who continue to inspire me.

It is also dedicated to the people of Buckinghamshire and the campaign against HS2: 'No backwards step'!

CONTENTS

Historic organisations:

CLWS - Church League for Women's Suffrage
CSWS – Central Society for Women's Suffrage
CUWFA - Conservative and Unionist Women's Franchise Association
FCLWS - Free Church League for Women's Suffrage
NCSWS - New Constitutional Society for Women's Suffrage
NLOWS – National League for Opposing Women's Suffrage
NUWSS - National Union of Women's Suffrage Societies
WCA - Women Citizen's Association
WFL - Women's Freedom League
WSPU - Women's Social and Political Union
WTRL - Women's Tax Resistance League
WLF - Women's Liberal Federation

Contemporary organisations:

CBS - Centre for Buckinghamshire Studies
PRO - Public Record Office
TWL - The Women's Library
WAS - Wycombe Abbey School

Historic Publications:

ASR - Anti-Suffrage Review, newspaper of the NLOWS
BEN - Bolton Evening News
BAAN - Bucks Advertiser and Aylesbury News
BE - Bucks Examiner
SBFP – South Bucks Free Press
BH - Bucks Herald
MBA - Middlesex and Bucks Advertiser
SBS - South Bucks Standard
VW - Votes for Women, newspaper of the WSPU

Contemporary Publications:

DNB - *Dictionary of National Biography*, Oxford University Press
WSM - Elizabeth Crawford's *Women's Suffrage Movement: A Reference Guide, 1866-1928*

List of Illustrations

Front cover
Oxfordshire, Bedfordshire and Buckinghamshire NUWSS Federation Banner. The latin inscription on the shield is a John Hampden family motto meaning, 'No Backwards Step'. From the Women's Library/Mary Evans Picture Library.

Back cover - Dove Window
The Dove Window, All Saints Parish Church, High Wycombe. The window features Emily Davies, who came to Wycombe to campaign for 'Votes for Women'. Two other women listed on the window also visited Wycombe to support women's suffrage: Millicent Fawcett and Maude Royden. Courtesy of All Saints, High Wycombe.

Courtesy of the Slusarczyk family & the Muriel Matters Society.

p. 117 Aylesbury Prison.

p. 120 A party of suffragettes from London, preparing to march from Aylesbury market square to the Prison. From the Buckinghamshire County Museum Collections.

p. 125 Aylesbury butchers along Cambridge Street, with advertising board featuring a stereotypical suffragette. From the Buckinghamshire County Museum Collections.

p. 127 Miss Elizabeth Annie Bell before Aylesbury County Court. From the Buckinghamshire County Museum Collections.

p. 129 Unveiling ceremony of the John Hampden statue, Aylesbury market square. From the Buckinghamshire County Museum Collections.

p. 141 A poster designed by Catherine Courtauld, highlighting the low wages and poor working conditions of the women chain makers of Cradley Heath. From the Women's Library/Mary Evans Picture Library.

p. 157 One of Catherine Courtauld's cartoons, lampooning the anti-suffragists. From the Women's Library/Mary Evans Picture Library posters.

p. 182, 2nd para, after 1st sentence. Mary Christie (23).

(caption: Painting of Miss Mary Christie, first Headmistress of Wycombe High School. Courtesy of Wycombe High School.

p. 189 Mrs Amy Scott and her family, outside Godstowe School, c.1905. Courtesy of Dorothy Ball.

p. 193 Wycombe NUWSS advert, South Bucks Standard, 1st January 1913.

p. 210 Foundation stone of High Wycombe Town Hall featuring Daniel Clarke, long-serving clerk and Mayor of High Wycombe Council. Photo: Colin Cartwright.

p. 211 Bust of Daniel Clarke Courtesy of High Wycombe Town Council and the staff of the Swan Theatre.

p. 217 One response to the Saunderton Station fire. *Bucks Free Press*, March 1913.

p. 230 Map of the 1913 NUWSS Pilgrimage, South Bucks Standard, 17th July, 1913.

p. 236 Pilgrims and local supporters gathered outside West Wycombe School. From High Wycombe Library.

p. 241 The banner of Godstowe school. Courtesy of Godstowe School. Photo: Colin Cartwright.

p. 259 The grave of Mrs Humphry Ward, St John the Baptist churchyard, Aldbury. Photo: Colin Cartwright.

p. 260 The grave of Sylvia Pankhurst, Adis Ababa. Courtesy of Neil Rees.

p. 260 The grave of Louisa Matilda Page, Chesham graveyard. Photo: Colin Cartwright.

p. 260 The grave of Annie Brooksbank, Chesham graveyard. Photo: Colin Cartwright (34).

p. 261 The grave of Countess Alice Kearney, St John the Baptist churchyard, Little Missenden. Photo: Colin Cartwright.

p. 261 The grave of Mrs Alice Pilley, St John the Baptist churchyard, Little Missenden. Photo: Colin Cartwright.

Foreword

By the Rt. Hon. Cheryl Gillan, Member of Parliament for Chesham and Amersham

INSPIRED by the discovery of a long forgotten newspaper interview with his great-grandfather on microfilm, Colin Cartwright has researched the history of a stirring time of change in our democracy: when women gained the right to vote.

It is a story of women – and of men – in central Buckinghamshire, who may not have hit the headlines as some of the proponents of women's suffrage did. Yet, in their tireless and patient dedication to the cause, in their efforts to persuade through every means available to them, they were part of the movement which led to women gaining the rights in the twentieth century which had been available to men for much of the nineteenth.

As a woman politician in the twenty-first century, I find it salutary. Nearly a century after women achieved the vote, many (like myself) find themselves the first woman to hold a particular post or office – and those landmarks are still there to be attained. Many women who cast their votes today still do so, partly, because they know of the sacrifices made by women in the campaigns to earn them that right.

Colin Cartwright reminds us of the women in Chesham, in my constituency, who formed a vital group, one of the first in the county, to debate and persuade others of the strength of their arguments. Incidentally, one of those ladies chose to keep her maiden name professionally – as I did – which even now is not necessarily an automatic option.

These links to the past are so important to us and to our democracy. I hope others will draw inspiration from them too.

Cheryl Gillan
House of Commons, London SW1A 0AA

By Richard Pankhurst

MUCH has been written over the years in general terms about the history of the early 20th century Votes for Women struggle in England.

Colin Cartwright's careful analysis is however both innovative and important, for he goes to the root of things in his careful reconstruction of the thinking on the issue in central Buckinghamshire. Personally, I find it almost incredible that Votes for Women, which we now take as the most normal thing in the world, should have been so bitterly contended; that a Liberal Government should have recourse to the forcible feeding of British women; and that the police in this great democracy of ours should have prevented my mother, only a couple of generations ago, from addressing a crowd in a market square in rural England.

The price of freedom, as has been said, is eternal vigilance.

Richard Pankhurst
Addis Ababa University, Ethiopia.

AS with archaeology, so with historical research: once the digging is underway, a 'new' and frequently surprising world begins to be revealed.

Surprise, for one reason or another, has been a common reaction when people have first heard about me writing *Burning to get the Vote*. Much of this reaction springs from the feeling: "I didn't think there were suffragettes in Buckinghamshire". Certainly, there were few militant suffragettes who actually lived in the county, but there was, before the outbreak of the First World War, an impressive and growing movement of women (and men) who supported the call for 'votes for women'.

I first started to get interested in this subject after some family history research into my great-grandfather un-earthed a long since forgotten newspaper interview with him in his bike workshop in Hove in 1897. My great-grandfather, Isaac Christmas, spoke about the new craze for women's cycling sweeping the nation around that time. This coincided, soon after, with reading about one woman cycling suffragist who joined the national pilgrimage for votes for women in the summer of 1913. I read about this anonymous woman, whom I subsequently discovered was called Mrs Mason, in the book, *Buckinghamshire Headlines* by Jean Archer. This revelation, coupled with the impetus of anticipating the 100th anniversary of the women's suffrage pilgrimage through Buckinghamshire in 1913, propelled me to the verge of starting to draft an idea for a book.

The final incentive I needed to go ahead with some initial research was provided by Elizabeth Crawford's mind-boggling books, *The Women's Suffrage Movement: A Reference Guide, 1866-1928* and the later, *The Women's Suffrage Movement in Britain and Ireland: A Regional Survey*. Both these books contain implicit and explicit encouragements for local historians to write local and regional studies, 'to breathe life back into these women'. (Crawford, Elizabeth - *Regional Survey*, p. 277)

I soon discovered that original sources for the women's suffrage movement in Buckinghamshire seemed very thin on the ground. However, there was a vast resource of local newspaper reports held at various places in the county. While the *South Bucks Free Press*, a Liberal newspaper, competed with Conservative *South Bucks Standard*, the *Bucks Advertiser and Aylesbury News,* competed with the 'recognised organ of the Church and Conservative

Party', the *Bucks Herald* in Mid-Bucks.[1] The *Advertiser*, boasting the 'largest circulation in Mid-Bucks', claimed to be, 'the only independent county paper'.[2] The *Examiner* too, arguably the most sympathetic to the suffragists, also competed for a readership in Mid-Bucks.

These newspaper accounts seem only to have been once referred to systematically on this topic, by Marion Burgin in her 1994 Review Article. This study provided a very helpful introduction to the bewildering array of characters and events which made up the movement, specifically in High Wycombe. Burgin herself rightly highlighted the political bias of these newspapers. However, both main political parties were divided on the issue of 'votes for women', so what was included may have depended on the view of each editor. The reporters tended to record verbatim much of what was said at these meetings, or even simply included reports sent in by the suffrage societies themselves. So these newspapers taken together, begin to help partially re-construct a fascinating picture of the women's suffrage movement in the county. The vast majority of information for my book is drawn from these newspaper sources, accessible at the Centre for Buckinghamshire Studies, the High Wycombe Library and Chesham Library The only gap in the newspaper record is in 1911, when curiously the *Standard*, *Examiner* and *Advertiser* are all missing. This has inevitably produced an even more incomplete account. I cannot pretend this is an exhaustive account. However, I do hope that, rather than being exhausting , it is at least comprehensive. I have inevitably had to introduce some constraints.

Geographically, I plumped for the vague and truncated area of 'central Buckinghamshire' for my study. This enabled me to include High Wycombe, along with the whole of the Mid-Bucks Parliamentary constituency. Wycombe was after all, where the 20th century women's suffrage movement was born. But the exclusion of the rest of South Bucks, including the stories of Marlow, Beaconsfield, Bourne End, Gerrards Cross, the Chalfonts and Slough, have enabled me to ensure the book did not become too much of a 'shaggy dog story'.

There were two geographical exceptions I allowed myself. Firstly, I chose to arbitrarily include the suffragette invasion of Bletchley Park in the north of the county, in the summer of 1909. I did this because this story helped not only to give some context to the kind of tactics the suffragettes were employing around this time in the rest of the country, it also demonstrated a significant development in WSPU tactics.

---

[1] *Kelly's*, 1911, advert.
[2] *Kelly's*, 1911, advert.

I also chose to include something of the story of the anti-suffragist, Mrs Humphry Ward. It is true that throughout this period, she lived a couple of miles across the border in Hertfordshire. However, that fact that this most celebrated of all the female anti-suffragists lived in the Chilterns, was I felt enough to warrant her inclusion here.

Chronologically, it seemed reasonable to begin in 1904, with what is apparently the first twentieth-century public meeting on women's suffrage in the county. While the outbreak of the war has provided the natural later boundary, I have also endeavoured, in my conclusion, to mention something of the story beyond 1914, including the significant milestones of 1918 and 1928, when women first won the vote, and then won equality of voting qualification with men.

The final constraint I placed upon myself was to exclude peripheral figures. For example, there were some characters who spent their earlier years in Buckinghamshire, who only became active in the movement later and elsewhere. Evelyn Sharp and Elsie Bowerman both fall into this category. The writer, Evelyn Sharp lived at Weston Turville Manor for a time.[1] Later, she was close to Emmeline and Christabel Pankhurst and took over as editor of the WSPU newspaper. Although Evelyn took holidays in the Chilterns and did speak once at a meeting of the United Suffragists in Chorleywood in March 1914, her suffragette activity was mostly confined to London.[2]

Elsie Bowerman, a pupil of Miss Dove's at Wycombe Abbey School and author of the first history of the school, has an even more intriguing story. She later formed a branch of the WSPU at Girton College. With her mother, she survived the Titanic disaster, going on to campaign with Emmeline and Christabel Pankhurst against trade union activity during the war and also witnessed the Russian Revolution in 1917.[3] However, there is no evidence she ever took part in the women's movement in the county of Buckinghamshire.

I have also excluded those who may have had homes in the county, but whose campaigning for the vote was conducted elsewhere. Princess Sophia Duleep Singh, lived from 1900 in Hilden Hall, Hammersley Lane, Penn. However, she sold copies of the WSPU newspaper on the streets of London and engaged in tax resistance at her London home.[4]

---

[1] Cox, Margaret - *The Manor House, Weston Turville*, pp. 40-1.
[2] John, Angela V. - *Evelyn Sharp: Rebel Woman, 1869-1955*.
[3] Crawford, Elizabeth - *WSM*, pp. 73-4.
[4] *The Vote*, 5th December 1913, p.86 and 6th February 1914, p. 245.

Finally, I have also not included those who came to live in Buckinghamshire after the vote was won. For example, the Drs Flora Murray and Dr Louisa Garrett Anderson, who both retired after the war to Paul End, close to the church in Penn.[1]

Some readers may be disappointed that this book features so little of the Pankhursts and other prominent suffragette leaders. However, all the Pankhursts are mentioned tangentially. There is some evidence, for example, that Mrs Pankhurst may have had a rural bolt-hole in the county. Christabel Pankhurst is mentioned in a Buckinghamshire Constabulary memo. Sylvia Pankhurst was the only Pankhurst to come to the county to speak at a meeting in the Aylesbury market square in 1912, but she was prevented from speaking on this occasion. One other WSPU leader, Mrs Emmeline Pethwick-Lawrence did spend time in close vicinity to the county. In 1910 she visited the John Hampden battlefield monument in Chalgrove and in February 1913 spoke at a meeting of the Chorleywood WSPU.

However, the story of the women's suffrage movement in Buckinghamshire, while it does indeed include several high-profile figures from the national movement, largely consists of the stories of an army of hidden heroines and heroes. They are the unlikely suffragists, whose sometimes bizarre antics over many years have mostly been forgotten. Hilda Kean's book, *Deeds not Words*, demonstrated that certain tight-knit groups of suffragists, like women teachers, tended to preserve the memories of their political struggles because of their continuing campaigning, but for most Buckinghamshire suffragists, once the vote had been won in 1918, that marked the end of their political campaigning.[2]

This is one of the curious features of the story of these women (and men) of Mid-Bucks and South Bucks. Their involvement in fighting for 'votes for women' has often been either accidentally overlooked, quietly ignored or deliberately denied, by family, friends, communities and, in some cases, even by the individuals themselves. Perhaps this is nowhere more evident than in the case of Elsie Bowerman and her history of Miss Dove and Wycombe Abbey School. Herself keen to put this past behind her, in her book, *Stands There a School*, Miss Bowerman nowhere mentions Miss Dove's passionate involvement in the struggle for women's enfranchisement.

---

[1] *Penn Village Voice* magazine, April/May 2010; *Miscellany* August/September 2001; Perrin, Robert - *No Fear, No Favour*, pp.180-186, *SBFP*, 1986. I am indebted to Miles Green for providing me with this information about Penn's links to these suffragettes.

[2] Kean, Hilda - *The Lives of Suffragette Teachers*.

Perhaps this is understandable, particularly in the light of the horrors of 'the Great War', which may have served to obscure much that immediately preceded it in popular memory. As Mrs Humphry Ward commented in a letter to a friend in 1917, 'Besides the war, what matters?'[1] However, even during the war there was a continuing *sotto voce* struggle over national priorities. Mrs Ward's book, *England's Effort*, published in 1916, was itself answered the following year by a little-known book, *Woman's Effort*.[2] This later book, written by a former government school inspector, attempted to carefully chronicle and celebrate the whole of the woman's struggle for the vote, including the militant actions of the suffragettes before the war.[3]

My hope is that *Burning to get the Vote*, will play some part in encouraging the people of Britain, both female and male, not to take for granted our democratic freedoms and never to forget how long it took and how much it cost to win the right to vote. This book may be about the courage and determination it took for women to win the vote, but this story has much to say to both genders.

Talking of not forgetting, I am indebted to many people in being able to complete this book. Firstly, I must mention the deacons and members of my church, who have humoured me in my obsession and allowed me permission to give time to this project. The Chesham4Fairtrade group has also been very understanding about the fewer hours I have given to this important campaign while I have been researching and writing this book. Most important, I must thank my family for putting up with my 'researcher brain' absent-mindedness, the evenings I have been glued to the computer screen, as well as the times I have slipped away to pore over old newspapers in libraries, instead of spending time with them elsewhere.

Many other people deserve my and a mention here: Christopher Low, Rachel Simon and all the staff at the Centre for Bucks Studies, William Phillips and the staff of the Bucks County Museum, Julie Anne Lambert of the Bodleian Library, Jackie Kay and thanks other members of the High Wycombe Society, Mike Dewey of the Friends of High Wycombe Library and the SWOP old photograph website, Diana Gulland and colleagues at the Bucks Archaeological Society, Peter Hawkes for his help in locating old photographs of Chesham.

---

[1] Sutherland, John - *Mrs Humphry Ward*, p. 362.
[2] Ward, Mrs Humphry - *England's Effort: Six Letters to an American Friend*.
[3] Metcalfe, A.E. - *Woman's Effort: A Chronicle of British Women's Fifty Years' Struggle for Citizenship (1865-1914)*.

Then there are the descendants of people featured in this book: Linda Price-Cousins, Dorothy Ball, Wendy Greenway and Sarah Richards have all been very helpful in providing information and encouragement.

Sam Hearn, Anthea Coles and all the Executive and members of the John Hampden Society, for their help with the previous booklet, *Walking with Buckinghamshire Suffragettes*, and their interest in the way John Hampden's example particularly inspired the tax-resisting suffragists. Andrew Clark, for his help with this booklet and for putting up with my talks to various audiences. Amanda Carroll and Rob Craig, who both helped with producing the booklet, and to Amanda specifically for designing the book's cover.

Mrs Cunningham, librarian of Wycombe Abbey School, Mr Gainer and Jennifer Thomas of Godstowe School, Rachel Sutcliffe of Wycombe High School, Darren Owers of Aylesbury Prison.

Frances Bedford, Australian MP, and for all the members of the Muriel Matters Society. Irene Cockcroft and Soroptomists everywhere. The staff of the Women's Library. Beverley Cook at the Museum of London. The staff of Chesham Library, Chesham Museum, the Bucks County Museum, the High Wycombe Museum, the Amersham Museum. Tony Sargeant and Rebecca Gurney of the Bucks Family History Society.

Historians and researchers of various stripes: Richard Ensor, Philip Walker, Michael Shaw, Keith Fletcher, Neil Rees, Bill Templeton, John Briggs, Ian Randall, Stephen Copson. Mrs Carolyn and Rev. Philip Thomas of Broadway Baptist Church, Chesham and Ken Peters of Union Baptist Church, Wycombe. Not forgetting Nigel Wright and John Colwell, my former Principal and tutor at Spurgeons College respectively, who both encouraged me in my writing.

My mother for the gift of *My Story*, Emmeline Pankhurst's autobiography and the rest of my family for their invaluable support. The priceless help of people like: Jill Liddington, Elizabeth Crawford, June Purvis and Hilda Kean. Thanks also to Cheryl Gillan, MP and to Richard Pankhurst for kindly agreeing to write forewords. To my publisher, Christopher Woodhead, for taking a chance and seeing the potential.

Colin Cartwright
Chesham, February 2013

'An old Buckinghamshire lace-maker carried her bobbins and pillow, supported on either side by young suffragists, and took a scarlet and white rosette home to wear like a veteran'.
Based on a report in the *Common Cause*, 6th May 1909. Tickner, Lisa - *The Spectacle of Women*, p.102.

AN elderly Buckinghamshire lace-maker took her place in a demonstration for women's suffrage, which wove its way through the streets of the capital on 27th April 1909. This event had been organised by the International Woman Suffrage Alliance, as part of its Quinquennial Congress in London. The proud spirit in which this anonymous woman from a traditional rural industry participated in this Pageant of Women's Trades and Professions, indicates how far the women's suffrage movement had reached into the homes and lives of ordinary people. It demonstrates how far the campaign for 'votes for women' had come since its earlier, faltering progress towards the middle of the previous century.

The story of the wider women's rights movement in Buckinghamshire could be said to date back to the signing of the Magna Carta, or even before. This significant document in British history, which was signed on the borders of Buckinghamshire, was certainly referred to by Buckinghamshire suffragists centuries later. Their extensive appeal to both momentous touchstones in British history, as well as lesser known examples, served to expose for them, the reality that women's rights, if only tentatively outlined in previous generations, were being routinely and blatantly ignored in their own experience.

The struggle for women's rights in this part of England, might be said to date back beyond Magna Carta, to the personal lives of women like the 12th century saint, Christina of Markyate. She had to flee an unwanted marriage by seeking sanctuary in the church. Her story was again pertinent to suffragists who lived in Buckinghamshire and across the country. Cicely Hamilton, who talked so pointedly of the 'marriage trade' and on one occasion engaged in debate with the Buckinghamshire anti-suffragist, G.K. Chesterton, would have clearly identified the ways in which the unbalanced

1

historical development of this ancient institution was continuing to impact the lives of women in the early 20th century.[1]

The emergence of the Lollard travelling preachers, encouraged by John Wycliffe from his 14th century living in Ludgershall and later from Leicestershire, could also be claimed as part of a gradual development in thinking about gender roles and the rights of women. There seem to have been female Lollard preachers and the movement was remarkably progressive in regard to gender relations.[2]

Perhaps the clearest early sign of the assertion of women's political rights came in the 16th century, with the involvement of Dame Dorothy Pakington in the 'election' of two MPs for Aylesbury. As a widow, Dorothy Pakington exercised the full powers of the lordship of Aylesbury, including nominating the Borough's two MPs in 1572. Pakington was referred to in the campaign of the Buckinghamshire suffragists, as evidence that before the 1832 Reform Act, women had been less excluded from the political process.

Suffragists in the county also made a particular point of celebrating the tax protest of the local and national hero, John Hampden, whose stand against King Charles I had been supported by four Buckinghamshire women. Remembering the names of these four women became a point of honour to fellow tax resisting suffragists in the county.

However, such exceptional cases as these highlighted how far ordinary women were from being treated equally with men, on a social, economic or political basis. Indeed, particularly in the 18th century, the closest women came to taking part in local or national electioneering was as prostitutes offering their service as part of an election bribe. The most celebrated so-called 'nymph of the pave' was Moll Smith of Aylesbury, who 'took an active part in the election of 1802 and again ... in 1804'. Moll would usually dress in the party colours and sit on the coach box, as the coach was drawn into town by the men.[3]

These kinds of election practices, along with more blatant bribery of electors was what eventually drove Parliament to introduce the Corrupt Practices Act in 1883. This legislation was arguably the most influential in the development of the women's suffrage movement at the end of the 19th century. Regulating the election process and limiting the amount of money which candidates could spend, meant that both the Conservative and Liberal

---

[1] Hamilton, Cicely - *Life Errant.*
[2] I am indebted to Bill Templeton, a local history enthusiast who has researched the Amersham Lollard Martyrs.
[3] Gibbs Collection, press cuttings, c.1841.

parties needed to find willing volunteers to help with the campaigning. The Primrose League and the Women's Liberal Association were both set up with the purpose of mobilising women to help their menfolk get elected to Parliament. While the Conservative party's Primrose League was effectively more a part of the social calendar, the WLA became a training ground for women organisers, many of whom went on to become women's suffrage campaigners.

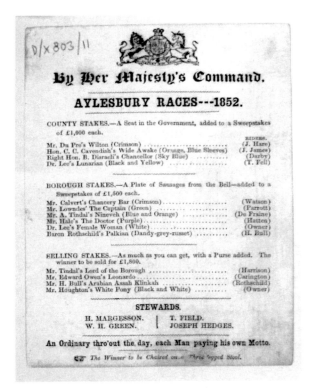

Aylesbury 1852 Election leaflet.
Reproduced with permission of the Buckinghamshire Archaeological Society.

However, 1852 is arguably the most significant year in this sketchy time-line of the women's suffrage movement in Buckinghamshire. This year may claim a historic first for Aylesbury and the whole county. Benjamin Disraeli had already stated his belief in women's suffrage at Westminster, a few years previously in 1848.[1] However, it was another, less famous Buckinghamshire resident who may have been the first candidate for Parliament to stand on a platform of 'votes for women'. In 1852, Dr John Lee of Hartwell House attempted to become MP for Buckinghamshire. His candidacy was supported by Quaker and early suffragist, Mrs Anne Knight. (see Appendix 1)

At the meeting for the nomination of candidates at Aylesbury Hall on 16th July, 1852, Dr Lee was received with 'discordance and cheers'. Watched by Lady Chandos, Mrs Disraeli and Mrs Compton-Cavendish and their friends from the ladies' gallery, Lee declared that he would, 'in Parliament vote for ... extending the suffrage to ladies.' He went on to pose the rhetorical question, '...upon what ground free-hold property excluded ladies from having its rights?' At a previous meeting in Newport Pagnall, Disraeli had joked that Lee presented unfair competition as 'he had enlisted on his side the whole of the fair sex'. Ever the consummate politician, Disraeli went on to encourage the electors to give him their second votes because '... if there is to be any alteration in the suffrage, I shall adopt the plan of Dr Lee'. He repeated his intention to support universal suffrage, including women, at the meeting in Aylesbury. Of course, Lee was defeated in the vote, and Disraeli never persuaded his party to support such a dramatic reform. According to one of those who nominated Caledon George Du Pre that day, such a step amounted to 'removing their wives and daughters from their proper sphere'.[2]

Despite such radical politics being openly discussed by two candidates at the 1852 election, it appears that the most significant 19th century milestone for the women's suffrage movement nationally, made little impact in the county. In 1866 a women's petition was presented to Parliament, by John Stuart Mill, which was soon followed the next year, by his unsuccessful attempt to amend the Second Reform Act to include women. These developments hardly seem to have registered in the Buckinghamshire newspapers.

The following decade, however, saw the beginnings of the first concerted campaign to persuade people in the county to support this reform. In 1870 'A petition from High Wycombe in favour of women's suffrage was presented in the House of Commons... by Mr P.A. Taylor, member for Leicester.'[3] The first women's suffrage Bill was presented to Parliament that

---

[1] Strachey, Ray - *The Cause*, p. 43.
[2] *BAAN*, 17th July 1852, pp. 4-5.
[3] *SBFP*, 26th February 1870.

year. This was followed by a number of meetings in the 1870s which indicate that the women's campaign was gathering more momentum and reaching beyond the capital and other urban centres.

However, the size of some of the meetings reported in the newspapers that decade indicate a certain lack of enthusiasm for this reform. High Wycombe Town Hall hosted an evening to promote the claims of the National Society for Women's Suffrage, but there was a 'very limited attendance'. Three councillors were present to hear talks given by Miss Beedy and Mrs Samuel Lucas of the Women's Suffrage Association. That week's editorial comment anticipated much of the future struggle, without foreseeing how difficult the fight would be:

'... there can be little doubt that the right they exercise in the municipal will soon be extended to the Parliamentary franchise. The broad principle on which they claim the franchise is that taxation and representation should be co-extensive; and that, as women are bound to obey the laws - and many laws specially affect them - they righteously claim to have a voice in the making of them. Thus far, we wish them all success; what they will ask for in the future, we leave for the future to decide'.[1]

The next year saw a 'well-attended' public meeting in Buckingham Town Hall, this time addressed by more well-known suffragists, like Miss Becker of the Manchester School Board, as well as Miss Lillian Ashworth. Miss Beedy, who also spoke, appears to have been awarded a Master's degree that year. The MP, Egerton Hubbard, chaired the meetings. Both resolutions of the meeting were carried amidst 'three cheers for the ladies'. The meeting proposed that a petition signed by the Mayor of Buckingham be sent to both Houses of Parliament. Also proposed was the sending of 'a memorial to Members for the County of Buckinghamshire' by Mr Hubbard, requesting them to support the Bill to remove the electoral disabilities of women, which was then before the House of Commons.[2]

In 1878, there was another meeting in High Wycombe, addressed by Miss C.A. Biggs and Miss Annie Young of the National Society for Women's Suffrage. While five representatives of the council were there on this occasion, the hall was only 'half full'.[3] A similar resolution to the Buckingham meeting was moved by Mr D. Clarke, presumably the Town

---

[1] *SBFP*, 6th March 1874.
[2] *BAAN*, 23rd October 1875.
[3] *SBFP*, 26th April 1878.

Clerk. It was passed with the support of the Rev. W.J. Dyer, who commented that, 'It was a question beyond argument and that what was wanted was the creating of an active interest in the subject'.

This 'active interest' does not seem to have been developed in the next decade, following the defeat of various women's suffrage measures which came before the House of Commons in the 1870s. The next time there seems to be a concerted effort to persuade others about 'votes for women' was the 1890s, through the South Bucks Liberal Association.

A town hall meeting organised by the South Bucks Liberal Association in Wycombe at the start of the political year, seemed to have been aimed at replicating the recent electoral success of the North Buckinghamshire Liberals in the south of the county. Lady Robinson of the North Bucks WLA chaired the evening. Liberal activist and temperance campaigner, Florence Balgarnie, was accompanied by Miss Ellen Chapman, Miss Arabella Shore, Mrs Dickson of Marlow and Mrs J. Thomas (later Lady Thomas). Miss Shore moved the resolution, 'That this meeting, while cordially recognising the growing prominence given in the Liberal Programme to measures of social and electoral reform, is of the opinion that the time has arrived when the political enfranchisement of duly qualified women should be included in that Programme'. In seconding the resolution, Miss Balgarnie declared that both 'caste prejudices' and 'sex prejudices' had broken down, and that, 'Mr Gladstone's axiom that "Men who live in a country should love that country, and it is the vote that stirs up their interest and fosters their love," applied also to women'. The resolution was carried unanimously.[1]

Throughout the 1890s, Countess Alice Kearney was very active in Buckinghamshire and other counties in support of the Liberal Party and their policy of Home Rule for Ireland. A member of the Women's Liberal Federation, she was also vociferous about women's suffrage. An article in the pro-Tory *Herald*, which no doubt was aimed at stirring up division within the Liberal Party, reported that the Federation had been accused of being an, 'extreme Female Suffrage party' by some leading Liberals.[2]

The 1890s were particularly notable as a period of in-fighting between the usually more ambivalent WLA and the WLF, which was formed later to campaign for 'votes for women' within the Liberal Party. Partly in an effort to revive the fortunes of the Liberal Party in Mid-Bucks, but not without

---

[1] *SBFP*, 25th April 1890.
[2] *BH*, 18th June 1892.

some controversy, Countess Kearney spoke at different places in the county, including meetings at Princes Risborough and Chesham, for example.[1]

The 1896-7 annual report for the South Bucks Liberals also recorded that Countess Kearney had spoken at several meetings. And it was at this positive, annual meeting in Slough where Kearney swayed the Liberal doubters, and the South Bucks Liberal Association adopted a resolution in favour of women's suffrage for the first time. Without reference to any particular Bill being considered by Parliament, this experienced speaker and campaigner drove home her arguments 'with much force and eloquence' on matters of principle. Countess Kearney wittily combined arguments for temperance reform, with arguments for electoral reform by quoting Edinburgh MP, Mr Herbert Paul. He said, 'he would rather go to the poll under the influence of the priest than under the influence of the publican'.

Kearney strongly objected to the commonly made assertion that 'women did not want the vote', because it was not based on any evidence. She roundly dismissed the argument that women could not fight for their country and therefore could not be treated as full citizens, saying that she could only understand that argument in a country which, 'had the conscription'. Long before she finished amidst 'Loud Cheers', she made this telling observation: 'The objection that the admission of women would be detrimental to Liberalism in a party sense was unworthy of a great party: she could imagine nothing meaner than to say a thing right and just in itself should not be done because it might be bad for a political party'.

After the Countess' speech, 'several delegates said they had come there with minds either indifferent or hostile, but had been quite converted by the eloquence of the speaker'. The resolution in favour of women's suffrage was carried with only one person present disagreeing.[2]

By the late 1890s, the South Bucks Liberals in particular, had developed a wider campaign, which included making the most of the cycling craze of the time. The Liberal Cyclists' Brigade was formed in 1899 to help, 'the great cause of Liberalism in this division'. Entertainment was put on at Lane End Assembly Rooms by the Marlow section of the South Liberal Cyclist's Brigade. Prospective parliamentary candidate for the constituency, Mr John Thomas (later Sir Thomas) spoke about his belief in 'women taking part in politics'. Warming to this theme and later declared in conclusion: 'Where

---

[1] *BH*, 18th June, 1892 and 5th December 1896.
[2] *SBFP*, 15th October 1897.

(women) occupy the same position as men, they should have the same qualification and ought to have the vote'.[1]

This meeting was followed up with others, including an open-air meeting at Lane End Temperance Hotel in the summer, held after a bike ride through the countryside.[2] This was followed the next week by a ride to Burnham Beeches, in 'delightful weather', where a crowd of people from Wycombe, Slough, Colnbrook and Farnham gathered at McCrow's Tea Gardens. Mr Victor Fisher gave a short speech, including a not entirely convincing call for 'Women's Suffrage'.[3] Fisher was a member of the Eighty Club, along with MPs like Herbert Asquith and Lloyd George. The Eighty Club was a small group formed in 1880 to celebrate and perpetuate the memory of William Gladstone's electoral victories.[4]

Other similar meetings were already planned, thanks to the, 'energetic secretary of the Brigade', Mr Norman Rivers. The following week's ride was to go through Beaconsfield and finish at Seer Green, where the Liberal cyclists were to be addressed by Dr. Charles Reinhardt of the Eighty Club.

While the political organisation of the South Bucks Liberals continued to gather strength, their candidate did not defeat the Conservative man until 1906. All the while, the Liberal women, many of them suffragists, continued to develop their own parallel campaign. In October 1899, the South Bucks Women's Liberal Association held a 'well attended' meeting in the Council Chambers of Wycombe Town Hall. The *Free Press* reporter observed that there were as many men there as ladies. Miss F. Embleton, organising secretary for Lady Carlisle, had already held a successful meeting in Marlow the previous day, when 20 ladies had joined the WLA. Miss Embleton spoke first of the work and dedication of her boss, only later declaring that she herself had been, 'a Liberal missionary for nine years'. She declared, 'It was quite unnecessary nowadays for women to apologise for speaking from platforms', and she looked forward to the day when women joined the men in being able to vote at Parliamentary elections. Mr John Thomas, who had been accepted as the next Liberal Party Parliamentary candidate for South Bucks, responded by endorsing what Miss Embleton had said about women's enfranchisement.[5]

---

[1] *SBFP*, 1st December 1899.
[2] *SBFP*, 9th June 1899.
[3] *SBFP*, 16th June 1899.
[4] Koss, Stephen - *Asquith*, p. 21.
[5] *SBFP*, 13th October 1899.

Given this kind of ongoing, low-level campaigning and the growing confidence of the local Liberal suffragists, it is perhaps not surprising that the woman who came to be the leading local suffragist in Buckinghamshire, Miss Frances Dove, was able to gather such an impressive and influential crowd to a crucial meeting in High Wycombe in 1904. The South Buckinghamshire constituency, in particular, had seen a consistent propaganda movement. Although this had not gained a wider more popular appeal by the turn of the century, there were positive signs which Miss Dove and other suffragists must have taken as encouragements to pursue a more active campaign.

There were perhaps two factors which were more significant than others in influencing the establishment of a successful campaign for 'votes for women' in Buckinghamshire.

The first was the continuing development of the railway network, which saw direct connections to London being established, like the one between Chesham and the capital in 1889, for example. This had two positive side-effects for the women's suffrage movement in Buckinghamshire. It meant, firstly, that it was easier for high-profile speakers to visit the area. This ease of access to the country helped boost the movement and reduced the isolation of the different branches. However, even more significantly, people from London were persuaded to either move out of the capital or to establish second homes. Many of the later recruits to the women's suffrage movement in the county were from this growing number of people who were either pioneering commuters, or those seeking to settle in a more rural location.

There was one draw-back to this development. It also meant that anti-suffragists could more easily arrive in numbers from wider areas to disrupt particularly high-profile events, as probably happened in Aylesbury in April 1912, and in High Wycombe in July 1913.

The second particularly crucial factor which determined the success or failure of the suffragist propaganda network was the ability to identify and train gifted volunteers. Like any other political movement, the cause for women's suffrage depended on people devoting time and energy to being local organisers. There were several occasions in the story of the Buckinghamshire suffragists and suffragettes where this became a determining factor in the growth or stagnation of the movement. The inability to find a local organiser was detrimental to the women's cause for example in Wycombe around 1906; in Chesham between 1909-12; in Aylesbury with the failed attempt to form a Church League for Women's

Suffrage branch in 1911; and ultimately with the Buckingham branch of the National Union of the Women's Suffrage Societies becoming moribund apparently after 1912.

Despite this particular difficulty, the women's suffrage movement did make significant progress in both Mid-Bucks and South Bucks. This was due to a growing army of dedicated and gifted women, who did so much to ensure that they and future generations of women would receive full political rights as citizens.

This is the story of the women - and men - of Buckinghamshire, who in different ways were 'Burning to get the Vote'.

Chapter 1: Miss Frances Dove and the High Wycombe Suffragists

'I see myself as a girl, skating with my father and brothers on the Serpentine, riding on the tops of omnibuses, rowing on the water in the Regents Park... I was merely doing what my younger brothers did... I was looked upon as a very extraordinary and exceptional specimen of girlhood... Again, I see myself as one of the earliest students at Girton College..., but at home I was virtually boycotted by all the young people of the neighbourhood... This prejudice has now entirely melted away.'
- *Free Press*, 20th March, 1908.

MISS Dove recounted these memories at one of the most significant public meetings in her long career. The nature of the evening itself marked an important development in the campaign for votes for women in Buckinghamshire. Instead of holding 'drawing rooms' in people's houses as in previous years, this was the first meeting in the Town Hall and marked the launch of a new local suffrage society, affiliated initially to the Central Society for Women's Suffrage. Having established Wycombe Abbey School in the preceding decade, Miss Dove was on the threshold of a wider, political role, having been elected to Wycombe Council just a few months previously. At this historic meeting, Miss Dove was responding to the speeches of Lady Knightley and Mrs Fawcett, leaders of the NUWSS, who were visiting Wycombe on that day to support the local campaign. To have received the public endorsement of the electors of Wycombe, followed a few months afterwards by the visit of these national figureheads of the constitutional campaign for votes for women, must have made Miss Dove feel that real progress was being made, and that some of the fruits of the women's emancipation movement were being realised in her own life.

The remarkable 1907 survey which Miss Dove conducted into the lives of the ex-pupils of Wycombe Abbey School, must have reinforced the feeling of progress in the advancement and achievements of women. From among the 800 replies she received from her postal survey, Miss Dove identified the following professions: 'several Doctors, a Head and many Assistant Headmistresses, Members of Education Committees, Authoresses, Hospital Nurses, Missionaries, the Principal of a Church Missionary Society Training Home, Housekeepers, Photographers, Gardeners, Charity Organisation Society Secretaries, Actresses, Journalists, Sculptors, Public

Singers, Artists in Stained Glass, Librarians, HM Inspectors of Schools, Inspectors of Boarded-out Children, Technical Teachers, Sisters, Superintendents of Inquiries of Investigation, A Solicitor's Clerk, a Portrait Painter and a teacher of Jiu-Jitsu'.[1] Miss Dove was later to declare, when she chaired another exciting meeting at the Town Hall in 1909, that, 'she did not think a hard and fast line could be drawn between men's and women's work'.[2]

Miss Dove in her formal councillor's garb, c. 1909.
Courtesy of Wycombe Abbey School

---

[1] Flint, Lorna - *Wycombe Abbey School, 1896-1986, A Partial History*, 1989, p.40; *Wycombe Abbey Gazette*, vol. III, no.9, November 1907, p.162.
[2] *SBFP*, 4th June 1909.

However, Miss Dove's earlier triumphant declaration of the 'melting away' of prejudice was shortly to be proved to be premature, as were any confident predictions of the imminent success of the women's suffrage movement. One of the lowest moments in Miss Dove's experience occurred in this same period, not long before her retirement as Headteacher of Abbey School in 1910. In November 1908 Miss Dove had been prevented, by the margin of just two votes, from being hailed as one of two of Britain's first female town mayors. Less than five years after this personal snub, Miss Dove was being chased through the streets of High Wycombe by an angry mob. A few months after this debacle, this indomitable woman failed to be re-elected as a local councillor by a wide margin

Nevertheless, by Miss Dove's own admission, she was often pleasantly surprised at the progress that was being made, in both the suffrage campaign and also more widely. The number and diversity of this list of occupations of the ex-pupils of Wycombe Abbey School serves as a vivid reminder of changing attitudes to women during Miss Dove's own lifetime. To begin with, there was no established system of schools for girls when Miss Dove was born. Nor were women allowed to work in a whole range of professions. Miss Dove's early life was lived in a very different era to the one she found herself in when she was elected to the Town Council of High Wycombe, just sixty years later.

Born in 1847, while her parents were on a tour of Europe, Frances Dove was the first of ten children in a relatively progressive family.[1] Her father was the Rev. John Thomas Dove. As curate of Rev. Llewelyn Davies of Christ Church, Marylebone, John was exposed early to the debate on women's education, being introduced to the vicar's sister, Emily Davies. Miss Davies was one of the most prominent figures in the growing campaign to widen educational opportunities for girls and went on to found Girton College, Cambridge in 1869.[2]

The history of her own education and training was outlined by Miss Dove in November 1904, at the presentation of a painting of her for display in the school library. Speaking in the third person about her experience, she said,

> She was born before the end of the first half of the century, when women's education was at its very lowest ebb. At that time there was a home for

---

[1] Perry, Kate - *DNB*, 2004-10; Bowerman, Elsie - *Stands There a School*.
[2] Bennett, Daphne - *Emily Davies and the Liberation of Women, 1830-1921*, Andre Deutsch, 1990.

governesses in Harley Street and Frederick Denison Maurice was a Professor at Kings College. Professor Maurice became interested in the struggles of governesses to obtain teaching for themselves, and as a result Queen's College was founded in 1848... She became a student at Queen's College in 1860... In 1871 she entered as a student at Girton College, lately founded by Miss Emily Davies... In 1877 she became a member of Miss Lumsden's staff at St Leonard's School, St Andrews and in 1882 was honoured by the Council by being asked to become its Headmistress.'[1]

Miss Dove was one of the first two women to sit for the Natural Sciences Tripos at Cambridge, which she passed in 1875. It was not until 30 years later that she was able to receive the degree, granted by Trinity College, Dublin, which had also been upgraded to an MA, in recognition of her subsequent achievements. In the summer of 1905, Miss Dove was one of over 700 'Steamboat Ladies' who crossed the Irish Sea between 1904 and 1907, in order to be awarded *quasi ad eundum* degrees at Trinity, because Oxford and Cambridge were still refusing to award degrees to women.[2]

Throughout her life, Miss Dove was passionately determined to see girls enjoying the same opportunities for education as boys. It was this which led Miss Dove to tender her resignation as Headmistress of St Leonards School, in 1895. She had identified a new challenge of establishing a new school in England, which she perceived as 'a great venture of faith'.[3] Miss Dove's uncompromising aim was enshrined in the Abbey School's original prospectus. This ambitiously stated, for example, that, 'The School is intended to provide for girls an education which, while moderate in cost and especially adapted to their requirements, shall be as complete on all its sides as that given to boys at the great Public Schools'.[4]

Miss Dove's desire to see equality between the sexes extended to her advocating a whole range of sporting activities, even those usually seen as a male preserve, like cricket. This unusually advanced attitude to female sporting prowess, found its ultimate expression in the chapter Miss Dove wrote for a book on the subject of 'The Cultivation of the Body'.[5]

Miss Dove arrived in High Wycombe in 1896, the year before the formation of the biggest suffrage society, the NUWSS. The year prior to her coming to the town, two pioneering women's football teams then touring

---

[1] *SBFP*, 2nd December 1904.

[2] Parkes, S.M. - *DNB*, Steamboat Ladies, 2004-10.

[3] *SBFP*, 2nd December 1904.

[4] Flint, Lorna - *Wycombe Abbey School 1896-1986*, p. 22.

[5] Beale, D., Dove, J. and Soulsby, L. *Work and Play in Girl's Schools*, Longmans, 1898.

the country, played at Loakes Park, High Wycombe.[1] And the year following Miss Dove's arrival marked the first public vote in support of women's suffrage, by the Liberal Association within the county.

Wycombe Abbey School pupils and staff, Christmas 1902.
Courtesy of Wycombe Abbey School

However, at this stage, Miss Dove clearly had other things on her mind. Losing no time in securing the funding and identifying the site for her future school for girls, Miss Dove was able to open the school, such as it was then, in September of that year. For the school premises, she had chosen prime real estate in the town, previously the residence of Lord Carrington. A close friend of King Edward VII, Carrington went on to be appointed as Minister for Agriculture in the Liberal government, first under Prime Minister Bannerman and then Prime Minister Asquith.[2] Both he and Asquith were to have public meetings in the county disrupted by militant suffragettes.

Forty pupils attended Wycombe Abbey School in September 1896, while the school was still being built around them. By the 1900 School Speech day, Miss Dove was able to announce 218 girls were attending Abbey School. Despite the huge amount of work involved in establishing Wycombe Abbey, Miss Dove was also involved in wider educational and social matters and was

---

[1] *SBFP*, 15th November 1895; Walker, Sam - *Mature Times*, January 2012, p. 13. I am indebted to Mike Dewey for this information.
[2] Adonis, Andrew - *DNB*, 2004-13.

instrumental in the establishment of the nearby Preparatory School, Godstowe, in 1900.[1]

As well as working hard to develop education for girls in the town, it seems that Miss Dove, from an early stage, was privately seeking to persuade prominent local people about the need for wider political emancipation for women. From a passing remark she made about the 'remarkable display of enthusiasm' which greeted a suffrage meeting in 1914, it is possible to conclude that Miss Dove may have started to raise this issue as early as 1899, only three years after she arrived in High Wycombe. She remarked that, 'Sixteen years ago, she could not have believed such a thing could have taken place'.[2]

If it was the case that Miss Dove began to be more vocal about votes for women from 1899, it is worth considering what in particular spurred her to action. It may have been the imminent advent of the new century, or perhaps the successful campaign of the women of Western Australia, who gained the vote later that year.[3] Not long afterwards, her former college principal, Miss Emily Davies decided also to throw her weight behind the women's suffrage campaign, apparently prompted by the death of Queen Victoria in 1901.[4]

However, having received little interest since the late 1890s, it was not until 1904 that the issue of women's suffrage first emerged into the public domain in High Wycombe. This event, which took place at Wycombe Abbey School, seemingly marks the opening of the Buckinghamshire campaign for 'votes for women' in the twentieth century. This may have come about partly through Emily Davies, who had taken on a strategic role in the suffrage issue as a leading member of the Central Suffrage Society in London. On the afternoon of Tuesday 21st June 1904, Miss Dove hosted a meeting at the school for all those who had expressed an interest in the issue of women's suffrage in the run-up to the general election.[5] The meeting, addressed by Miss Davies, agreed to form a society to promote the cause of women's suffrage in Bucks, affiliated to the Central Society for Women's Suffrage.

Those present numbered over 40, including a doctor and a number of clergymen. The vicar of All Saints, High Wycombe's parish church, Rev. E. D. Shaw, was there, as well as Miss Dove's future successor at WAS, Miss

---

[1] Basker, Mrs Russell A. - *Godstowe, The First 100 Years, An Informal History.*
[2] *SBFP*, 6th February 1914.
[3] Cockroft, Irene – *Art, Theatre and Women's Suffrage*, p. 108.
[4] Bennett, Daphne *Emily Davies and the Liberation of Women, 1830-1921*, p. 220.
[5] *SBFP*, 24th June 1904.

Whitelaw. Two women also came from other parliamentary constituencies. One woman, Miss A. B. Allnutt, had been working with the University Extension movement in Wycombe for the last six years.[1]

A committee was formed at the end of the meeting, comprising the following: Mrs Commeline (Beaconsfield), Mrs Dunbar Dickson (Marlow), Miss Hadfield and Miss Reid (Bourne End), Miss Raleigh (Loudwater), Miss Stevenson (Hedgerley), Miss Dove, Mrs Peachall and Miss B. Wheeler (Wycombe). Mrs Sarah Peachell was the widow of the Headteacher of Wycombe Grammar School.[2] Miss Bertha Wheeler was later appointed Treasurer of the High Wycombe suffrage society, but at this first meeting it appears there were no volunteers for the roles of Secretary or Treasurer.

Several of the women from other parts of South Bucks went on to play a key role in later forming their own, more local NUWSS branches: Mrs Magdalen Commeline, for example, went on to form the Beaconsfield NUWSS, and Miss Ethel Stevenson, from Hedgerley Park, helped to form the Gerrards Cross NUWSS.

Suffragists from the Gerrards Cross area, being further away from High Wycombe and with a good number of influential figures involved, had plenty of incentive to establish their own branch. As early as May 1909, there was a 'large attendance' at a meeting held in Gerrards Cross Schoolroom, when Miss Ethel Stevenson presided.[3] Miss Alice Lee, BSc, BA., was one of the speakers. At a later meeting she was named, Dr. Alice Lee.[4] Despite someone letting off a stink bomb in the Schoolroom, the vote was 'carried by acclamation'. The *Free Press* describes this as a meeting of the 'Buckinghamshire branch of the NUWSS', but the Wycombe society itself had not become affiliated to the NUWSS at this stage. More confusingly still, the NUWSS Federation Third Annual Report states that the Gerrards Cross branch was only formed in 1914. The President for that year was named as Miss Stevenson, the Secretary Mrs Barnard Davis, and the membership was numbered at 54.

Other networks of women who did not identify themselves with the NUWSS were later involved in establishing branches in South Buckinghamshire which were affiliated to other suffrage organisations, like

---

[1] *SBS*, 12th January 1906: Formation of a Wycombe Branch of the Workers Educational Association.
[2] Burgin, Marion - *The Women's Suffrage Movement in High Wycombe and some Neighbouring Towns, 1907-1914*, p. 50.
[3] *BFP*, 28th May 1909.
[4] *SBS*, 22nd February 1912.

Mrs Sargant Florence and Miss Edith Hayes from Marlow, who belonged to both the WFL and the WTRL[1] Miss Kate Frye, from Bourne End, was an organiser of the New Constitutional Society for Women's Suffrage and established a branch there.[2]

This first public meeting of suffragist campaigners in 1904, took place well over a year before the militant WSPU set up headquarters in London. It certainly seems that there were no other women's suffrage initiatives in twentieth century Buckinghamshire before this. While the women's suffrage movement had been relatively quiet in the 1890s, these national and local developments highlight the renewed impetus for votes for women which would come to rage across Buckinghamshire and across the nation over the next ten years.

Later in 1904, during the presentation of a portrait of Miss Dove for the school library, she was to make another reference to votes for women. This was in the presence of Dr Burge, President of the School Council and Headmaster of Winchester School, the pupils and their parents and the school staff. In referring to the founding of Queens College in 1848, and with the struggle for women's education, Miss Dove commented: '...so the stone was set rolling which resulted in the whole present system of schools and colleges for women - (applause) and must culminate sooner or later in obtaining for them the rights of citizenship by the bestowal of the franchise (Hear, hear).'[3]

It is difficult to discern much further suffrage campaigning activity in Wycombe in the years immediately following 1904. However, it seems likely that in these first two years Miss Dove and others conducted a series of 'drawing rooms'; meetings in homes which sought to quietly win people to the cause and build up a movement of committed volunteers.[4]

However, the original plan to put some pressure on the local parliamentary candidates at the next election seems not to have come to fruition. From the lengthy newspaper accounts of the 1906 elections, it does not seem that the original committee had managed to organise any events or produce any propaganda to encourage the candidates and the electorate to consider the question of 'votes for women'.

---

[1] *The Vote*, 4th April 1913, p. 385; *BFP*, 20th February 1914, p. 8.
[2] Crawford, Elizabeth - *Campaigning for the Vote: Kate Parry Frye's Suffrage Diary*.
[3] *SBFP*, 2nd December 1904.
[4] Burgin, p. 7.

Mrs May Scott, first Headmistress of Godstowe School.
Courtesy of Godstowe School

One indication of the difficulties experienced by the local suffragists in the early years is revealed in a letter written by Miss Dove, several months after the 1906 General Election, which swept the Liberals into power (See Appendix 2). Miss Dove replied to a previous letter from Miss Palliser of the CSWS, which may have raised the issue of the level of the group's activities. In the letter Miss Dove wrote to reassure Miss Palliser, that 'we are still much interested in Women's Suffrage here'. However, Miss Dove had not been able to find a Secretary for the Society from supporters outside of the school, ever since the previous summer. All of which suggests that Miss Dove had found plenty of allies among her fellow teachers, but that at this early stage the campaign was struggling to widen the movement much beyond the local schools.

Many of the women named at the first 1904 meeting went on to form the backbone of the local campaign for votes for women. A significant proportion of the early supporters were either teachers or members of the teaching staff of either Wycombe Abbey School or Godstowe School. Miss Dove's most active fellow campaigner was Mrs May Calder Scott, first Headmistress at Godstowe, whom Miss Dove had initially employed as an

19

English teacher at WAS in 1897. Mrs Scott later became as much associated with the cause of 'votes for women' as Miss Dove.[1]

Miss Anne Whitelaw.
Courtesy of Wycombe Abbey School

Miss Anne Watt Whitelaw succeeded Miss Dove as Headmistress of Wycombe Abbey School. Brought up in Auckland, New Zealand, she studied at Girton College. Joining the staff as Head of Mathematics in 1897, Miss Whitelaw later became a Housemistress.[2] Like Miss Dove, she was also awarded her MA at Trinity College, Dublin. In 1907, having returned to her native country to take up a post as Headmistress of Auckland Girl's Grammar School, she must have witnessed first-hand the changes that women's suffrage had brought to New Zealand, which in 1893 was the first

---

[1] From the booklet, *Godstowe School: An informal story of the beginnings*, Godstowe archives, nd., p. 1; Basker, pp. 3-5; Burgin, pp. 53-55 biog. I am indebted to Dorothy Ball for much information about Mrs Scott and the Gillie family.
[2] *SBS*, 25th March 1910.

country to give women. Following Miss Dove's retirement in 1910, Miss Whitelaw returned to High Wycombe, having been unanimously elected as the new Headmistress. Like her predecessor, Miss Whitelaw hosted suffrage meetings at the school.

Miss Constance Daniel, 1911.
Courtesy of Wycombe Abbey School

Two other WAS teachers seemingly present at the meeting in 1904, were Miss Constance Daniel and Miss Anna Maria Scott. Miss Scott was originally from Melbourne, Australia, and was one of Miss Dove's pupils at St Leonard's School. Having attended Girton College, she left her post as an Assistant Mistress at the City of London School for girls to become an Assistant Mistress at the very beginning of the founding of WAS. Miss Daniel also studied at Girton College and joined the staff at WAS in its first year. Both took *ad eundem* MA degrees at Trinity, Dublin in 1907. Alongside their Headmistress, as well as forming an important part of the backbone of the school from its early days, they clearly shared Miss Dove's views on women's suffrage and wider emancipation.

Miss Anna Scott, 1908.
Courtesy of Wycombe Abbey School

Miss Eliza Parker, while not a teacher, was a member of Godstowe's staff who was a convinced suffragist from an early age. A Miss Parker was certainly named as being present at the original women's suffrage meeting in 1904. If this was Eliza, she would probably have been 15. Born in High Wycombe and aged 22 in 1911, Eliza was a cook in Mrs Berney's household, 'Ulverscroft', one of the houses of Godstowe School[1]. She later became Secretary of the register of local 'Friends of Women's Suffrage'. Mrs Berney was later to talk enthusiastically of Miss Parker's involvement over several years.[2]

It seems clear that, despite the significant numbers of suffragist teachers and staff at WAS and Godstowe, in 1906 Miss Dove did not want to over-burden already busy staff with the role of Secretary of the local suffragist branch. That year had been a particularly busy one for Miss Dove and her

---

[1] 1911 England & Wales Census.
[2] *SBFP*, 7th February 1913.

fellow teachers. Miss Dove had assumed a wider community role by helping to form the Central Aid Society.[1] This organisation offered financial and practical help to those who were disabled in the district and to poor local families suffering unemployment.[2]

Also in 1906, Mrs Scott became involved with the newly formed town branch of the Worker's Educational Association, launched by the vicar of All Saints, Rev ED. Shaw.[3] The branch was to become affiliated with the National Union of Teachers, the Progressive League, the Educational Committee of the Co-operative Society and the Esperanto Society.[4] According to the account of a Wycombe WEA activist, the idea for the WEA originally sprang from the idea of, 'a group of university men who felt they were in danger of being divorced from the great world of life and action and from the common life of the people'.[5] The WEA 'clubrooms' at no.1 White Hart Street, later went on to become the central office for the local suffragists and venue for a series of educational talks about women's suffrage.

Miss Dove and Mrs Scott's attention towards matters of social concern indicate a certain sympathy with socialist thinking, demonstrated, for example, by Mrs Scott's attendance at a series of Fabian lectures in High Wycombe.[6] The vicar of All Saints, Rev. Shaw presided at some of these meetings. And Miss Dove and Mrs Scott together attended a branch meeting of the local Church Socialist League.[7]

The close association between female teachers, socialism and suffragism was also indicated by the visit of Mrs Ethel Snowden to High Wycombe in 1907. Mrs Snowden was a writer, lecturer and temperance campaigner, whose background in teaching and then women's suffrage in Yorkshire and the north-west, earned her a name as a gifted speaker.[8] Her marriage to Philip Snowden in 1905, who was soon elected as a Labour MP for Blackburn, afforded her a bigger platform for her blend of socialism and

---

[1] *SBFP*, 12th March 1915.

[2] *Memories of High Wycombe*, True North Books Ltd, p. 102; Pearce, Olive - *Wycombe Rebel: The True Story of Ted Rolph, 1892-1972*, 1982, p. 62.

[3] *SBS*, 12th January 1906.

[4] *SBFP*, 12th April 1912.

[5] *BAAN*, 28th September 1912, p. 12.

[6] *SBFP*, 15th March, 11th and 18th October 1907, for example.

[7] *SBFP*, 19th March 1909, p. 3.

[8] Hannam, June - *DNB*, 2004-13.

morality. She was first invited on a speaking tour of the United States that same year.

Snowden had been invited to speak at the Guildhall by the WEA on the topic of 'Woman – The Educator'.[1] Introduced by Miss Florence Dring, Mrs Snowden opened by describing how disappointed she had been by the recent national conference of the Association in Manchester, where there had been no speeches about the education of working women. She was, however, on the basis of the audience before her that evening, pleased to see that 'the women were well catered for by the High Wycombe Branch.' Repeating a saying in circulation at the time, Snowden declared that, 'a nation never rose above the level of its women'. So, she went on to condemn the fact that the average wage of working women was less than half that of men at seven shillings a week. While she declared the teaching profession as 'the noblest of all', her talk became more a diatribe about women's suffrage than a talk on education both by and for women.

Snowden's appearance in Wycombe was shortly after the NUWSS' first large-scale London demonstration on 9th February, which was dubbed 'The Mud March'. She honoured those who took part, because they were 'fighting not for themselves but for the emancipation of their sisters... (Loud applause)'. Referring to the lack of time given to the Women's Enfranchisement Bill introduced to the Commons by a Liberal MP following the march, she was scathing about the spectacle of men coming out of Parliament, 'laughing and chuckling at the defeat of heart-broken women, who, for 40 or 50 years, had struggled for equal terms with men.'

Calling for a holistic socialism which included not only land nationalisation, but the growth of 'the social spirit' which placed women on the same terms as men, Snowden launched into an overview of the women's emancipation movement internationally. Speaking of recent developments for women's rights in China, Japan and India, she questioned whether the women of England were really free. Snowden went on, 'It was always a painful experience to her to speak at drawing-rooms in London to ladies well dressed and supposed to be well bred, but there the women were economically bound to their husbands, and not allowed to develop their own talents, being merely considered graceful table heads and entertainers'.

The Anti-suffragists had not yet organised themselves into a formal organisation at this stage, but it is clear from Snowden's comments that many of their arguments were already widely heard. She commented, 'They

---

[1] *SBFP*, 15th March, 1907.

waxed eloquent on the vastness of their Empire... but they would not really be great unless they admitted women in the scheme of things'. In closing, and in response to a question about whether women would 'overwhelm' the men, Snowden uttered this prophetic observation: 'It might take perhaps another 20 or 30 years to get women the vote, unless they had a more businesslike House of Commons.'

While a high proportion of suffragists in High Wycombe were teachers, a woman's involvement in the teaching profession did not of course guarantee a persistent commitment to women's suffrage. The Wycombe High School science teacher, Miss Mary Bowers was reported to have taken part in one of the women's suffrage processions in London in 1908 wearing her graduate gown.[1] This was the 'Great Demonstration' on the 21st June organised by the WSPU, who had aimed for a gathering of 250,000 people in Hyde Park. According to Mrs Pankhurst, the *Times* reported that this number may have been doubled or even trebled.[2] It was on this occasion that the suffragettes first sported their colours of purple, green and white. However, it does not appear that Miss Bowers had much subsequent involvement in the movement locally, although she was still teaching at the High School several years later.[3]

The same week of Mrs Snowden's visit, Miss Mabel Hope of the GPO Telegraph Department also came to Wycombe. She spoke about women's wages to a meeting organised by the local Labour Party at the Speed's Hall. The low pay endured by women employed by the government at the time was widely seen as a scandal by many women campaigners. In 1906, the Association of Post Office Women Clerks had just produced evidence for the Hobhouse Parliamentary Committee on this issue.[4] The report recommended an increase of wages for certain classes of male employees, but no increase for female workers. Simmering resentment among female staff of the GPO, may well have led to the attacks against pillar boxes as early as 1908, which were retrospectively attributed to the suffragettes, although they probably did not adopt this as a means of protest until later. (see Appendix 8). There was a case of an arson attack on a pillar box in Chesham in 1909, although it is impossible to tell whether this was just an ordinary case of mischief.[5]

---

[1] *SBFP*, 19th June 1908, 'Gossip'; Burgin, p. 18.

[2] Pankhurst, Emmeline - *My Own Story*, pp. 112-115.

[3] *SBS*, 2nd January 1913.

[4] Records of the Association of Post Office Women Clerks.

[5] *BE*, 12th November 1909, 'District Pars'

Miss Hope told her audience that she felt the best way forward was both for more women to join trade unions, as they had been doing, and also for women to be given the vote. But when questioned directly at the end of the meeting, Miss Hope, 'said that she herself was for adult suffrage'.[1] This highlighted one of the biggest tensions between the labour movement and the women's suffrage movement. Most suffragists and women's suffrage organisations argued that a measure to enfranchise a proportion of women, should be given priority over any legislation to enfranchise more men.

This may have been one of the reasons why Mrs Scott and Miss Dove may have been wary of being too closely associated with the Independent Labour Party. Miss Dove in particular was keen to stress that women's suffrage was a 'non-party' issue. However, it does seem they both believed their support for women's suffrage was consistent with socialist sympathies, and probably felt they had a more ready audience for their progressive views among ILP members and sympathisers. Local Labour party supporter, Ted Rolph, obviously respected these suffragist women.[2] Furthermore, Miss Dove and Miss Scott's mutual friend, Dr Jane Walker, was not only patron of both WAS and Godstowe, but as well as being renowned for having pioneered an early treatment for people suffering from tuberculosis, she also seems to have held socialist views.[3]

The leading suffragists' leaning towards socialism, may help to explain why the local women's suffrage group recruited two ILP sympathisers around this time: Miss Florence Dring and Mrs Mary Boutwood. These two women took on some of the organising duties for suffrage meetings in High Wycombe. Mrs Boutwood was the first secretary for the Wycombe branch of suffragists.[4] The suffragist ranks were later swelled by other women with socialist views, like Mrs Matheson, from Beaconsfield. In 1910 Mrs Matheson, who was born in Russia, addressed an ILP meeting at the Speed's Hall in High Wycombe.[5] However, she may not have joined the suffragist campaign until 1913.[6]

So, when the growing alliance between the NUWSS and the ILP was formerly ratified in mid-1912, it may well have caused some heart-searching and even division within the ranks of these Wycombe suffragists. However,

[1] *SBFP*, 15th March 1907.
[2] Pearce, Olive - *Wycombe Rebel*, pp. 43 and 61-2.
[3] Cohen, Susan L. - *DNB*, 2004-13.
[4] *SBFP*, 20th March 1908; Burgin, p. 50.
[5] *BFP*, 18th March 1910
[6] *SBFP*, 7th November 1913.

this shift towards the Labour Party had been anticipated by much of the suffragist leaders' earlier activities, and would have been wholeheartedly welcomed by some of the Wycombe suffragists.

Other earlier leading supporters of the cause were not teachers, but nonetheless may have become involved through the determined persuasion of Miss Dove and her fellow teachers. Those present from the first public meeting included Mrs Davenport Vernon and Miss Bertha Wheeler. Mrs Davenport Vernon was married to a leading businessman in the town, who was a close supporter of Miss Dove and an enthusiastic suffragist. A prominent churchman and county magistrate, Robert Davenport Vernon had been elected church warden of All Saints in 1899.[1]

Miss Bertha Wheeler was perhaps one of the most notable suffragist figures native to the town. Having identified herself with the suffragist cause at the 1904 meeting, it was only much later that she became prominent in the movement, being appointed Treasurer of the Wycombe NUWSS branch, probably in 1912. Miss Wheeler was the daughter of Thomas Wheeler, previously Town Mayor and an influential businessman in Wycombe, involved in both brewing and banking.

Members of other professions, such as doctors, were early supporters of the movement. Dr Bell was there at the first meeting. Later, Dr Eva Meredith became associated with the local suffrage movement some time after 1906. She was involved both as Medical Officer for the Central Aid Society and probably had a role in overseeing the health of the pupils of both Godstowe and Wycombe Abbey Schools.[2] Dr William and Mrs Ethel Fleck joined the suffragists later on. Mrs Fleck became a regular supporter for women's suffrage meetings from the 1908 branch launch. And with their 'Tudor House' in the High Street, the Flecks were probably chosen as hosts for many visiting suffragist speakers, including the overall organiser of the NUWSS pilgrimage in 1913, Mrs Katherine Harley.[3] Clergymen were also evident among suffragist ranks, not just later on, but from the beginning. Rev. E.P. Baverstock was named at the 1904 meeting. And the Vicar of Taplow, Canon Garry, contributed to this significant meeting. Alongside Rev. E.D. Shaw, the Rev. J. Rushby Smith, Vicar of Christ Church, Wycombe, was also an early supporter of votes for women.

As well as the growing local support, there was a further sign of progress towards equality for women at this time, which would have cheered the

---

[1] *BAAN*, 29th June 1912, p. 5.
[2] Burgin, p.12; Godstowe speech day: *BH*, 27th June 1914.
[3] *SBFP*, 23rd February 1914, obit.

Wycombe suffragists. This was the passing of a measure by Parliament in 1907, which granted women the right to stand as candidates in town and borough council elections. This included the right to stand for election as mayor. Given her prominent role as Head of Wycombe Abbey School and her growing involvement in the wider community, Miss Dove was persuaded to stand for election as a local councillor in 1907. Her list of seconders and proposers totalled 34 people, including seven women.[1] She also received the public approval of leading figures in the town, including Mr Charles Raffety, who wrote a letter recommending that the people of High Wycombe vote for Miss Dove.[2]

Miss Dove was elected at the head of the poll for the East Central Ward, gaining 360 votes out of over 1,100 votes cast for four candidates. A 'great roar' went up at the announcement of the result and Miss Dove accepted her appointment amidst scenes of great elation.[3] There was particular interest that year in the Corporation procession from the parish church that Sunday, with Miss Dove among the councillors, wearing her Girton College cap, gown and hood.

The account in one history of Wycombe Abbey School describes the reaction of the Wycombe Abbey pupils on local election day, once they had heard the result:

> 'The wildly excited girls were allowed to stay up on that All Saints Day to wait for the result and when the news came through at nine o'clock, they flocked to the Rupert Gate to cheer her home to Big School. Eventually she was able to respond.... "If you'll only stop that horrid noise you shall all have a whole holiday tomorrow". Whereupon there were more cheers and a spontaneous outburst of "For she's a jolly good fellow".'[4]

A few months later, public enthusiasm was again particularly marked at the unprecedented meeting which welcomed national leaders of the NUWSS to High Wycombe. It seems that the local suffragists were perhaps already considering transferring their allegiance from the Central Society for Women's Suffrage, to the more successful NUWSS. Despite this sense of forward momentum, the women did not feel confident enough of their audience, or of having sufficient interest to go fully public. At the last

---

[1] *SBS*, 25th October 1907.
[2] *SBS*, 1st November 1907 - see Appendix 3.
[3] *BH*, 9th November 1907.
[4] Flint, p. 42.

minute, the venue of the meeting was changed from the Town Hall itself to the smaller Red Room. The meeting was made a ticketed one. According to one report, this caused 'considerable disappointment' for some townspeople, with significant numbers unable to gain admission.[1]

Drawing identified as 'Constance Westmacott, Mrs Dixon Davies', nd. Courtesy of Sarah Richards

The meeting was opened with the reading of the society's annual report, by the Secretary, Mrs Boutwood. This was as much a call to arms as a report. The local suffragists had clearly been busy in the last year, even if their efforts had been largely invisible in the local press. The Secretary made a point of thanking by name those who had helped with six drawing room meetings during the year. Those who had hosted were: 'Mrs Bleek Leech,

---

[1] *SBFP*, 20th March 1908.

Miss Dove, Mrs Dunbar Dixon, Miss Houghton, Mrs Peachall, Miss Reid.' Those who had read papers were, 'Mrs Dixon Davies, Mr Hakluyt Egerton, Mrs Lehmann, Miss Eden Lewis, Miss Stevenson and Mr Stooke-Vaughan.' Those who had chaired the meetings were: Mrs H. Dale, Miss Dove, Mr Meakin, Mr Shaw, Miss Stevenson and Lady Thomas.'

This in itself was an important development in the campaign and indicates both an increase in numbers of people from different backgrounds getting involved, as well as a growing awareness of the wider implications of women being given the vote. Unfortunately, no titles for the papers presented were mentioned, but the range of subjects addressed was probably reflected in the variety of topics which Wycombe suffragists discussed in later years.

One of the lecturers mentioned for the first time in relation to the local suffragists was Mrs Constance Davies. Mrs Davies (referred to in the newspaper accounts as Mrs Dixon Davies), was an experienced activist and philanthropist, who lived previously in Chesterfield, Derbyshire. Mrs Davies was involved in other campaigns, including being Secretary of the Church Anti-Opium Committee.[1] She appears to have become involved in campaigning for votes for women after moving to Buckinghamshire, in or possibly before 1907. Constance was married to Mr Dixon Davies, a solicitor, JP and Liberal Party activist.

At the 1908 annual meeting, Mrs Boutwood issued a four-fold appeal: for people to join the society; to donate money; to form discussion centres in their immediate neighbourhoods; and finally for three people to volunteer to become secretaries. The Wycombe suffrage society was already planning to form new societies in South Bucks, both to address the issue of 'isolation' experienced by current members living in 12 scattered villages, and to spread their message.

Concluding her report, Mrs Boutwood stated that none of the present committee were young and appealed to younger people in the audience, 'who will benefit from what we are sowing'. Referring to the Biblical story of the Good Samaritan, she finished on a confident note, that as Britain had already emancipated slaves, Catholics and Jews, it would not be long before women gained emancipation also.

Following a speech by Lady Knightley, Mrs Millicent Fawcett moved the resolution in favour of women's suffrage, 'in the cause of justice and for the

---

[1] *Manchester Courier and Lancashire General Advertiser*, 13th July 1907. Here she is described as living in Beaconsfield. I am Indebted to Sarah Richards for much of this information.

well-being of the whole community'. She then addressed the meeting. Mentioning several encouragements, including the example of New Zealand and the launching of a men's league for women's suffrage, Mrs Fawcett spoke of the overwhelming majority the previous women's suffrage Bill had received in the Commons, despite the spoiling tactics of the 'antis'. However, she also remarked on the continuing and surprising ignorance of some concerning their constitutional movement, singling out Lloyd George for particular comment. While receiving an NUWSS deputation, he had apparently scolded the women for their tactics of breaking up meetings.

Mrs Fawcett's resolution was then seconded by Earl Russell, with supportive statements by Liberal party activist, Mr Wallace Atkins, who went on to become the unsuccessful Mid-Bucks Liberal Party candidate for the January 1910 General Election. Others who expressed their support were Mrs Commeline from Beaconsfield, and the vicar of All Saints, High Wycombe, Rev. Shaw. Miss Dove, invited to address the meeting by Earl Russell, spoke of her encouragement at the progress of the movement. She mentioned the 100 years that it took before the slave trade was abolished and expressed the hope that it would not be that long before, 'women received their full heritage of citizenship'. Thanking the speakers, she gave special mention to the Secretary, Mrs Boutwood, who she said had, 'worked patiently through much discouragement'.

The proposition was put to the meeting and 'carried by acclamation'. The excitement of that March 1908 event was matched by the mood of suffrage campaigners across the country. The women's suffrage movement seemed to be building an inexorable momentum.

Even school speech days at WAS became an occasion for raising the issue of 'votes for women'. With the exception of her portrait unveiling at the school in 1904, Miss Dove was usually careful to separate school activities from campaigning for women's suffrage. However, Mrs Edward Micholls from Campden Hill, a school patron and member of the School Council, spectacularly broke with this protocol in 1908.[1] Although her brief was to propose a vote of thanks to the assistant mistresses from the platform, she made this comment:

'She could hardly refrain from mentioning the question of the Franchise being extended to women. (Laughter) In any such case she was quite sure of one thing that they were unanimous in their desire that their girls should be worthy of the vote, whether they were anxious to receive it or not. To

---

[1] Bowerman, Elsie - *Stands There a School*: 'List of Patrons', p. 84.

paraphrase a well-worn quotation, she would say "Tis not in women to command the vote (at any rate in the present Parliament), but we will do more, we will deserve it".[1]

The vicar was more diplomatic when he later accepted that people in the audience might not share Mrs Micholls enthusiasm. His view was that, 'nothing should drag from him on that platform his opinion as to certain claims that were advanced by women'.

However, for all the excitement of the 1907 council elections and the significant milestones in the local campaign for the vote in early 1908, the desire of Miss Dove and many local women to establish greater equality between the sexes, was thwarted later that year. Miss Dove narrowly and controversially missed becoming Mayor of the town. Despite strongly asserting that she had not herself sought this office and only responded to the requests of her peers, this must have come as a bitter blow to Miss Dove. The conduct and tone of the discussions surrounding her appointment must have been deeply disappointing for someone who believed in both the justice of her cause and the need for progress.

There was extensive local and national newspaper coverage given to the dramatic events surrounding Miss Dove's nomination and last minute rejection. The *Herald*, which usually did not feature much news from High Wycombe, devoted a column to these proceedings and commented that, 'the sole topic of conversation in Wycombe has been the decision of the Town Council to nominate Miss Councillor Dove...'.[2]

Miss Dove was nominated at a private meeting of the council on the 20th October. She was nominated by a previous Mayor, Alderman Arthur Vernon, a Conservative councillor, who ran a well-known local business with his father, as a land agent and surveyor. The nomination was seconded by Councillor Charles Elsom, one of the early patrons of Godstowe School. In a letter he wrote to 'clear the air', Mr Elsom talked of giving Miss Dove's nomination his 'hearty support'.[3] However, there must have been heated debate as the meeting, which originally included 24 of the 31 councillors, lasted over five hours, so some councillors left early before the final vote was taken. Thirteen councillors voted for Miss Dove at this nomination meeting.

Following Miss Dove's nomination being made public, a protest meeting was hastily arranged at the Town Hall on Tuesday 27th October. The *Herald*

---

[1] *SBFP*, 3rd July 1908.
[2] *BH*, 31st October 1908.
[3] *SBS*, 30th October 1908.

reported that large posters were displayed across the town, both by the opposition to advertise the protest, and also by those supporting Miss Dove.

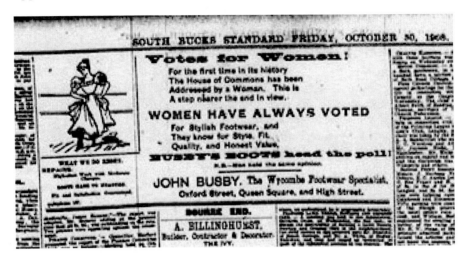

Advertisement in the *Standard*, 30th October 1908, referring favourably to Muriel Matters' speech in the House of Commons

The poster produced by supporters of Miss Dove was addressed to the voters of the East Central Ward. Reminding local voters that just last year they had returned Miss Dove to the Council at the head of the poll, the poster urged them to 'rally round the member of their choice, to attend the meeting... and see fair play'.[1] There was a significant number of both local residents and people within and beyond the county who had cheered Miss Dove's original election and sent her telegrams of congratulation. However, there was probably a division of opinion within even these people, as to whether it was best to elect a woman to be Mayor of High Wycombe.

The *Standard* estimated 1,500 people were present at the meeting called in the Town Hall, a venue which accommodated 1,300 people seated.[2] At the start of the meeting, three balloons were released from the gallery, to which was attached a placard bearing the slogan, 'Votes for Women'. The gallery was 'filled with ladies'.[3] The *Herald* reporter described the response of the

---

[1] *BH*, 31st October 1908.
[2] *SBS*, 30th October 1908.
[3] Ibid.

crowd as 'mild excitement', while the *Standard* claimed the excitement was 'intense', partly due to rumours of suffragettes from London planning to attend the meeting.[1] The police were apparently on high alert for 'suspicious females'.

Amidst cheers and laughter, the balloons' pointed flight was ended when Mr W. Dickson, near the platform, jumped up, smashed the balloons and tore up the placard.

Both opposition and supporters of Miss Dove received cheering and derision as they entered the hall. The loudest ovation was reserved for Miss Dove herself, who came in during the Chairman's opening remarks. Miss Dove was widely applauded for her 'pluck' in being ready to enter 'a more or less hostile assembly'.[2] The Chairman, Alderman Walter Birch, explained that he had not initiated the protest meeting. But having been invited to chair the meeting via a telegram, he pronounced that he had been pleased to receive the invitation.

After Mr Birch's introductory remarks, Alderman Charles Deacon addressed the assembly. Deacon was a businessman and sportsman, a Liberal and a local Methodist preacher.[3] He moved the first resolution of protest against Miss Dove's nomination and then addressed the crowd. His comments raised the issue of Miss Dove only having been a councillor for a year and that, as a woman she would not be able to sit as a Chief Magistrate, or recommend someone else to sit in her place. Deacon disagreed that her 'mental capacity' and philanthropy recommended her for this post. He also commented that he felt that appointing Miss Dove as Mayor would be a 'disgrace' to the town. And he objected to the public appeal made to the voters of the East Central Ward to support Miss Dove, while the views of the voters of the other three wards, the 'town proper' as he called them, were in danger of being overlooked.

Councillor William Gomm, a chair manufacturer, then seconded the protest resolution and concluded his remarks with a poem:

'Our beautiful Dove, has fallen in love,
With thirty-one men round a table;
She wants to sit in the Mayoral chair,
But I doubt whether she is able'.

---

[1] *BH*, 31st October 1908 and *SBS*, 30th October 1908.
[2] *SBS*, 30th October 1908.
[3] *BE*, 28th February 1912, obit.

Shortly after this, Alderman Arthur Vernon attempted to intervene to propose an amendment to the motion opposing Miss Dove's nomination. However, the apparent attempt by him to take over the platform, was not welcomed by most of the audience, who began jeering loudly. He was unable to receive a hearing for several minutes. After having spoken with the Chairman and also Miss Dove, Vernon attempted to speak to the audience once again, without success.

Somehow, during this furore, a vote was taken on the original protest resolution and passed by a 'tremendous majority'. Still standing before the meeting throughout these proceedings, Councillor Vernon was asked to resume his seat by the Chairman.

Councillor A.W. Nash then spoke to the meeting. For some reason, he produced a baby's comforter at this point, declaring it 'ready for use'. Nash declared his support for women's suffrage, but 'he was not in favour of a woman sitting in the chair and ruling 31 men'. He repeated earlier arguments that the existing Mayor, Robert S. Wood, had not been given due recognition at the nomination meeting and that he should have first been given the opportunity to stand again, before Miss Dove's name was put forward. He successfully proposed a deputation to the current Mayor, to see if he would stand again.

Despite this display of vocal opposition, Miss Dove asked to address the meeting. She was received with 'loud cheering and the waving of hats and handkerchiefs'. Miss Dove refused to withdraw from the Mayoral elections, saying that she had been duly chosen as Mayor-elect at a properly constituted meeting and she did not feel they were 'playing the game in holding that protest meeting and raising an opposition to her'.[1] She objected to the protest posters having been headed by the words, 'Borough of Chepping Wycombe', as though they had official Council approval.

The protest meeting was brought to a conclusion with some closing remarks by the Chairman, Councillor Deacon. Reflecting on nearly 27 years in business and in public life, he declared that, 'so far as the business capacity of ladies was concerned, there was not one of them to which he would give as much credit, as a fourth standard boy in our elementary schools'.

The local controversy provoked plenty of national newsprint, some animated local correspondence, as well as some unusual adverts. John Busby's Footwear Specialist, which had shops in Oxford Street, Queens Square and Wycombe High Street produced an advert. Their position was

---

[1] *BH*, 31st October 1908.

unequivocal and referred to the recent demonstrations in the House of Commons, including the speech by Miss Muriel Matters. The advert read: 'Votes for Women! For the first time in history, the House of Commons has been addressed by a Woman. This is a step nearer to the end in view. Women have always voted for stylish footwear...'.[1]

Correspondence on these events, which appeared in the next two issues of the *Free Press*, seemed fairly evenly split. There were two letters which deplored, for example, the 'unsportsmanlike manner' and 'infantile arguments' of those protesting against Miss Dove's nomination.[2] Both of these were anonymous, being signed, 'Disgusted' and 'As it Struck Me', reflecting perhaps an awareness of the degree of opposition in the town.

In contrast, Charles E. Skull of 'Enderly', High Wycombe put his name to his letter and declared that appointing a female Mayor would make the Borough look 'ridiculous'.[3] Mr J. Bailey of White Lodge, Amersham Hill managed to negotiate a middle way, stating that while he would have opposed Miss Dove becoming Mayor, on the basis that she could not sit as a magistrate, he felt it would make the town look ridiculous if it now decided not to appoint her, following her nomination having been accepted by a properly constituted meeting.[4] Other councillors contributed to the debate on the opposition side, including John Furness, a builder and undertaker and Robert Joseph Howland, a chair manufacturer.

The following council meeting to vote on Miss Dove's nomination was held in the Guildhall, on Monday 9th November. The Corporation's procession to the building threaded its way through large crowds. Once the building was packed to capacity, policemen were posted on the doors to restrain the crowds from forcing their way in. Hundreds gathered and waited outside in the High Street for the Council's verdict. Alderman Vernon tried in vain to persuade his fellow councillors to support Miss Dove's nomination. According to the *Examiner* report of 13th November, Alderman Deacon 'led the opposition'.

Alderman Vernon opened the debate. When he charged Miss Dove's opponents with 'prejudice', there was a particularly loud and sustained reaction. However, the *Examiner* reporter commented that, 'there were a certain number of speakers who had little to advance by the way of

---

[1] *SBS*, 30th October 1908.
[2] Ibid.
[3] *SBS*, 6th November 1908.
[4] *SBS*, 30th October 1908.

argument, but who seemed to feel strongly the primordial disinclination of man to be ruled by woman, and whom no amount of talking could shake'.[1]

Councillor Elsom again seconded Vernon's proposal of Miss Dove as Mayor. He commented that some years ago, he too would have been of the same opinion as Miss Dove's opponents, but that he had been gradually persuaded of the case for women holding public office. He then ventured the opinion that much of the opposition had arisen from the tactics of the 'suffragettes', but he was confident that Miss Dove had no sympathy with such tactics. Similarly, he was confident, from his experience of sitting on the Wycombe Abbey School Council, that 'he had never known one more business-like or capable of presiding over the deliberations of a Council which was composed of men.'[2] He urged the opponents to become 'passive resisters' and abstain from voting against Miss Dove that day.

After speeches, from both sides of the argument, by councillors and aldermen Deacon, Flint, Fleck, Nash, Taylor, Cox and Gomm, the meeting had lasted over three hours. The decision was taken to vote on the matter, without hearing further speeches and the vote in favour of Miss Dove's nomination was lost: 14 in favour, 16 against. Miss Dove just failed to become one of the nation's first female mayors by a margin of only two votes. However, 1908 still marked a significant milestone in the progress of the women's movement, as Dr Elizabeth Garrett-Anderson gained this first for women, by being voted the mayor of Aldeburgh, Suffolk.

At the end of the meeting, Miss Dove was asked by some of her enthusiastic supporters about standing again another year. But she shook her head and with a 'kindly smile' said she was 'growing old'.[3]

The meeting was adjourned until the next day, to try to meet the council's deadline for appointing a new mayor. During the meeting, Councillor Walter Birch, who had been proposed as the new Mayor by Alderman Deacon and seconded by Alderman Nash, made a thoughtless but perhaps deliberate remark, which provoked a strong reaction from Miss Dove. He commented that 'they would be able to keep the Council in order, even if they had half a dozen suffragettes there'. Miss Dove responded by saying, 'That is a most personal remark. I am not a suffragette and I wish that to be thoroughly understood. (Applause).'[4] The *Examiner* report on the

---

[1] *BE*, 13th November 1908.
[2] *SBS*, 13th November 1908.
[3] *BE*, 13th November 1908.
[4] *SBS*, 13th November 1908.

same day observed that Miss Dove had 'protested against her name being so frequently associated with those of the militant suffragettes'.

At the conclusion of the meeting, Councillor William Wharton, the owner of a chair factory, was nominated and then elected as Mayor for 1908.

It seems that Miss Dove lost the vote to become Mayor not simply because she was a woman, but because she was a woman who was prepared to stand up for women's rights. Those opposed to her election were keen to make capital out of the strong feeling against the suffragettes, especially following the disruption of a meeting of Lord Carrington's in the town earlier that year, as well as the suffragette rushes on the Houses of Parliament the previous month. Despite Miss Dove's constant disavowal of law-breaking tactics, her association with the women's suffrage movement automatically condemned her in the eyes of some of her council colleagues, as well as in the mind of the local population.

Although Miss Dove lost this particular battle, she did not allow this defeat to discourage her for long. There were too many exciting developments in the women's suffrage movement, both nationally and locally.

In April 1909, Miss Dove hosted a party of 70 international suffragists from some 20 different nations at the Abbey School.[1] They were attending the Fifth International Women's Suffrage Alliance Conference in London. Learning from the experience of successful suffrage campaigns like those in New Zealand and Australia, as well as some of the U.S. States, the women of Britain increasingly saw themselves as part of an international movement in favour of women's enfranchisement. And the visit of such a notable party to Wycombe shows what an influential figure Miss Dove had become within the ranks of the suffragist movement.

Miss Dove's involvement with the international suffragist movement, probably led directly to the arrangement of the next high-profile event on 2nd June, 1909.[2] In contrast to the annual meeting the previous year, and in view of the anticipated crowds a small venue was exchanged for a larger one, in. According to the *Free Press* reporter, the decision to move the meeting from the Red Room to the Town Hall itself, proved justified. Another notable feature of this meeting is the close co-operation between the NUWSS and the WFL in South Bucks. This desire to combine forces probably led soon after to Miss Dove being invited to write a short article for the WFL's newspaper, *The Vote*.

---

[1] *SBFP*, 30th April 1909.
[2] *SBFP*, 4th June 1909.

Miss Dove opened the meeting and spoke both about men and women's complementary gifts and about the changing gender roles and expectations. Although Miss Dove had, from an early age, objected to the common notion of the 'separate spheres' of the sexes, this may be the first time she makes this point so forcefully, perhaps encouraged by the more radical feminism of her friends in the WFL. The meeting was mostly composed of women, so she raised a laugh when she mentioned a boy she knew who had just made his own shirt. But her observation that it was not necessarily women who should always be expected to do the household cookery, received a loud interjection, revealing the presence at the meeting of some opponents to the campaign.

Miss Dove then introduced Mrs Lillian Hicks of the WFL, as someone who 'had worked hard and made some very great sacrifices for the cause of Women's Suffrage'. Lillian Hicks may well have been known to Miss Dove through her earlier involvement with the Central Society for Women's Suffrage. Having left the WSPU for the WFL, she later re-joined the WSPU and was twice arrested by the police, but on both occasions acquitted of militant actions. She also joined the WTRL and resisted paying her taxes twice. Her daughter, Amy Hicks, was one of the leading suffragette hunger-strikers held in Aylesbury Prison in 1912.[1]

Mrs Hicks began by tackling the common 'antis' objection that 'women could not think imperially'. She then addressed the need for reform at home, including the issue of equal pay for women, arguing that, 'their inferior position could only be altered by the possession of political power'.

Sir John Cockburn was then introduced by Miss Dove. As the ex-Premier of Southern Australia, which had introduced women's suffrage some years before, Miss Dove joked that 'he is still alive and looks well and flourishing'. Sir John reflected upon his knowledge of High Wycombe. As a medical student at London University forty years previously, he used to visit the town to see a friend and fellow medical student, Mr William Rose. In those days medicine had been a male preserve, but he went on to describe his pleasure at recently witnessing women receiving their medical degrees at Westminster Abbey.

This experienced speaker dealt humorously with someone in the audience who performed a dramatic yawn, and Sir John later confronted some interruptions to his speech by observing that those not prepared to listen to argument were proving themselves unfit for the vote. Then,

---

[1] Crawford - *WSM*, pp. 284-5.

mentioning what may have been a WFL or WSPU event in Caxton Hall, London, Sir John described how a woman only five feet tall had demonstrated her grasp of ju-jitsu by throwing a much taller policeman. He concluded this part of his speech by observing that, 'If it was said that, despite physical exercises, women were still the weaker sex, the reply was that it was all the more reason why they should have the privilege of choosing champions who could guard their rights'.

Sir John went on to argue that, 'Women should have the vote on the principle that there should be no taxation without representation; and he could not help thinking that if women would adopt a little passive resistance in the matter of taxation it would be difficult for politicians to withstand that argument.' At least three women in Buckinghamshire were later to heed this advice.

Observing that women gaining the vote in Australia had not, 'brought women off their pedestal... or detracted from the sweetness of their disposition', Sir John closed his speech by asserting that women gaining the franchise was inevitable.

Miss Lamond, from the NUWSS national office, then delivered an 'eloquent and closely reasoned speech', which echoed many of the previous arguments. No questions being raised at the end, the meeting was closed, following a vote of thanks made by Mrs Scott.

There was another high-profile meeting later that year on Saturday 6th November at 'Witheridge', Knotty Green.[1] This was not quite the launch of a new Beaconsfield branch of the NUWSS. However, with Mrs Constance Davies chairing the meeting, and given the large number of prominent citizens present previously not known to be associated with the campaign, this meeting was a new departure and demonstrates the growing influence of the women's suffrage movement in the area. The meeting closed by recommending the women's case be presented to the current Liberal MP for South Bucks, Mr Arnold Herbert.

Despite the personal set-back of the previous November, Miss Dove reflected the optimistic mood of many women's suffrage campaigners, when she commented in the Christmas 1909 edition of the Women's Freedom League newspaper:

'The whole status and ideal of womanhood must be lifted into a region that it has not hitherto occupied. It must, in fact, occupy the same place as the best of men... Now this will never take place until women have the

---

[1] *SBFP*, 12th November 1909.

franchise... The perfect work can only be accomplished in church, or State, or home, where the gifts of both men and women, working together in an equally responsible manner, are combined to attain it'.[1]

However, her experience of being rejected as Mayor may have partly prompted her opening negative comment. Since childhood, Miss Dove had felt a 'keen sense of the injustices that I endured and saw others enduring, merely because we were not men.'

The next year marked something of a high-water mark for the constitutional campaign, with the much-anticipated Conciliation Bill being first considered by the House of Commons. The passing of this Bill would have allowed over a million women property holders to have a vote in Parliamentary elections. Before the end of the year, Mrs Fawcett was able to claim that 4,000 NUWSS meetings had been held nationally between July and November to support the Conciliation Bill. That same year in April, Miss Dove led a delegation to visit one of the most prominent opponents of women's suffrage in Buckinghamshire, MP for Mid-Bucks, Lord Lionel de Rothschild.

1910 also marked a significant personal milestone for Miss Dove. She retired as Headmistress of Wycombe Abbey School. This development coincided with other women increasingly taking a more prominent role in the local suffrage movement. Consequently, 1911 became a watershed for the movement, and appears to have been a period of consolidation and re-organisation after the extra activity prompted by two general elections in 1910. The WSPU's declaration of a truce following the death of King Edward VII and the seeming proximity of a government measure for women's suffrage may have actually led to a lessening of activity amongst the constitutional campaigners. Fewer meetings were certainly reported during 1911, in the *Free Press* at least. But, if this was the case, the events of late 1911, when the government refused to introduce women's suffrage legislation in preference for putting forward a new Manhood Suffrage Bill, certainly re-invigorated any suffrage campaigners who may have started to become complacent.

The sweltering summer of 1911 witnessed the coronation of King George V. Local suffragists took part in the excited celebrations which swept the Empire, as well as seeing them as an opportunity to continue to press their case for a larger vision of the role of its citizens, both male and female, for sharing in the democratic government of this global enterprise.

---

[1] *The Vote*, 9th December 1909, p. 74.

One of the teachers from Wycombe Abbey School took part in the London demonstration for women's suffrage on 17th June, and wrote anonymously of her experiences in the school's magazine. Whoever it was, commented of that memorable, seven mile long demonstration: 'the pleasure of seeing the procession was small in comparison with the joy of taking part in it.' (See Appendix 6)

High Wycombe joined in the extended national festivities.[1] This included a procession of 6,000 children representing local schools and Sunday Schools. They marched from the High Street to Daws Hill Park, where music, refreshments and entertainment had been arranged. Many of the children wore fancy dress, including Alice Darvill and Elsie Barter, who were dressed as suffragettes, carrying a banner reading, 'Votes for Women'.

Photograph by Edward Sweetland. Reproduced with the permission of Hazel Langford. The original caption to the photo states: "Suffragettes' parade and crowds in Queen Victoria Road. View from upstairs window of White House, Sweetland's photographic studio, Coronation Friday 1911'.

---

[1] *SBFP*, 30th June 1911.

While it was true that local suffragists were not as busy organising meetings in 1911, they were busy re-organising, with two branches being launched within the constituency. There was the birth of a branch of the New Constitutional Women's Suffrage Society in the area south of High Wycombe, based around Bourne End. The NCSWS was partly started as an attempt to persuade constitutional women to adopt a more sympathetic approach to militancy.

Then, towards the end of 1911, another women's suffrage branch was launched in Beaconsfield, which initially was not affiliated to a larger suffrage organisation. Among the leaders of the Beaconsfield group were Mrs Constance Davies, Mrs Commeline who was married to the local vicar, and Mrs La Pla, who was married to the minister of the Congregational Church there.[1]

Like the Wycombe suffragists, they too decided later to come under the umbrella of the NUWSS. A meeting at the 'Redlands' home of Dr and Mrs Whitfield was called to chose between three groups: the NUWSS, the NCSWS and the Federated Council of Women's Suffrage Societies.[2] Miss Rochfort's proposal of joining the NUWSS won a two-thirds majority, despite Mr Gower arguing for the NCSWS, on the basis that they did not insist ona government measure. In letters read out to the meeting, both of these national organisations offered operational freedom to the local branch, saying that they would not be obliged to support their election policies, which is probably why the Beaconsfield and District suffragists had initially preserved their independence. At the end of the meeting, Mrs Olave Snow of 'Carngray' and Mrs Whitfield were appointed secretaries of the new branch of the NUWSS.

A new High Wycombe NUWSS emerged in 1912, which, despite an inevitable dip in numbers from the development of other branches, was soon mounting an impressive educational campaign to win over waverers and to persuade those who had been traditionally opposed. A new generation of suffragists emerged from the disappointment of the abandoned Conciliation Bill, who set about organising a regular and varied programme of meetings on an unprecedented scale and over an extended period. Many key suffragist speakers were involved, alongside local activists. These meetings were also for the first time, consistently advertised on the front page of the *Free Press*, as well as occasionally in the *Standard*.[3] The

---

[1] Burgin, p. 51.
[2] *SBFP*, 18th April 1913.
[3] *SBS*, 2nd January 1913.

advent of significant numbers of people who had moved to the town following the development of High Wycombe's direct rail link to London, certainly seemed to help swell the suffragist ranks. And the closer relationship developing between the NUWSS and the ILP led to the involvement of a wider cross-section of the local population, including working women and men.

So, in 1912, with Miss Dove appointed as their President, the High Wycombe NUWSS emerged with greater confidence and determination, which was later greatly bolstered by the idea of a national pilgrimage for women's suffrage in 1913 which would take in Buckinghamshire. It is no wonder that, later on, Miss Dove was excited by the unprecedented numbers of enthusiastic supporters. While she commented that she felt she was at times 'pushing against a brick wall', the fact that she said this to a meeting in Aylesbury, shows that she was more determined than ever to encourage a wider audience to give their all to the just cause of 'votes for women'.[1]

---

[1] *BH*, 25th January 1913.

Chapter 2: WSPU - The Longdown Farm Summers: the Suffragettes reach Buckinghamshire

'Votes for Women sold splendidly, the meetings were most enthusiastic and one new member signed her card in a country lane in the middle of a pool!' - *Votes for Women*, 3rd September 1909, p. 1136.

THE Women's Social and Political Union was launched in the Manchester area in 1903. In 1906 the WSPU moved its centre of operations to London. Emmeline Pankhurst and her daughters, with their firebrand preaching and eye for publicity, managed to recruit many women. Before the move to the new Clements Inn Headquarters, WSPU organisers had been active in Canning Town, for example, recruiting working-class women. However, partly due to a need to generate funding, in 1907 the WSPU leadership took a conscious decision to recruit from among the wealthy London elite.

So, the story of the WSPU in Buckinghamshire may well begin in the West End, in the salons and drawing rooms of Chelsea, Kensington and elsewhere. Any women who had holiday homes in the Chilterns would have been actively encouraged to consider using them to widen support for the cause of fighting for women's freedom. Alternatively, some may have been encouraged to lease properties as new, regional centres of operation. Later, when more suffragettes became deliberate about law-breaking, there were many hunger strikers who needed places to recover or places to hide. So, the WSPU needed an extensive, informal network of rural retreats for exhausted and wounded suffragettes. Later still, some of these places were used as safe-houses for travelling WSPU arsonists and bomb-makers. It is unlikely that Longdown Farm was ever used in this way.

One of the many ladies recruited by the Pankhursts and their fellow suffragettes was Mrs E.M. Casserley of Muswell Hill. It appears that in the summer of 1909, and probably the year before, she was renting Longdown Farm, on the Hampden Estate, from the Earl of Buckinghamshire. Mrs Casserley is the named person in reference to the property in the brief article in the 3rd September, 1909 *Votes for Women*. This farm is in a particularly secluded, wooded valley in the Chiltern escarpment, perhaps chosen for both its remoteness and its location, fairly close to Chequers.

The earliest WSPU forays into provincial Buckinghamshire were, however, less strategic. It seems the first time WSPU actions are featured in local newspaper reports in 1908 and 1909, they show militant suffragettes engaged in 'hit and run' tactics. The policy at this stage was, following similar tactics employed in Manchester, Scotland and elsewhere, to create as much disruption as possible to any political meetings involving the Prime Minister or any government ministers, and to gain publicity for their demand for justice for women.

However, WSPU tactics were always evolving. They soon adopted a longer-term approach, which included establishing local branches, even in apparently unpromising places for political activism like Buckinghamshire. However, one branch was briefly established, in a town in the heart of the Chilterns with a history of religious and political dissent: Chesham.

Those involved in the establishing of the WSPU branch in Chesham were not numerous or well-known. However, the pattern from other Home Counties shows that provincial women were clearly active in the more militant wing of the suffrage movement. Indeed, in some cases the WSPU found it difficult to restrain some individuals and branches from taking initiatives not backed, initially at least, by those at the heart of the WSPU leadership.

The first prominent militant suffrage campaigner to visit Buckinghamshire was Mrs Charlotte Despard, a saintly socialist, renowned for choosing to live in the Battersea slum area of Nine Elms.[1] Being tall and wiry, with an unusual and 'rational' dress sense, Mrs Despard was hard to miss or mistake. The outspoken leader of this new group already had an enthusiastic following and a reputation as a passionate and persuasive speaker. Earlier the same year, Mrs Despard had achieved some national notoriety by taking part in the WSPU's first attempt to 'rush' the House of Commons, following the King's speech on 12th February 1907. She was arrested with many others and, having refused to pay her fine, Mrs Despard was sentenced to a month's prison term in Holloway. She was released early.

When Mrs Despard came to High Wycombe in December 1907, however, she was no longer part of the WSPU. Only three months previously, she and other prominent women leaders had decided they could no longer stomach the authoritarian nature of the WSPU leadership and formed a breakaway organisation, which eventually was named the Women's Freedom League. The WFL had similar aims and attitudes to its mother organisation, but being more socialist and pacifist in its philosophy was less enthusiastic about more extreme forms of militancy. Thirteen WFL branches

---

[1] Mulvihill, Margaret - *Charlotte Despard: A Biography.*

were quickly established in London by November. The WFL continued to see growth in its number of branches, to 53 in 1908. However, while it remained one of the smaller suffrage groups, with an estimated membership of 4,000 in 1908, the WFL arguably had an influence out of proportion to its size.

Perhaps Mrs Despard felt, given the proximity of Marlow, which had become the solitary branch of the WFL in Buckinghamshire, that Wycombe was a strategic location to extend the reach of the WFL in the area. Mrs Despard would have been aware of the added encouragement of Miss Dove having been elected as a Wycombe councillor the previous month. Furthermore, there were some prominent WFL members in the county, like Mrs Mary Sargant Florence, whose house, Lord's Wood in Marlow, was later used as a place for recuperation by suffragettes.[1]

Judging by her closing remarks on the night, Mrs Despard was clearly hoping that her visit would serve as the impetus for the establishment of a branch of the WFL in the town. It appears this hope was never realised, possibly because the WFL constitution stated that 'no WFL branch can consist of less than 12 members'.[2]

According to the *Free Press* report, Mrs Despard had been invited to speak at the High Wycombe Guildhall by the local branch of the Independent Labour Party.[3] This meeting formed part of a wider propaganda campaign by the local Labour Party. Miss Florence Dring, in the absence of Mrs Mary Boutwood, struggled to maintain order. Mrs Boutwood may have already agreed at this point to be Secretary for the Wycombe suffragists. She had certainly accepted this position in early 1908, but if so, she clearly saw no conflict of interest in her chairing a meeting organised by the ILP, in support of the leader of the WFL. She lived in Bledlow, so it was the more practical issue of her train being late, which prevented her from being there.[4]

The hall was crowded with both men and women, including a group at the rear of the hall, who had come along simply to disrupt the meeting. Mrs Despard appealed for a hearing amidst constant interruptions, but barely finished her opening remarks. Her plea to them as Englishmen to give her a fair hearing, failed to have any effect on the hostile element in the audience, who responded with jeers and various popular songs. The Mayor, Alderman

[1] Crawford - *WSM*, p. 223-4
[2] *The Vote*, 29th July 1911, p. 170.
[3] *SBFP*, 13th December 1907.
[4] Burgin, p. 8.

Robert Wood, who was present in a personal capacity, was asked to intervene and was eventually prevailed upon to do so. But even his appeals fell on deaf ears.

By 8.25pm, the decision was taken to adjourn the meeting to the Speed's Hall, in the nearby Paul's Row, where the rowdy element in the crowd were not allowed entrance. In this new venue, Mrs Despard praised the Labour Party for having gained representation for workers in Parliament and expressed the hope that women would soon also gain the vote. She affirmed the contribution which women already made to the nation, through the payment of taxes. She paraded her militant credentials and demonstrated the already existing motivation for the later launch of the Tax Resistance League with the following declaration: '...when her next taxation papers came in January, she intended to write across them, "Taxation without representation is tyranny"'. Her comments were interspersed with enthusiastic applause.

The people of Wycombe did not have to wait long for the next visit of suffragettes to the town, this time from the WSPU. A group of militant campaigners visited Wycombe from London for the day on 3rd April, 1908. They had been drawn by a large public meeting arranged in support of the Government's Licensing Bill recently presented to Parliament. The meeting was due to be addressed by local landowner, Minister for Agriculture, Lord Carrington, and had been arranged by local Temperance and other 'kindred societies'.[1] Suffragette courage in the face of public hostility was already well-known. However this example of disrupting a meeting demonstrates how easily the WSPU could alienate potential supporters, like the ranks of women temperance campaigners represented there that day.

This visiting group of suffragettes were later named in the newspaper account as Miss New, Mrs McCloud, Miss Stephens and Miss Gye. Edith New, formerly a teacher, had made national headlines by chaining herself to the railings in Downing Street earlier that year. Having joined the WSPU in 1906, Edith had been appointed an Organizer for the Hastings by-election in March and was fresh from her campaigning there. Elsa Gye had only been with the militants for a year when she took part in the protest in Wycombe, but she went on to become a WSPU Organizer in Derby, as well as taking part in campaigns and protests in Scotland, Birmingham and London.[2]

Part way through Lord Carrington's address one of the four shouted out, 'Votes for Women', which prompted the expected response of 'Chuck her out!' She was escorted from the Town Hall. Not long afterwards another of

---

[1] *SBFP*, 10th April 1908.
[2] Crawford - *WSM*, p. 446 and p. 254; Kean, Hilda - *Deeds not Words*, p. 13.

the suffragettes shouted from the gallery, 'Why don't you give the women the vote?' She too was ejected.

Lord Carrington persisted, but tempted fate when he referred to both the presence of women on the platform and in the hall, giving their support to the Licensing Bill. Another suffragette, this time at the end of the Hall shouted out, 'Why don't you give them the vote?'. Stewards led this woman to the entrance. Shortly afterwards, there was one final interruption to the meeting, from the middle of the Hall. This time, unlike the previous militants, this suffragette declined to listen to the stewards' request for her to leave. As the *Free Press* reporter described this 'scene', 'She clung to her chair, but the stewards were determined and after a brief struggle she allowed herself to be escorted to the door'.

Undeterred, the four women attempted to hold a meeting outside in Victoria Road, but were prevented from doing so by Head Constable Sparling, who recommended that the ladies move to Frogmoor Gardens. According to the local newspaper reporter, having taken up a position on a piece of waste land opposite, 'Miss New spoke for something like an hour on "Reasons why women should get the vote". The proceedings were... not altogether free of good natured chaff, which the speaker did not appear to object to. When the meeting terminated, 'a considerable number of the spectators accompanied the champions of "Women's Rights" to the station, where they entrained for London'.

A more significant development in the local campaign was the attempt that summer to establish a base of operations within the county. This new phase in WSPU tactics in Buckinghamshire was first signalled by the appearance of a Holiday Campaign advert in the pages of the 20th August 1908 issue of the WSPU's *Votes for Women*.[1] The advert mentions the address of 'The Ark, Longdown Farm', with an appeal for others to join in helping Miss Jacobs and Mrs Caprina Fahey during what was left of the summer. Mrs Fahey was a masseuse, living in North West London. She had only just joined the WSPU at a Hyde Park demonstration in June 1908.[2]

It seems that the WSPU leadership wasted no time in encouraging new recruits to recruit others. It also indicates the success of WSPU leaders and other activists in fanning into flame a high level of enthusiasm within those new to the movement, coupled with the readiness of many women to suffer for their cause. Women hearing about the suffering of other women at the hands of the male authorities, often provided the initial impetus for

---

[1] *VW*, 20th August 1908, p. 1087.
[2] Crawford - *WSM*, p. 212.

provoking a deeper level of commitment among audiences of suffragette marches and meetings. There was a similar response among some of the male WSPU supporters too. This was certainly true for Cambridge undergraduate Hugh Franklin, whose second family home was just outside Chesham. The WSPU leadership had correctly concluded that the experience of imprisonment would help to further radicalise the movement and create an alienated army of women ready to not only speak up for women's equal rights, but commit 'deeds of daring' too.

Just a few months later, in February 1909, Mrs Fahey was arrested as a member of the deputation sent by the very first Women's Parliament in Caxton Hall to the House of Commons. After her trial, she refused to pay a fine, in keeping with WSPU policy, and was imprisoned for a month. By the summer, she was back at Longdown Farm, helping to organise a series of meetings across central Buckinghamshire. Before this though, there was another confrontation with the government, unusually in the north of the county, involving a different team of suffragettes.

Bletchley Park was the home of the Leon family, who had managed to secure quite a coup by persuading Prime Minister Asquith to come to an event hosted by them and the North Bucks Liberal Association on Friday 13th August 1909. This summer rally was described by the *Free Press* reporter as 'unique' in that it was 'the first time Mr Asquith had addressed what might be described as a rural audience in defence of the Budget'.[1] The audience of 2,000 people, including many landowners, dignitaries, clergymen, local MPs and prospective candidates, were hardly comfortably accommodated in a marquee in the grounds on what turned out to be a sweltering day.

The WSPU could not resist this opportunity for challenging the Prime Minister. However, compared to their one day hit-and-run tactics in Wycombe the previous year, a more sophisticated campaign, over several days, seems to have been developed. They used the publicity surrounding Asquith's visit to arrange meetings on several days prior to the event, to appeal to the local population and win a hearing for their cause. Open-air meetings in Bletchley and Fenny Stratford were arranged during the week running up to the Prime Minister's visit. Reports in *Votes for Women* claimed that the four evening meetings were well-attended and well received. What may have drawn a crowd was the notoriety of the suffragette speakers. Miss Maud Joachim, for example, had been imprisoned in Maidstone Prison the previous autumn.[2] Katherine Douglas Smith was the other speaker.

---

[1] *SBFP*, 20th August 1909.
[2] Crawford - *WSM*, p. 310.

The writer of the report in *Votes for Women* could not contain her glee at the way suffragettes were able to breach the local Liberal Party's careful security arrangements.[1] According to a Liberal steward present on the day, Mr Asquith had only agreed to come as long as they could guarantee no suffragette interruptions. The WSPU newspaper reported how, supported by an anonymous team of men, four women gained access to the grounds the night before and slept in a plantation of pines near the marquee (Miss Marsh, Miss Ainsworth, Miss Wurrie and Miss Hall). Nellie Hall's mother had been a close associate of the Pankhursts in Manchester and was one of the original nucleus of six women who formed the WSPU in 1903. In 1909, Nellie was 'still a schoolgirl'. Charlotte Marsh became active for the WSPU just the previous year and was sent to prison in June 1908 on a charge of obstructing the police in Parliament Square.[2] Charlotte was later to re-visit Buckinghamshire as an inmate of Aylesbury Prison.

Having gained access to the grounds of Bletchley Park undetected, these four women then had to remain still, where they were, throughout that day until early evening. Around 6pm the Prime Minister made his appearance in the tent, to a rousing chorus of 'For he's a jolly good fellow'. Armed with megaphones, the four women rushed forward, raising various shouts like, 'When are you going to give justice to women?' Nellie Hall managed to chain herself to a tree. The WSPU correspondent went on:

'In an instant there was uproar. Some people cheered and some roared in helpless fury... At last.... stewards reached the women and attacked them in proportion of about six to one. Some of the liberal men completely lost their heads... Others pushed the women into the bushes, using such bad language that their calmer friends remonstrated. Pushed and hustled, the women were driven out of the grounds into the road, where a large and sympathetic crowd raised a hearty cheer. Miss Douglas Smith, who had been outside, dashed over the wall and made for the tent, chased by 12 men and was eventually caught'.

The women continued to hound Mr Asquith when he left Bletchley Park, although they were prevented by police from catching the same train as the Prime Minister. Mr Asquith was not only booed by a crowd as he left Buckinghamshire, but, 'on his arrival at Euston, a pertinacious male suffragist who had travelled in the same train, once more asked him the

---

[1] *VW*, 20th August 1909, p 1085.
[2] Crawford - *WSM*, p. 259 and p. 381.

question which he is never allowed to forget.' (The initials of the anonymous male suffragist were F.R.).

This one report demonstrates very clearly the courage and determination of these suffragettes, who were such a persistent nuisance to Cabinet Ministers and to the Liberal government as a whole. It is no surprise that while the *Free Press* reporter manages to confuse his language in calling them 'Suffragists', he also has no qualms about describing them as 'redoubtable'.

A different group of women were engaged in similar activities that summer, in the heart of the Buckinghamshire countryside. In the previous week's issue of *Votes for Women* appears an advert appealing for, 'Local members and sympathisers encouraged to contact Mrs E. M. Casserley (Muswell Hill) about two weeks of propaganda work in the district'.[1] Mrs Fahey and Miss Jacobs are again mentioned, based at Longdown Farm. In the 3rd September edition, there is this excited report:

> 'Glowing accounts from Miss Annette Jacobs, who with Mrs Keeling has been organising a fortnight's campaign which included Chesham, Aylesbury, Great Kimble, High Wycombe and elsewhere. Votes for Women sold splendidly. The meetings were most enthusiastic'.[2]

The 27th August, 1909 edition records what it proudly called, 'the first suffragette meeting ever held in Aylesbury.[3] The account describes how a crowd of 200 was present, even though the meeting had only been advertised by chalking the town's pavements ten minutes before. There seems to have been little disruption at this meeting, compared with other more widely advertised meetings in the town. The speakers were even 'congratulated and cordially thanked'.

On Wednesday 25th August, the same team of women visited Chesham, having advertised a meeting the day previously, using brown paper handbills. An identical summary report of this meeting, lifted from the pages of the 28th August *Votes for Women* was reproduced in both the *Examiner* and the *Advertiser*. The *Examiner* also includes details of the address given by Miss Jacobs, which is almost identical to the words of her talk in Wycombe two days later.[4] The reporters may have drawn on a press release previously supplied by the formidable WSPU propaganda machine.

---

[1] *VW*, 13th August 1909.
[2] *VW*, 3rd September 1909, p. 1136.
[3] *VW*, 27th August 1909, p. 1112.
[4] *BE*, 27th August 1909.

Miss Jacobs is described as 'engaged in school work' and elsewhere as a 'pupil teacher'.[1] Her arguments centred around the unfairness of continuing to deny women the vote, coupled with the contribution that women could make to legislation. She mentioned two recent examples of laws passed by Parliament, which would have made better legislation if women had been involved in the debate: the Children's Charter and regulations for teachers and women workers. She went on to describe how and why the WSPU developed its militant methods in Manchester and finished by answering questions, including why suffragettes were not willing to wait for the introduction of a private members Bill in Parliament.

That evening Miss Jacobs drew a 'tremendous crowd' in the Broadway. Mrs Keeling, chairing the meeting, was clearly alarmed by the two ugly rushes towards the platform by members of the crowd during Miss Jacobs' address. However, Miss Jacobs insisted on continuing and won grudging respect for her determination.

At the close of the meeting, she was asked questions, including what improvements she would suggest making to the housing question. Perhaps she did not feel confident enough to be drawn on this particular matter, as she countered with a well-worn theme of suffragette propaganda, that women were classed among criminals and imbeciles and their opinions were not considered valuable. She then adroitly answered the question of why suffragettes were not pressing for adult suffrage, instead of limited household suffrage, a contentious issue which divided the ranks of the suffrage movement. Miss Jacobs simply replied that the women were not so presumptuous to ask for more than the men had. Finally, she fielded another controversial question when she was asked whether women would sit as MPs in Parliament. She replied that with potential future female voters being outnumbered by male voters by six to one, she thought it was unlikely there would be a flood of women MPs.

Wycombe was the venue for a similar meeting later that week, organised by this same group of suffragettes.[2] On the morning of Friday 28th August, in typical WSPU fashion, pavements were chalked to advertise the meeting in Frogmoor Gardens. This was a common venue for open-air political meetings and was often used by the local branch of the ILP.

---

[1] *SBFP*, 3rd September 1909.
[2] Ibid.

Frogmoor, High Wycombe, scene of many political rallies and of several lively open-air meetings organised by both suffragettes and suffragists. From High Wycombe Library

Wearing purple, white and green sashes and selling *Votes for Women* newspapers, the group also included Mrs Keeling and also Mr Hugh Franklin of Chartridge Lodge, near Chesham. The reporter contrasted their 'good humoured' reception, with the hostile reception received by Mrs Despard at the Guildhall meeting in 1907. Miss Clayton introduced the two speakers, Miss Jacobs and Miss Fahey, who carried on regardless, despite some amusement when the box supposed to create a platform gave way beneath them. Miss Annette Jacobs, although 'a novice at public speaking', spoke for over three-quarters of an hour and was not 'disconcerted in the least by the laughter and good-natured chaff'. Finishing her talk, the crowd responded with 'Bravo!' and applause.

Many in the audience apparently wanted to know why the women had not made a nuisance of themselves before, when the Tories were in power. This seems to indicate that those present were mostly Labour or Liberal supporters, who shared a common concern at the time, that giving propertied women the vote would present an unfair advantage for the Conservative Party. The suffragettes' answer was that it was only in the last few years that women had realised that quiet campaigning over 50 years had got them nowhere and that they needed to adopt more extreme methods in order to see some response to their demands. The suffragettes argued that this militancy was particularly justified in view of the government's refusal to receive WSPU deputations or to give assurances about introducing government legislation.

Mrs Fahey declared that 'in order to obtain equal rights for the women of this country they were prepared to sacrifice their lives'. She described her time in prison and how some other WSPU members had started a hunger strike. Amidst constant interruptions, Mrs Fahey concluded her address to the audience and questions were invited. The matter of the women's attitude to divorce was raised and Mrs Fahey replied that it was 'horrible' and assured the crowd that, 'if women were given the vote, they would do their utmost to get the law changed'.

It seems after this fortnight, Mrs Fahey left the area and by January 1910 she was campaigning prior to the General Election as WSPU Organizer for Middlesex, based in Harrow.[1] Miss Annette Jacobs may have stayed in the area, being named 'pioneer' for the movement in Chesham, presumably as the first suffragette to speak publicly in that town.

Following the two summer campaigns organised by WSPU activists in 1908 and 1909, it would appear campaigning was then based in local centres. Perhaps the prominence of both the NUWSS and the WFL in Wycombe and the Labour sympathies in the town help to explain why no attempt to establish a local WSPU branch seems to have been made here. Local suffragettes were more active in Chesham and to a lesser extent in Aylesbury.

The conclusion of these two 'Longdown Farm summers', when temporary teams were drawn together for a fortnight of meetings across a wide area, marks a significant turning point in the story of the WSPU in Buckinghamshire. There were other, similar, short-term campaigns, organised by other groups. For example, the one in Aylesbury in 1911, organised by the CLWS; the caravan tour of the county in the summer of 1911 by Muriel Matters on behalf of the WTRL; and the by-election campaign in High Wycombe in 1914, organised by the NUWSS. But, given its lesser emphasis on local organisation and its insistence on militant activity, the later years of the WSPU in Buckinghamshire are characterised by a small number of isolated individuals or very small groups across the county. Later, there were also small teams of militants who paid fleeting visits to the area with a very different purpose. These came to the area, not with the intention

---

[1] Crawford - *WSM*, p. 212.

of persuading others to their cause, but only with the aim of carrying out headline-grabbing attacks on property. The only exception to this came in April 1912, with a much larger prison protest meeting arranged by both the WSPU and the WTRL in Aylesbury.

There were clearly tensions between the various women's suffrage groups active in the county. On several occasions, letters were published in local newspapers, in which constitutional suffragists of the NUWSS, distanced themselves from the tactics of the WSPU.[1]

However, there is also ample evidence of individuals from different groups working together, which was often a necessity in the less populated, rural areas of Buckinghamshire. Certainly, the stories of Wendover and Aylesbury and even Wycombe, all demonstrate a remarkable ability at times for co-operation between the various groups, despite their strongly-felt differences. The story of Buckinghamshire suffragists and suffragettes supports the view that many women belonged, often at the same time, to more than one suffrage group, if not to several. The experience of campaigning for the vote gave these women a common bond which was hard to ignore, despite differences of opinions over tactics, or over whether to seek adult suffrage or a more limited electoral qualification.

---

[1] Eg. *SBFP* 29th April 1909 and 19th November 1909; *BE* 9th August 1912: 'Condemnation of Violence'.

Chapter 3: Chesham and Buckinghamshire's WSPU Branch

'When a man is responsible for having women knocked about and physically injured by others... he deserves a whipping... It is because I held Mr Churchill guilty... that I determined to punish him in the only way that was open to me.'
- Mr Hugh Franklin in *Votes for Women*, 9th December 1910.

THE earliest indication of local people in Chesham pressing for votes for women came in 1908, some time before most other places in the county. The High Wycombe campaign was already well underway by this stage, but Chesham stands alone as being scene of the only branch of the Women's Social and Political Union in the county. Not only can Chesham justifiably claim its very own 'suffragette', this town was also the second home of arguably the most infamous male sympathiser with the suffragette cause. But this story starts in 1908, when a short article appeared in the *Examiner*: 'We hear it on good authority that there is a scheme on foot to form a Suffragette Party in Chesham, and that a lady residing in the town has been invited to become the secretary of the party. Further developments are awaited with interest'.[1]

From subsequent newspaper reports, it is likely that the woman being referred to here is Mrs Emily Brandon of Khartoum Avenue (now Eskdale Avenue). It also seems likely that it took Mrs Brandon several years before a fledgling branch of the WSPU was established in the town. Not surprising perhaps that this campaign was often less dramatic compared to events which unfolded in Aylesbury and High Wycombe, for example. However, the unique developments of this campaign give a fascinating insight into the experience of a suffragette in a small provincial town.

The first time the issue is more widely raised in the *Examiner* is in the overview of 1908, under the title, 'The Year of Women Suffrage'.[2] The summary gives some details of suffragette protests surrounding the House of Commons in February, June and October of that year. Based on Mrs Brandon's own part in subsequent demonstrations, it is possible she may have already been involved in some of these London protests.

---

[1] *BE*, 6th March 1908.
[2] *BE*, 1st January 1909.

Eskdale Avenue, which led to Khartoum Avenue, where Chesham's suffragette Mrs Emily Brandon lived, 1907-1912. Courtesy of Peter Hawkes

For whatever reason, Mrs Brandon did not join in trying to evade the 1911 census along with some of her fellow suffragettes. As a result, it is possible to glean the following information. Mrs Brandon appears as Mrs Emily Charlotte McMahon Brandon on the census form. Having married Albert Brandon, an upholsterer from Tring, in 1900 or 1901, they moved to 'Bankside' in Chesham in 1907. From something she probably wrote later, Mrs Brandon ran a small business of her own, although this is not recorded on the census form. Her decision to retain her maiden name, quite unusual at the time, shows both her independence of mind and her desire to celebrate her Irish ancestry. An Irish exile born in London, Mrs Brandon probably joined the WSPU after going to hear one of the Pankhursts soon after they moved their headquarters to London in 1906.[1]

It seems that during 1908 and 1909 Mrs Brandon may well have been visiting house to house, trying to drum up support. From other events in the area, it is clear that the issue was becoming a live one. In December 1908, for example, an evening is devoted to the question of 'Should Women have Votes?' at The Lee Guild Debating Society. The meeting was chaired by the

---

[1] I am indebted to Paulin Meier for some of this information.

well-known local businessman and landowner, Arthur Liberty, who had launched the first 'Liberty's' shop in London in 1875. Mr Liberty went on to become a prominent figure in a local anti-suffrage group. That evening the 80 members of the Guild who took part in this debate voted by a large majority against the proposal brought by Mr Elliot Pearson.[1] This is just one indication of what an uphill struggle it was for people like Mrs Brandon, sometimes to even win a hearing among the local population.

The following year was significant for one other key figure in Chesham's brush with the suffragettes. This area of the Chilterns had become Hugh Franklin's second home, ever since his family bought a cottage and poultry farm with 25 acres in 1889, the same year the railway came to Chesham. The Franklins, a wealthy Jewish family with interests in banking and publishing, developed this plot into Chartridge Lodge. Hugh probably spent many childhood summers in Chartridge before 1908, when he went to Caius College, Cambridge, initially to study Engineering.

Hugh's move to university prompted a rebellion against his Jewish faith and a shift towards more radical politics. In short order, the following year, Hugh became a member of the Labour party and also joined the swelling ranks of those passionate about gaining votes for women. This was a result of having gone to hear Mrs Emmeline Pankhurst speak at the Queen's Hall, London, along with an undergraduate friend, Albert Lowys.[2]

Around this time, Hugh started a project to build a ground-breaking new aeroplane, with Albert and two other engineering students 'in the field opposite Chartridge Lodge during spring vacation'. This project must have been prematurely abandoned in favour of Hugh's new passion. He campaigned for women to get the vote, by selling newspapers and chalking pavements in London, Cambridge and also in Buckinghamshire. Franklin helped out with the August 1909 open-air meetings in the area. But he was more active at Cambridge. Having joined the male equivalent of the WSPU, the Men's Political Union in February 1910, he was disciplined by the college authorities for his attempts to publicise a meeting for Mrs Pankhurst at the Cambridge Guildhall in May 1910.[3]

Chesham was one of the suffragette's natural targets for their 1909 summer campaign. 'The Suffragette movement has reached Chesham' is how the local newspaper announced it. The evening open-air meeting in the

---

[1] *BE*, 18th December 1908. Other speakers mentioned: Mr May, Mr George Lewington, Miss Britton and Miss Marjorie Griffin.

[2] Hugh Franklin and Elsie Duval's Papers, Autobiographical Notes, 1911.

[3] Crawford - *WSM*, pp. 229-30; Doughan, David - *DNB*, 2004-10.

Broadway certainly attracted a 'tremendous crowd'.[1] No mention is made of Mrs Brandon or of Mr Franklin in this article, but they may have both played a role in helping to organise the visit.

The following year brought a significant breakthrough. A local suffragette was invited to write an anonymous column in the *Examiner* newspaper. Other local newspapers also demonstrated that they were sympathetic to the women's struggle: for example, the editorial in the *Free Press* of 15th July, 1910. However, the *Examiner* was the only newspaper in the county to give a suffragette such an opportunity. Frank David Hiddleston had been appointed Editor of the newspaper in 1904.[2] While 'FDH' or 'Spec' was critical of the more extreme activities of the suffragettes, he displayed sympathy for the women's struggle, as well as for the wider campaign for universal suffrage.[3]

Seven articles appeared in the paper, between January and July 1910, with various titles: 'The Importance of the Vote - Do the women of Chesham want it?', 'Why every woman should be a Suffragette' and the last three are simply entitled, 'Chat by "Suffragette"'. There is a strong case to be made that the writer is Mrs Brandon, who on the 1911 Census, retained her Irish maiden name, McMahon. It emerges in one of the later articles that the writer is of Irish descent. There are few other personal details. But, in other articles in the paper, Mrs Brandon's home is the only one mentioned as being used for a women's suffrage meeting in the town. This, coupled with the fact that she is the only prominent local person closely associated with the suffragettes, makes it reasonable to conclude that she penned these words herself, with a little help from the WSPU propaganda machine.

Early in her first article, based on her experience of house to house visitation, Mrs Brandon makes an honest assessment of the balance of opinion locally. She estimates that 20 per cent are against women's suffrage, with only 10 per cent in favour and the rest indifferent. It is no wonder this lone campaigner found it so difficult to establish a WSPU branch in the town. This also helps to explain why the local anti-suffrage campaign was able to quickly muster so much support in later years.

Several common objections to women getting the vote were noted in Mrs Brandon's opening article. First up was the common cry, and the bane of many a suffragette, that 'A woman's place was in the home'. Mrs Brandon responds particularly fiercely to this statement on the lips of two local

---

[1] *BE*, 27th August 1909.
[2] Fletcher, Keith - *Chesham People*.
[3] *BE*, 29th May 1908, Editorial.

tradesmen: 'When I had called at these shops I had particularly noticed what the wives of these men were doing, if not all the work, best part of it. What were these women doing in these shops? Their place was in the home, their husbands said so!'[1]

Other objections were that, 'A woman had no place in the political sphere'; or that by entering the political sphere women would lose the love and respect of their husbands. More personally, one woman had commented, 'Yes, I do endorse all that you say, but my husband is opposed to it, and I dare not show any sympathy'.

The final objection Mrs Brandon mentions is the militant tactics of the suffragettes Locals had cited the recent Bermondsey election incident, when a vote counter was injured by militant suffragettes using vitriol to sabotage the count. She responds by asserting: 'I have heard many an ardent suffragist denouncing the militant tactics, who would never have heard of votes for women... had it not been for the very original methods of the WSPU'. This writer betrays an impatience with the non-militant suffragists, shared by many Pankhurst devotees: '... very little would be accomplished if our women were to invite, say a few friends to tea, "Just to have a chat, dear, on Women's Suffrage"'. However, this kind of approach is one she herself employs later on, perhaps out of desperation.[2]

In common with her fellow suffragettes, Mrs Brandon saw attack as the best form of defence. She went on to condemn the unbalanced nature of the legal system and the disgraceful treatment of suffragette prisoners by the government in not allowing them political status. Mrs Brandon then quoted Mrs Pankhurst:

'The vote first of all is a symbol, secondly a safeguard, and thirdly an instrument. It is a symbol of freedom, a symbol of citizenship... It is a safeguard of all those liberties which it symbolises... an instrument, something with which you can get a great many more things than our forefathers who fought for the vote ever realised as possible to get with it'.[3]

She concluded with the words, '...while you have a representative government for men, you have a despotic government for women', and urges other women to join her in this worthy fight for their rights.

---

[1] *BE*, 14th January 1910.
[2] *BE* 7th October 1910.
[3] *BE*, 14th January 1910.

In her second article the following week, Mrs Brandon went to great length in detailing the way present laws were unjustly weighted against women, particularly in regard to marriage, divorce, child maintenance and inheritance. Poor pay and little advancement for women is another injustice she highlights. It seems she is quoting from a book on women's suffrage by Arnold Harris Matthew, one of many publications well thumbed by suffragette campaigners. But the piece finishes on a more passionate note as she turns to the attitude of the present Liberal government and Prime Minister Asquith in particular:

> 'The Prime Minister says before women shall have the vote, the majority of men must show they support the proposal. But... our claim would be good although not a man in the country were with us. Did anyone wait before giving votes to men to see if the women approved of it? ... The present Prime Minister it is quite obvious will not give us the vote until he is badgered into it.'[1]

These comments demonstrate the personal animosity already existing between Asquith and the suffragettes. They also show the difficulty the women's suffrage movement faced, in that they were aware that even the majority of female opinion was not necessarily with them at this time. Here, as other suffragettes did, Mrs Brandon insists that demonstrating a majority in favour of electoral reform was seen as superfluous by William Gladstone in 1884. These comments also reflect the thinking of the Pankhursts, who had already convinced themselves that ever more dramatic means of protest were the only way they were going to eventually change the minds of their political leaders.

The third article again shows the 'mixed reception' this particular suffragette is getting on the doorsteps of Chesham. Mrs Brandon describes herself as being 'disheartened' after another day canvassing people, feeling that, 'prejudice was over-ruling commonsense' and that few people seemed to understand the movement. While there were those who apparently signed her petition with 'very little hesitation' and those who welcomed her warmly, the more common reaction she witnessed that day ranged from amusement and horror to being told that she should be ashamed of herself.

At one point she is taunted by a, 'small army of very dirty, disreputable children', who form a mock procession behind her, shouting, 'votes for women!' The incident reveals a significant level of awareness in the town

---

[1] *BE*, 21st January 1910.

regarding the movement, if young children are able to readily identify what she is doing from what she is wearing and to copy suffragette behaviour. Mrs Brandon responds rather pompously by reflecting:

'What a pity the mothers of these children were not suffragettes; had they been those mites, instead of tramping the damp and dreary streets, would have been washed and brushed up and put into their little beds quite two hours before and those ragged garments neatly repaired. You know friends, a suffragette makes a speciality of the training and educating of children.'[1]

Mrs Brandon then describes encountering an unemployed man just outside the police station, who refuses to sign her petition and then challenges her with the familiar charge that, '...too many men are workless because women are willing to work for next to nothing'. However, as someone who runs her own employment agency, she has a ready response. She places the blame for his situation with his own sex: 'You have made it a tradition that women of your own class shall be overworked and underpaid and then you dare complain'. This dejected man is left with this ringing call, 'You men have got every good thing by standing together and we want you to help us instead of hindering us. If you won't help us for the sake of justice, do it for the sake of your own bread and butter'.

It is easy to see the truth of this woman's declaration that, 'I was never more proud in my life than when I wore the colours for the first time'. This is a reference to the WSPU colours of purple, white and green, which she may have worn at an earlier suffragette event in London, or perhaps the previous summer in Chesham. Since the previous article, Mrs Brandon claims to have been inundated with enquiries for more information. She writes,

'Any number of women have told me that they had no idea what votes for women really meant until they read that article. They thought women really wanted to sit in Parliament and take the management of affairs out of the hands of the men. As I have endeavoured to explain before, we women do not want to rule the country... but what we do want is to be consulted in questions appertaining to woman and also help to make laws which apply to woman.'[2]

---

[1] *BE*, 11th February 1910.
[2] Ibid.

However much interest there has been, it is clear from the next paragraph, the difficulties she faces in persuading others to don the WSPU colours:

> 'No woman, if she becomes a Suffragette, need neglect any single one of her home duties. She is not bound to march in processions, carry flags, wave banners, assault Cabinet Ministers, break windows, have tussles with burly policemen or go to prison. She need do nothing of the sort... yet take an interest in our cause and be an ardent supporter. All are welcome, old or young, single or married, rich or poor, dairymaids or duchesses.'

The second half of the piece under the heading, 'Why every woman should be a Suffragette' appeared in March. It deals largely with the issue of domestic abuse and the inability of women to get a just response from the existing legal system. The question of greater financial equality in marriage soon follows. Mrs Brandon makes the suggestion that, '... there should be a law to compel every man to contribute a fair per cent of his income to the upkeep of his home, wife and children'.[1] The article concludes:

> 'The Suffrage movement has sprung up to champion the cause of freedom based on equity. Everyone knows that partnership in mentality is almost the surest way to improve relations between husbands and wives. It is this ideal which is writ large over "votes for women"'.

The next article does not appear until June. It is not clear whether this signifies a lessening interest on behalf of the newspaper, or simply that Mrs Brandon has been too busy to write more frequently. On this occasion her mood is much more positive and she declares that '... victory for the women's vote is now in sight'.[2] She mentions Lady Eva McLaren's 'Women's Charter', introduced to the House of Commons in March by Sir Charles McLaren, which detailed nine specific grievances among the campaigners for women's enfranchisement.

The mystery columnist is most excited by the prospect of a Conciliation Bill being debated by Parliament, which will feature a modest measure to include £10 women householders as Parliamentary voters. This, she asserts, is viewed by the WSPU as just a beginning, a way of establishing the principle of female enfranchisement. She expresses the hope that the

---

[1] *BE*, 11th March 1910.
[2] *BE*, 3rd June 1910.

government will not prevent the Bill's passage and so 'frustrate' the current truce between the WSPU and the Liberal government. Then, having briefly touched on the experience of her employment agency and the variety of people she has met through it, Mrs Brandon returns to a familiar theme of husbands needing to give their wives a fair allowance.

Mrs Brandon continued with this theme in her next 'Chat by "Suffragette". She mentions an issue, raised in Lady McLaren's 'Women's Charter' which has since been established in law, but in 1910 was far from being the case: 'A wife who devotes her whole time to house-keeping and the care of the children, should have a claim upon her husband during his life and upon his estate upon his death'.[1] On education, Mrs Brandon also champions Lady McLaren's principle that, '... the amount of money spent upon each girl... in elementary schools should be equal to that expended on each boy'. However, it is her final statement in this article which stands out. It seems that her frustration at the lack of practical support from other women in the town is beginning to tell. She writes:

> 'I know many (ladies) in this town and yet "NOT ONE" will come forward and give a hand, and help fight this heartbreaking battle. To stand outside the Union and let other women do the fighting argues to my way of thinking a lack of self respect and personal dignity - I am reminded, however, of a contributor to one of our well-known weeklies, who advises one to put it mildly or not at all, so I think under the circumstances I had better say no more.'

After campaigning in Chesham for possibly over two years, Mrs Brandon has yet to see even one other woman join her in the struggle. This indicates the massive inertia weighing against significant social change. More than that, it reveals not only how costly it must have been to publicly support the suffragettes. The cause of this, despite the suffragettes' formidable expenditure on propaganda, may have been a disconnect with ordinary people, partly or largely due to the WSPU's extreme tactics. However, the WSPU had not finished in its attempts to win over public opinion. In May, Mrs Brandon used the pages of this newspaper to invite local women to join her at a London demonstration. She encouraged the women of Chesham to 'wear white dresses, walking length, and carry

---

[1] *BE*, 17th June 1910.

bouquets of flowers'.[1] It is unclear whether anyone from the town joined her that day.

However, the final article in Mrs Brandon's series is full of breathless excitement as it centres on her description of the part she played the 'great demonstration' in London on 18th June.[2] On that Saturday, Mrs Brandon joined with an estimated 10,000 other suffragettes from across Great Britain and the world. Together they converged on the Albert Hall, coming from the Embankment, Whitehall and Claridges. This event coincided with the end of the formal period of mourning for King Edward VII and a carnival atmosphere was created by the display of 700 colourful banners, flowers being held by each suffragette, and by the forty marching bands which took part. Here was a multi-faceted army of women in earnest.

The seriousness of this joyful occasion was particularly evident from the presence of over 600 women, all wearing white, representing the number of prison terms already served by suffragettes. Their banner read, 'From Prison to Citizenship'. Charlotte Marsh, later to be imprisoned in Buckinghamshire, carried the WSPU colours at the head of the procession, to honour her recent 3 month imprisonment with force feeding.

Had there been a similar march in 1912, Mrs Brandon could herself have been included in this part of the procession. However, she was particularly proud to be a banner bearer for the Irish contingent that day (see Appendix 5).

The marchers crowded into an overflowing Albert Hall to hear Mrs Pankhurst and Lord Lytton, who was chair of the Conciliation Committee which had drafted the new Bill for Parliament. After the speakers, a collection of over £5,000 was received.

Mrs Brandon also described the two deputations of women who visited the Prime Minister shortly after this march. Mrs Fawcett of the NUWSS was one of the key representatives of the women that day. A summary of what she is reported to have said to Asquith is recorded by Mrs Brandon:

'(Mrs Fawcett) reminded him of his promise made at the Albert Hall that the new government ought to have an opportunity of expressing an opinion upon Women's Suffrage. She continued: "Great hopes have been raised by the introduction of this particular Bill, and I know there will be great disappointment if it is not carried...".'[3]

---

[1] *BE*, 19th May 1910: 'Women's Day',
[2] *BE*, 1st July 1910.
[3] Ibid.

It is clear that Mrs Brandon's hopes at least have been raised, even if others in the movement were far more sceptical. Lady Eva MacLaren, also part of the deputation to the Prime Minister, challenged him to ensure the Bill had a second reading in Parliament. Then referring to the demonstration on 18th June MacLaren said that, 'I doubt that we have all quite realised how strong these 10,000 women have at heart the cause which they advocate.' This particular quote provides the spur for the outpouring of Mrs Brandon's own feelings about this historic opportunity:

'No friends! I do not think one-sixteenth of the population have realised how much this cause is to us. Some of us have lost the love of father, mother, brothers, sisters, sweethearts... Women have shown their demand for the vote by petitions, by great public meetings, by willingness to undergo imprisonment for the sake of the cause. These are the only methods available for the unenfranchised.'

While anticipating imminent victory, her closing remark is as ominous as it is prophetic: 'If the Government should thwart or postpone that victory now, "God help them in the times that are coming"'.

The Asquith government did allow a second reading of the Conciliation Bill, which was passed by a significant majority. But towards the end of the year, the Bill was sent to Committee and therefore shelved. This provoked a further outburst of protests and WSPU law-breaking, which possibly explains why Mrs Brandon is not given further opportunity for writing a column in the *Examiner*. However, she does adopt different tactics and in October 1910 is reported to have held a 'drawing-room meeting' in her home. After a debate, chaired by Miss Katherine Raleigh of Uxbridge and attended by both suffragists and 'antis', the decision is taken to launch a WSPU branch in the town. The short article concludes with an appeal for any ladies interested to get in touch with the 'secretary' at 'Bankside' and that, 'A speaker and leader are urgently needed.'[1]

At no stage is there any indication of Mr Brandon's attitude towards his wife's views. But it is hard to avoid the conclusion that he must have had some sympathy, even if he did not entirely agree with what Mrs Brandon ended up doing for the cause.

Later in 1910, public opinion became even more polarised and the political climate turned darker. Hugh Franklin was caught up in this febrile

---

[1] *BE*, 7th October 1910.

atmosphere. Having been one of the key organisers for the London demonstration in June, he took the WSPU call for 'Deeds not Words' very personally. Mr Franklin was arrested on 18th November, along with many others during the infamous 'Black Friday' protests in London. He was released without charge on this occasion, but the scenes he witnessed that day were to change the whole course of his life.

One incident at Downing Street seems to have particularly incensed Hugh Franklin that day. One of the WSPU leaders, Mrs Anne Cobden Sanderson, was there, 'faint from exhaustion' from the struggle between the suffragettes and the police, according to Franklin's account.[1] She is immediately led away under protest, on the direct orders of the then Home Secretary, Mr Winston Churchill. Franklin overheard Churchill telling a Police Inspector to 'Turn that woman away!' Most likely well aware that Mrs Cobden Sanderson was an old family friend of the Churchills, Hugh felt this to be high-handed and ungentlemanly conduct on behalf of the Home Secretary.

Winston Churchill's remark that day, coupled with other reasons he lists in his *Votes for Women* article, provoked a strong personal animosity in Hugh Franklin. He held Churchill responsible for injuries sustained by the suffragettes and tried to take the matter up with Churchill in person. At some point Hugh bought a dog whip. And in the next few days, Hugh Franklin pursued Winston Churchill first to his club, The Athenaeum, and then to a speaking engagement in Bradford. On 26th November, Franklin was ejected from the meeting at Bradford, along with a friend, Mr Hawkins, who had his leg badly broken after he was thrown twice down some stairs, probably by some over-zealous Liberal stewards. Afterwards, apparently by accident, Hugh found himself on the same train to London as the Home Secretary. He took this opportunity to try to attack the Home Secretary. Seizing Churchill by the throat, he cried out as he raised his dog whip, 'Take that you (dirty) cur!'[2] He was restrained by Inspector John Parker and Sergeant Sandercock who were travelling with Churchill, and arrested.

Mr Franklin's court case received nationwide publicity and was reported in the *Examiner*.[3] Hugh was sentenced to 6 weeks imprisonment in Pentonville. As his appeal to be treated as a political prisoner was refused, he engaged in his first hunger strike and was force-fed. The next year, Franklin was arrested a second time, on 8th March, for trying to break the windows of

---

[1] *VW*, 9th December 1910.
[2] *BE*, 9th December 1910
[3] *BE*, 2nd and 9th December 1910.

Churchill's London home, again being imprisoned and again resorting to the hunger strike.

The story of the 'votes for women' campaign in Chesham is at this point hard to follow, as there are no surviving copies of the *Examiner* for 1911. This was, however, the year of the first women's suffrage caravan tour of the 'John Hampden county'.[1] From 5th to 19th July, Miss Muriel Matters and Violet Tillard in the WTRL caravan, held an itinerant campaign, which included three meetings in Chesham. The tour finished with a garden meeting on 18th somewhere in Chesham, when the Secretary of the WTRL, Mrs Kineton Parkes, motored over to Chesham with Mrs Fagan. The WTRL committee subsequently agreed that the two women had, 'done excellent work for the cause'.

The most notable development for 1911 was that Chesham's own suffragette campaigner, Mrs Brandon, was herself sent to prison. This is revealed in a snippet of news in the *Herald*. On 21st November, 1911, Mrs Brandon took part in a demonstration outside the Houses of Parliament. This was specifically to protest that the government was now proposing that the Conciliation Bill from last year be replaced with a Bill for Manhood Suffrage. This legislation, it was suggested, could be easily amended the following year, to include women.

Arrested along with 220 other women, Mrs Brandon was charged with obstruction. At Bow Street Magistrates Court, she was fined five shillings, which she refused to pay on principle consistent with other convicted suffragettes. Her brief comments to the court are recorded: 'The Manhood Suffrage Bill is an insult to the women of England and I did it as a protest'.[2]

Not long after her spell in prison, Mrs Brandon was busy organising another suffragette campaign in Chesham. In recognition of her imprisonment, this campaign involved some higher profile speakers. Mrs Cobden Sanderson visited Chesham in February 1912, leading a small team of suffragettes, including Mrs Katharine Gatty, Miss Amy Hicks and Annette Jacobs, returning to the town after her visit in 1909.[3] Mrs Gatty, described as a 'lady journalist' was a close friend of Emily Wilding Davison.[4] Miss Amy Hicks had recently rejoined the WSPU, after a period in the WFL and was a member of the committee of the WTRL.[5] Mrs Cobden Sanderson had been

---

[1] WTRL Committee Minute Book, 1909-13, 9th June – 18th July 1911.
[2] *BH*, 9th December 1911.
[3] *BE*, 2nd February 1912.
[4] Crawford - *WSM,* pp. 241-2.
[5] Crawford - *WSM*, p. 285.

one of the first prominent defectors from the NUWSS into the ranks of the WSPU in 1906.[1] She also joined the WTRL when it was launched in 1909, and was perhaps responsible for first suggesting the 1911 census boycott. Her visit to Chesham came shortly before her participation in the Aylesbury prison protests, under the banner of the WTRL, partly to express her support for Amy Hicks during her imprisonment there.

Two day-time, outdoor meetings were held in the Broadway, while the Chesham Co-operative Equity Hall hosted a meeting on Friday 9th. This was followed by an evening meeting at the Corn Exchange in the market square, which concluded the weekend's events. The *Examiner* reporter described the series of meetings as 'successful', although the opening evening only saw what was called a 'fair assembly'.[2]

Chesham's Co-operative Society building in the Broadway (long, two storey building, centre right), c. 1910. The Equity Hall, scene of several meetings for women's suffrage, was behind the semi-circular window on the first floor. Broadway Baptist Church, were Rev J.H. Brooksbank was minister is opposite. Courtesy of Colin Seabright / Keith Fletcher

---

[1] Crawford - *WSM*, pp. 615-7.
[2] BE, 16th February 1912.

Mrs Gatty spoke first, with a witty account of her imprisonment. Then Mrs Sanderson gave a speech which listed three reasons for campaigning for the vote. Firstly, because, 'the time was ripe... In Ireland and India there was a demand for representation with taxation and the Government was giving heed to the cry. Then why slight the women in their demands?' Secondly, because, consistent with her fellow suffragettes and contrary to popular opinion, 'she believed in the home'. At this point, Mrs Sanderson mentioned how her work as a Poor Law Guardian in London often inspired her to see a change in the, 'present industrial system'. She described a meeting just the previous day, when her fellow male Guardians had expected a woman with six children to be earning enough to support her family. Thirdly, she was convinced that now was the time for women to be allowed to play a part in administering, and if necessary, changing the laws of the land.

At the final meeting in the Corn Exchange, Miss Hicks gave a 'witty' and 'pertinent' speech. The reporter mentioned that several of the women taking part had 'suffered imprisonment', including, '...Mrs Brandon, who made the local arrangements and whose persistence and energy went largely towards the success of the campaign.' It was also stated that the aim of the meetings was to establish a branch of the WSPU in the town.

It is possible that a branch of the WSPU was established directly after this meeting. However, not long after this a different women's suffrage group entered the fray in Chesham. The fact that three different women's suffrage organisations arranged three separate meetings to discuss the same theme in the town that summer, shows both what a hot topic this was for the public at the time, and also how keen both suffragists and suffragettes were to make capital of this public groundswell.

In May the Church League for Women's Suffrage publicised a meeting at the Equity Hall, with Miss Canning of London due to speak on, 'the White slave traffic and rescue work in connection with Women's enfranchisement'.[1] 'White slave traffic' was the polite way of referring to prostitution. This development in Chesham's story, signals not only that there were many other women and men in the town sympathetic to the women's suffrage movement, but also indicates a new phase in the growth of the movement.

The three years before the outbreak of war witnessed an upsurge in the extreme tactics of the suffragettes, as well as a corresponding growth in anti-suffrage activity. They should also be seen as a period when a groundswell of people attempted to reclaim the middle ground in the debate. Many of these

---

[1] *BE*, 3rd May 1912.

people were from the churches and were aiming to explore the moral and spiritual dimensions of the movement.

While there may not have been any CLWS branches formed in the county, there were certainly significant numbers in each Buckinghamshire town who simultaneously supported the bigger suffrage societies, as well as either the CLWS or its Free Church equivalent. Indeed, the formation of a FCLWS branch in Beaconsfield in 1913, reflects this development in the wider campaign.[1]

A sympathetic campaign against prostitution, viewing the women caught up in the trade as victims of male lust and conspiracy, had been evident since the latter part of the nineteenth century, led largely by Mrs Josephine Butler. In later years the journalist, Mr W. T. Stead, highlighted the evils of prostitution. However, in April 1912, just weeks before the meeting in Chesham, he was among those who died at the sinking of the *Titanic*. So, coinciding with impending Parliamentary debates on this issue in 1912, there may have been a growing urge within the churches to carry on the work Stead had done. His name was mentioned by speakers at the various meetings on this theme and cheered by the large crowds attending.

At the CLWS meeting on 7th May, Chesham resident, Mrs Louisa Matilda Page, introduced the first speaker that evening. Mrs Page was known for her campaigning in the town on a number of issues. Married to Herbert Page, Managing Director of a local printing and publishing firm, she lived with her husband along Stanley Avenue in 1911, subsequently moving to 'Lyndhurst' at the top of White Hill. Both Louisa and Herbert had been born in St Pancras, London. Louisa's obituary stated that she 'was in keen and active sympathy with those of advanced thought who were looking to a new world and were not afraid to take a stand against some of the things which were generally accepted, but which they regarded as wrong.'[2] Her campaigning work, often through letters written to the local papers under the initials of 'L.M.P.' ranged widely from temperance and religious matters, but clearly included the struggle to gain votes for women.

The first speaker, Mrs Webb, spoke about 'this great evil' and the legislation being debated by Parliament. It is not clear whether this is a Mrs Webb from Chesham, of which there were several, or perhaps a case of a journalist mis-spelling a name, as Mrs Webbe spoke at a later meeting on the same subject.

---

[1] *Free Church Suffrage Times*, November 1913, pp. 78-79.
[2] *BE*, 16th March 1934, obit.

At this first meeting on the subject, Mrs Webb spoke at length about the groups of men and women who would 'lurk round the railway stations in large towns' and would profit by luring young women into prostitution. She drew the obvious point that female enfranchisement would allow them a say in framing legislation regarding the widespread abuse of women. Miss Canning then spoke about women and sweated labour, another issue often close to the hearts of churchwomen, with its echo of the previous fight against the slave trade. After some questions, one of the leading Chesham suffragists, Mrs Samuel proposed a vote of thanks to the speakers. [1]

Mrs Mary Samuel, always referred to in the papers as Mrs Denton Samuel, lived at 'Hildesheim' on Eskdale Avenue and ran a school and kindergarten at Khartoum Avenue.[2] It is quite likely she knew Mrs Brandon and while she may have been influenced by her fellow suffragist, Mrs Samuel does not appear to have joined the WSPU. It appears she never wavered from her commitment to the constitutional methods of the NUWSS. She is the woman most likely to be carrying the Chesham bannerette in the photograph of the NUWSS pilgrims at West Wycombe (see Chapter 10). Mary's husband, Benjamin Samuel, was Head Postmaster in the town and they both came originally from Liverpool. (1911 England and Wales Census)

This May meeting arranged by the CLWS provided the spur for two more much bigger meetings. These aroused the interest of a much wider section of the town's population than previously, combining the efforts of local supporters of both the WSPU and also the NUWSS. Chesham was unique in the county for having three women's suffrage organisations actively campaigning at the same time.

Later that same month, Monday 20th, Miss Muriel Matters was invited by the Mid-Bucks NUWSS to speak at Chesham's Equity Hall. A wider social and geographical representation at the meeting is specifically mentioned in the newspaper report, including local landowners, Mr and Mrs Wm. F. Lowndes, along with Mr and Mrs Stafford-Webber, Mrs Donkin and Mrs Gamlin. Also attending were Miss Alice and Miss Hilda Webb, close relations of Mr George and Mary Webb who owned a large brush factory in the town. Equally significant was the presence of members of the nearest WSPU branch in Chorleywood, like Mrs Offer.[3]

These and other interested women and men were mentioned alongside Mrs Brandon and the Misses Williams. One of these Williams sisters was to

---

[1] *BE*, 10th May 1912.
[2] *BE*, 14th January 1910.
[3] *BE*, 17th May 1912 - Mrs Offer chaired a meeting of the Chorleywood WSPU.

play her part in the next instalment of the local WSPU story. Miss Kathleen A. Williams was the youngest daughter of a clergyman, John Alfred Williams, who had previously had livings in Worcestershire and Bedfordshire. Kathleen appears to have been living with her widowed mother, Mary Williams in Amy Mill House probably since 1908, following her father's death.[1] Miss Williams may have been Mrs Brandon's first and perhaps only 'convert' to the WSPU cause in the town.

Miss Catherine Courtauld, the Secretary of the Mid-Bucks NUWSS branch, living near Great Missenden, was joined on the platform by Chesham suffragists, Mrs Page, Mrs Samuel and Miss Barrett. Miss Courtauld opened the evening with remarks about the history and extent of the non-militant NUWSS. She went on to directly challenge anti-suffragist fears by asserting that 'She did not believe they could have a strong and healthy nation unless every citizen felt they had some influence in the life of that nation'.[2] Miss Courtauld finished by moving the resolution which Miss Matters was due to speak about: 'That this meeting considers woman's suffrage an urgent reform, and calls upon the Government to enfranchise women this session'.

Miss Muriel Matters, an Australian suffragette, started by putting the question of 'votes for women' into a wider context of a national and international spiritual movement towards freedom. She quoted Ibsen's play, The Doll's House, to which some suffragists attributed their 'conversion' to the cause.

Continuing by teasingly challenging Lord Cromer's assertion that, 'if women had the vote, they would have a revolution', Miss Matters called these scare tactics 'nonsense'. Muriel went on: 'The revolution had taken place years ago when they first educated women, and Lord Cromer, like Rip Van Winkle, had been asleep and had not noticed'. It is easy to see why Muriel was such an engaging and popular speaker.

Following this humorous aside she drives home the serious point of her overall theme that 'Many women in England were in the same state as the slaves in the United States, when Wilberforce went to inquire into their condition... From a political point of view (women) were in a state of slavery, because they were taxed without their consent and legislated for without their point of view being considered'. More specifically, she urged that Parliament should pass the current Criminal Law Amendment Bill, which would allow, 'anyone to arrest at once, anyone suspected of that trade,

---

[1] I am indebted to Bill Templeton for this information.
[2] *BE*, 24th May 1912.

without the need of going for a warrant, during which time they could escape'.

The fact that at the end of the meeting the resolution on votes for women was passed with only one dissentient, suggests that there was a much wider sympathy for an immediate measure to enfranchise women than indicated by Mrs Brandon's previous experience of campaigning for the WSPU.

Mrs Brandon followed up this meeting with another on the same theme at the Corn Exchange in July, which attracted an even bigger audience. Moreover, the publicising of this meeting reveals a WSPU branch now in existence in the town. Miss K.A. Williams, of Amy Mill House, wrote a letter to the Town Council, encouraging them to 'give a lead to public opinion and attend the meeting' and signed herself as WSPU 'Honorary Secretary'.[1] Coupled with a later letter in which Mrs Brandon signs herself as 'Honorary Organiser, pro-tem', this certainly suggests the beginnings of a local WSPU committee, even if Mrs Brandon is still awaiting someone to step into her new self-designated role. The WSPU were not hampered by any constitutional rules, like those of the WFL or NUWSS.

The short article detailing the response of the Council to Miss Williams' letter shows a variety of responses, including the suggestion of sending along the Town Clerk to represent the Council. Councillor Reynolds, who loudly asserted that everyone on the Council was in sympathy with the objects of the White Slave Traffic meeting, seemed to imply that it was not necessary for most of the councillors to attend. However, the Chairman of the Council and JP, Mr F. E. Howard, countered this and concluded the discussion by saying that 'he hoped it would be possible for many members of the Council to be present and support him'.[2]

An open letter was apparently circulated before the meeting, which stated, 'It is not a question of whether you are a Conservative or a Liberal, suffragist or anti, militant or non-militant sympathiser, but whether you approve of a right or a wrong thing'.[3] This all adds up the local WSPU's clearest attempt to rally people to a moral crusade and bring persuasion to bear on the issue of votes for women, instead of the increasingly common approach of confrontation and militant action.

The report of the meeting itself mentions the hall being 'full to the doors' and several people having to stand by the entrance. The Chairman,

---

[1] *BE*, 21st June 1912.
[2] Ibid.
[3] *BE*, 28th June, 1912.

Mr F. E. Howard made a rallying cry of his opening remarks. He said that, 'Men of every shade of religious and political opinion were united with women in prosecuting the campaign... (to) ... wipe out one of the stains, which marred our fair name as a nation'.[1] He went on to introduce the two speakers. The first was Mrs A.J. Webbe, of the National Vigilance Association, an organisation that was devoted to keeping vulnerable women out of prostitution. The second speaker was Mr Shallard, a Fabian lecturer, and had been a member of the National Administrative Council of the Independent Labour Party from its early days.

Mrs Webbe laid out the case for a change to the existing law and asked the rhetorical question, 'what connection had the woman suffrage question with the campaign against the White Slave Traffic?' She answered by asserting that, 'If women had co-operated with men in making the laws no such laws would have been possible, and if women had equal voting power with men at the present time there would be no difficulty in passing the Bill now before the House'.

Making the connection between women's low income and the temptations to prostitution, Mr Shallard threw out a challenge to the government to increase the pay of its women employees, specifically mentioning the poor wages of the female office workers in the War Office under Lord Haldane.

The meeting agreed unanimously to the resolution that Parliament pass the current Bill designed to help the police take action against those who profited from prostitution. The Rev. J.H. Brooksbank of Broadway Baptist Church, having been asked to move the vote of thanks, took this opportunity to declare that, '...he had been a supporter of women suffrage from early manhood'. Rev. Brooksbank was actively involved in a number of social issues in the town, including temperance, protecting vulnerable bar-maids, as well as supporting local trade unions. His wife, Annie, took part in meetings of the local Liberal Party. And when appointed President of Chesham's Baptist Women's League in 1909, shortly after the launching of the national BWL network, Mrs Brooksbank talked of its aim: 'the enfranchisement of Baptist women'.[2] The immediate context of this remark seems to be in reference to women's work within the churches, but a wider implication is clearly also intended, as she disavows 'militant means'.

---

[1] *BE*, 5th July 1912.
[2] *BE*, 19th February 1909.

It is possible to conclude from these brief remarks, that the work of the WSPU in Chesham was at least responsible for drawing out sympathisers who may otherwise have remained silent on this vital issue.

Following this meeting, Mrs Brandon subsequently wrote a letter to the *Examiner* as local WSPU 'Honorary Organiser (pro-tem)'. In her letter she relates that the Prime Minister had sent acknowledgement of the resolution passed at the 'great protest meeting against the White Slave Traffic'.[1] The *Advertiser* reports that the petition bore the signatures of 100 people.[2]

After this high-point of her campaigning, the Chesham WSPU trail in the local newspapers goes cold. On one level this might seem puzzling, in view of an apparent growing momentum towards women's suffrage in the towns of central Buckinghamshire.

However, in May 1913, the Brandons sold their 'Bankside' home and may have moved out of Chesham at this time. It is also possible, with the increased outlawing of the WSPU from 1913, that Mrs Brandon with her prison record, perhaps under pressure from her husband, may have thought it wise to discontinue her campaigning role. In February of that year, the Police Superintendents of each Division in Buckinghamshire were asked to forward a list of all known suffragettes living in their area to the Chief Constable.[3]

There are other possible and potentially complementary explanations. One is that Mrs Brandon may herself have become disillusioned, either with her lack of success at gaining local support, or perhaps with WSPU tactics themselves. These tactics came to include arson attacks upon buildings including churches, railway stations and houses in Buckinghamshire. Alternatively, Mrs Brandon may have assumed a lower profile so that she could play a role in supporting the travelling teams of women who carried out these attacks. Finally, there may have been other factors involved, perhaps as simple as having to move with her husband's job.

What needs no conjecture is the story of Chesham's other 'suffragette'. Towards the end of 1912 Hugh Franklin himself took up Christabel Pankhurst's call to use arson as the next weapon in the WSPU armoury. The thinking was to embarrass the government and to bring financial pressure to bear on the government and nation through the increased cost of insurance.

Hugh Franklin's choice of target was an empty railway carriage in Harrow station. Having lit a piece of canvas soaked in paraffin and thrown it

[1] *BE*, 26th July 1912.
[2] *BAAN*, 6th July 1912, p. 2.
[3] Bucks Constabulary Memoranda Books, 25th February 1913.

into a carriage, Franklin left the scene, but not before he was detained and was recognised by the station guards who promptly doused the fire. Hugh was well known at the station, as the station is on the Metropolitan Line through to Chesham. Managing to slip away from his captors, Franklin then went on the run for two months, going into hiding in London. But he was unable to avoid arrest. He was tried and sentenced to nine months imprisonment. At the Middlesex Sessions Court, he remained defiant:

'Whatever sentence is passed upon me, I shall feel that the acceptance of such a sentence would be the admission of my guilt. Therefore, it is my intention to refuse all food after I get into prison. Whatever my sentence, it will not be served all its length. Otherwise it would be a sentence of death.'[1]

True to his word, Franklin once again resorted to hunger-striking at Wormwood Scrubs, and on this occasion was force-fed over 100 times. He was the first to be released under the new 'Cat and Mouse Act' designed specifically for hunger-striking suffragettes.[2] Under the terms of his release, he was supposed to promise no further attacks and to report to Wormwood Scrubs again on 12th May to continue his sentence, having regained some strength. However, Hugh went on the run, along with three other suffragettes: Elsie Duval, Phylis Brady and Ella Stevenson.

The warrant for Franklin's arrest was mentioned in local police communications: 'He may be arrested at sight and conveyed direct to Wormwood Scrubs Prison.'[3] But Franklin evaded re-arrest, and under the alias of 'Henry Forster' escaped to the continent, along with his future wife, Elsie Duval. Hugh only returned to England once an amnesty was announced by the government on the outbreak of the First World War.

The rest of Chesham's story is less dramatic in comparison to Hugh Franklin's escapades. However, there are further developments in the campaign which are worth noting. What seems clear is that the NUWSS and other non-militant women's suffrage groups attempted to take over the vacuum left by the militants. While at times discouraged by the extreme tactics of their near cousins in the movement and also by popular fury, they seem ever more determined to widen their appeals. Suffragists in Chesham particularly, must have been cheered by the sympathetic approach of the

---

[1] *BE*, 14th March 1913.
[2] Crawford - *WSM*, pp. 228-30.
[3] Bucks Constabulary Memoranda Books, 14th May 1913.

Examiner newspaper. A regular column of 'Women's Suffrage Notes' was introduced from 1913, which was decidedly pro-suffrage in tone.[1]

The determination of local campaigners was largely met with admiration and growing support among the people of Chesham, despite the mushrooming of anti-suffrage groups in this period.

Mrs Ethel Snowden, was one well-known minor celebrity to visit Chesham later that year. Mrs Snowden was a renowned socialist writer and lecturer. An article in the *Free Press* stated that in 1913, she had the honour of being the first woman to address the House of Representatives in Ohio.[2]

Invited by the Educational Branch of the Co-operative Society to speak at the Equity Hall, she came ostensibly to talk about child welfare and education. However, in closing her long speech, she inevitably echoed the common call of her fellow suffragists to include the women's viewpoint when framing government legislation.[3] Presiding over the event was Miss Violet Mary Woolf, headmistress of Whitehill Girls' School. The second speaker was Mr L. Steele, a local Labour activist, working with the Worker's Union among those employed in the local woodenware industry. He spoke about the evils of child labour. He echoed Miss Woolf's call for a change to the school leaving age in Bucks, which at 13 was lower than many other parts of the country.

The following year the Mid-Bucks NUWSS opened its winter campaign with a 'social evening' at the Equity Hall.[4] Mrs Page chaired the evening and introduced local speaker, Mrs Savory, from Wendover. She started with a uniting call to all women, whatever particular persuasion, and concluded the evening by stating: 'In Australia, within six months of the passing of the Act giving votes to women, the White Slave Traffic was completely abolished'.

Using a local speaker for such an event is in itself a significant development, which shows the movement was developing its own leaders, confident in speaking to a range of audiences on a number of subjects related to women's suffrage. Until 1913, local branches in the county tended to rely on high-profile speakers from beyond the district to be able to draw a crowd. It seems that increasingly, the local suffrage groups saw this as

---

[1] *BE*, 23rd January 1914, for example.
[2] *SBFP*, 13th March 1914.
[3] *BE*, 26th October 1912.
[4] *BE*, 24th October 1913. Those listed as present among a 'good audience' were: Miss Catherine Courtauld, Mrs W. F. Lowndes, Mrs Stafford-Webber, Mrs H. J. Gamlin, Mrs G. E. Rice, Mrs Denton Samuel, and Mrs Johnson, Mrs Maple and Mrs Saunders.

unnecessary and not only presided at meetings but also provided experienced speakers from their own ranks.

From the beginning of 1914, the Mid-Bucks NUWSS set out with the intention of organising a series of monthly lectures in Chesham. For the first time, Mrs Denton Samuel is named as 'hon. correspondent' for Chesham.[1] This was a training role for a future branch secretary and is a clear indication that the Mid-Bucks NUWSS were planning to launch a separate branch in the town.

At the first of these meetings, on 14th January in the Co-operative Society's Equity Hall, Mrs Samuel outlined the plan 'setting forth the principles and objects of woman suffrage among working women'. A range women speakers was in mind, who could from their work in 'industrial associations, health centres, or social and preventative work, or children's courts', would show why, 'the vote would... be of incalculable benefit to the country morally and spiritually'. Mrs Samuel asserted, 'Women were no longer content to be legislated for without being consulted'. Miss Courtauld also gave details of the work of the local branch in the area, which was followed by a tea.

The second meeting in the series did not attract such a large audience. Blaming poor attendance on the inclement weather, the reporter commented that the enthusiasm of those present more than compensated for the low turnout. Chairing the meeting on 11th February, 1914, Mrs Page opened the meeting with some remarks which reveal some of the related campaigns close to her heart:

'Mrs Page spoke on "How the Vote would benefit Working Women," and showed how at every turn domestic legislation was shelved and ignored while men paid attention to things like increased armaments and things of interest to themselves. She instanced Temperance Reform, which was admitted on all hands was a long overdue measure ... as well as other items which touched the working woman very closely.'[2]

Mrs Samuel followed with an address on 'The Women's Movement'. In giving a short history of the movement, Mrs Samuel mentioned how the surplus numbers of women at the end of the last century had driven some women into 'sweated labour'. While increased education for women had provided more opportunities it had also opened their eyes to many social

[1] *BE*, 16th January 1914.
[2] *BE*, 20th February 1914.

injustices, including the 'economic slavery' of 'the marriage market' and the lack of legal protection for unmarried mothers. Before they broke for refreshments, Mrs Samuel issued a rallying cry: '...side by side with the men... we shall work unceasingly, untiringly until our long struggle shall end in triumphant victory.'

However, it would appear that the Chesham suffragists may have decided not to continue this series of monthly meetings. There are certainly none reported in the *Examiner* from March onwards. Perhaps they had struggled to find the necessary speakers, or the low turn-out for the second meeting had discouraged them. Whatever was the case, there was a lecture organised by the Mid-Bucks NUWSS, but this took place in Missenden on 12th March. Miss Penrose Philp, from the State Children's Association, spoke about Poor Law Children. There was little of immediate relevance to the suffrage question, but those present reportedly 'listened with great appreciation to the lecture, and questions were asked at the end'.[1]

About this time, another local suffrage society came into being, belonging to a new network called the 'United Suffragists'. It covered both Chesham and Amersham and seems to have been driven by Mrs Drinkwater of 'Fieldtop' in Amersham-on-the-hill, who was secretary of the branch, and also by another Amersham resident, Mr J. H. Jackson.[2] At the end of March, Mr Jackson chaired a United Suffragists meeting at Chorleywood Town Hall, when Miss Evelyn Sharp and Henry Harben spoke.[3] At the end of the meeting, the vote was declared narrowly in favour of the suffrage resolution.

The United Suffragists represented a new attempt to re-unite both men and women and the two wings of the movement, militant and non-militant, under the wings of one organisation. Its national launch in February 1914, supported by some well-known figures, like the Pethwick-Lawrences ejected from the WSPU in 1912, was an attempt to win wider appeal to the cause by reclaiming some middle ground in the debate. The Amersham/Chesham branch was one of the first three to be formed in the country, probably due to the close support of Mrs Agnes Harben of Newland Park, Chalfont St Giles.

Members of the local branch were responsible for organising events in May 1914 in Amersham, in a meadow at Grimsdell's Lane. The Amersham Town Brass Band played to attract a crowd, which was then addressed by George Lansbury, former Labour MP for Bow, and suffragette sympathiser.

[1] *BE*, 20th March 1914.
[2] Crawford - *WSM*, p. 694.
[3] *BE*, 3rd April 1914.

Another meeting was held one Friday evening in July in Chesham Broadway, which was a more lively affair, partly due to the crowd swelling during the course of the meeting. People finishing work and perhaps others emboldened by a beer or two from their local pub, asked several questions of the speaker, a clergyman from the East End of London. Rev. J.M. Maillard's main argument was that 'women voters could aid the men in the fight against present day evils'.[1] Questions asked mostly centred around WSPU militancy. One man, however, stated the anti-suffragists frequent claim that, most of the 'thinking women' he knew did not want the vote'. Mr Maillard simply retorted that from his own experience he could not agree with this assessment.

The debates that raged around this issue did not seem to move on a great deal. But, as elsewhere, the women's suffrage movement in Buckinghamshire was clearly showing signs of growth, just as the news of the war broke across Europe. While the proliferation of different suffrage groups may have served to diffuse some energy and also to cause some confusion among the populace, it is also true that increasing numbers of people were proclaiming themselves convinced suffragists, in spite of seemingly relentless waves of suffragette attacks up and down the land.

One of these prominent women was Caroline Franklin of Chartridge Lodge, Hugh Franklin's mother. The friends, who wrote a retrospective tribute to this woman who worked for many years to improve education and the situation of the poorest classes, were keen to distance her from the memory of the excesses of the women's suffrage movement.[2] However, Caroline Franklin was supportive enough of the movement to become an executive committee member of the Jewish League for Women's Suffrage in 1913.[3]

Some people, including non-militant suffragists, were indeed inspired by the courage and sacrifice of the suffragettes. But increasing numbers of people seem to have been won over by the persistent persuasion of the suffragist campaigns and their insistence that the issue should not be judged solely by prejudice, nor by the practical difficulties of party politics, nor on the basis of the behaviour of a minority of militants, but on the basis of the principle of the equality of men and women before the law.

---

[1] *BE*, 24th July 1914.
[2] '(Caroline) took no part in the political movement for women's suffrage', *Caroline Franklin, 1863-1935: Tributes to her Memory*, p. 7.
[3] Crawford - *WSM*, p. 229.

In Chesham, the WSPU campaign may have eventually run out of steam, after a decidedly uphill struggle. But, the story of the growth of several other groups campaigning for women's suffrage in Chesham, is clear evidence of a steadily growing, if not overwhelming, groundswell in favour of 'votes for women'.

Chapter 4: Wendover: Tax Resisters, an Australian Suffragette and the Mid-Bucks NUWSS

'Just as John Hampden offered first passive resistance to authority, then active resistance, so the women had their course clearly marked out before them'.
- From 'No votes, no Taxes', an article written by WSPU leader, Emmeline Pethwick-Lawrence, following her visit to the Chalgrove battlefield monument to John Hampden. *Votes for Women*, 7th October 1910, p. 4.

THE story of the women's suffrage movement in Wendover is particularly unusual. For example, the twists and turns of this tale feature a woman who appears to be the only tax resister for votes in central Buckinghamshire. It is also true that a notorious Australian suffragette stayed for a fortnight in Wendover in 1911, which is why she is included in this chapter. Although Muriel Matters came to live just outside High Wycombe around this time, although she usually spoke at meetings in other parts of the county and elsewhere across the country.

Another distinguishing factor in Wendover's women's suffrage account is that, initially at least, the unofficial headquarters of the Mid-Bucks branch of the NUWSS was also here. The Mid-Bucks NUWSS was also very active in Aylesbury, Chesham, Great Missenden and later even in some of the smaller villages. But it is clear from local newspaper accounts, that, with the exception of High Wycombe, the non-militant NUWSS initiatives were earlier here than anywhere. There were suffragist meetings here in May 1909. This would seem to indicate that, outside of Wycombe, Wendover had the strongest representation of women, and men, who supported women's enfranchisement.

The name of St Teresa's Holiday Home for Girls, along Dobbins Lane, Wendover, is inextricably linked with the women's suffrage movement in this area. St Teresa's is featured possibly for the first time in the local newspapers in 1906, when the people of Wendover were invited to 'A Pound Day', in order to raise local awareness and to raise money for the home.[1] St Teresa's was established to provide a place in the country for poor girls living

---

[1] *BH*, 30th June 1906.

in London slums, whose families would not have been able to afford a holiday for them.

Postcard showing St Teresa's. Courtesy of Philip Walker

Message from the founder of St Teresas', Mrs Katie Sichel on the reverse

Plans for the home must have begun several years earlier, when Miss Katie Solomon, moving out of Hampstead, bought a cottage with large grounds on Chiltern Road, near to Dobbins Lane.[1] The new home was built in the grounds of the cottage, and later a chapel, St Agnes' Mission Church. The designs for St Teresa's, drawn up by Miss Solomon, were subsequently displayed at the Mid-Bucks NUWSS art exhibition at Missenden in 1914.[2] Katie may have been related to Lady Leon of Bletchley Park, as her mother's maiden name was Leon, and Lady Leon visited a St Teresa's Pound Day in 1912.[3]

Miss Leonore Sichel, Katie's future sister-in-law, became Matron of the home. Leonore was Alfred Sichel's younger sister: they were both born in Highbury, London, three years apart.[4] Katie married Alfred Sichel in 1911 and lived next door to St Teresa's, at 'Lindholme', 34 Dobbins Lane. Alfred Sichel, like his German father, was involved in the dress trade. Both Katie and her husband were enthusiastic supporters of votes for women and Katie was a leading figure in setting up the society. She was still acting as Chair for the Mid-Bucks suffrage society in 1914.[5] The first Annual General Meetings of the Mid-Bucks society met at St Teresa's, certainly in 1911 and 1912, although there seems to be no newspaper record of the first annual meeting in 1910.

When women engaged in charitable work, they both became more generally aware of wider social and political issues and came into contact with other progressive-thinking women. This is probably how Miss Leonore Sichel and Mrs Katie Sichel and many other local women initially joined the ranks of the women's suffrage movement. Similarly, another local suffragist, Mrs Florence G. Hamilton, was 'honorary secretary' of the Church of England Society for Providing Homes for Waifs and Strays.[6]

How long these three women and others in the town had held suffragist views is not known. At the meeting reported at St Teresa's on Wednesday 26th May 1909, the main speaker from the NUWSS opened by saying that women's suffrage was 'no new idea, and they had been working for a very

---

[1] *Kelly's* - 1899, 1903.

[2] *BH*, 25th July 1914.

[3] *BH*, 7th June 1912; I am indebted to Philip Walker for many of these details, as well as the photograph of St Teresa's.

[4] 1911 England and Wales Census.

[5] *Third Annual Report*, NUWSS Federation, p. 18.

[6] *BH*, 30th June 1906 - mistakenly referred to here as '*Miss* Hamilton of Chestnut Cottage' (my italics).

long time'.[1] While Miss Lamond was referring to the national campaign, it does seem likely that there had been low-level activity in the town for some time also.

Various apologies were received at the meeting: from Lady Battersea, Mrs E.J. Payne, Miss Savory and Mrs Lauriston Shaw. Lady Battersea was a member of the Rothschild family who lived nearby in Aston Clinton House. She was a temperance and prison campaigner who had previously been President of the National Union of Women Workers.[2] 'Miss Savory' probably refers to a resident of the High Street, Miss Mary Anne Savory, who had lived in Wendover all her life and had been District Visitor and church worker for many years.[3] Mrs (May) Shaw lived at 'Icknield Cottage' with her husband, Lauriston, a 'consulting physician'. They both came originally from north London.[4]

The number of apologies suggests that this may not have been the first of such meetings. It also indicates the reasonable success of the strategy employed by the Mid-Bucks suffragists, which was later described by Mrs Hamilton in a letter published in the *Advertiser*:

> '... for the last three years in Mid-Bucks, ... the Bishop and Member had been asked to receive deputations of church workers and municipal voters and others, that notable residents, the clergy, doctors and other professional people had been approached...'[5]

In Wendover, a considerable number of local women were sympathetic to the cause of women's enfranchisement, and a degree of organisation was already in place quite early on. Miss Mackenzie was referred to as 'secretary' of the new society. However, Dr Leonard H. West had been persuaded to chair the meeting in the unfortunate absence of Mrs Hamilton and Miss Mackenzie. He confessed to having been initially reluctant, partly due to the association of 'militant actions with women's suffrage meetings'.

Equally aware of the possible anxieties of some of those present, Miss Lamond went out of her way to reassure her audience that if women were enfranchised on the same basis as men, the female vote would only amount to around 2 million, compared to the current male electorate of 7 million.

---

[1] *BH*, 29th May 1909.
[2] Davis, John - *DNB*, 2004-13.
[3] *BAAN*, 1st December 1917, p. 5, obit.; 1911 England and Wales Census.
[4] 1911 England and Wales Census.
[5] *BAAN*, 27th April 1912, p. 9.

She finished her talk with the common cry that, because Parliament was regularly enacting legislation which affected women, and because, 'women had to pay for them, they thought that they ought to be able to register their opinions about these laws'.

Mr Mallon then spoke about 'sweating', or the widespread abuse of women through poor pay and poor working conditions. A member of the audience, Mrs Horwood, then added her support. This is quite likely Mrs T. Horwood, mentioned in association with the Church League for Women's Suffrage mission to Aylesbury in 1911. The resolution, proposed by Miss Lamond, was that 'suffrage should be extended to women on the same terms it is extended to men'. This was passed with one or two dissentients and Mrs Hamilton was thanked in her absence for the 'arrangements in connection with the meeting'.

This 1909 event pre-dated the formal launch of the Mid-Bucks branch of the NUWSS, supposedly in January 1910, which coincided with the general election. The new society was organised enough to arrange a voters' petition in the area. Miss Katie Solomon, who signed herself as 'Secretary' of the Mid-Bucks branch at this point, detailed the appeal for signatures which was made to voters in Aylesbury, Wendover, Great Missenden and Chesham.[1] The questioners made it clear that suffragists were not asking for women to sit in Parliament and that only women who already had the municipal vote were being proposed for the vote. Given these qualifications, 274 Buckinghamshire men had signed the suffragists' petition. Miss Solomon observed that the 'vast majority' of those approached were willing to sign. Her only regret was that the small number of workers had limited the potential size of the petition.

What is equally notable is the fact that the local anti-suffrage league in Wendover, was formed even before this, in May 1909, the same week as the St Teresa's public meeting in favour of women's suffrage. Members of this newly formed group of 'antis' must have turned up in numbers to a debate organised by the Wendover Literary Institute Debating Society at the schools, in February 1910.[2] Chaired again by Dr West, Mrs Ruckham of Cambridge proposed a resolution to the meeting in favour of votes for women, while a Miss Lindsay spoke against. From among the large number of lady members and visitors attending the resolution was 'lost by a very large majority'.

---

[1] *BH*, 19th February 1910.

[2] Ibid.

It is possible that the presence of suffragette campaigners in the area, in the summers of 1908 and 1909, may well have spurred some local people to form organised opposition. Equally, their presence may have encouraged others to take a stand for 'votes for women'. There is no evidence that any women of Wendover were directly recruited to the WSPU, although there was clearly one example of a Buckinghamshire woman joining the WSPU on the spur of the moment, in the summer of 1909.[1]

At some point, Mrs Florence Hamilton must have decided to take up the challenge of playing a major part in persuading the local population of the justice of the suffragist cause. By this time, Mrs Hamilton, originally from Scotland, appears to have been a resident of Wendover for several years.[2] In the summer of 1910 she was living in Chestnut Cottage, which had a prime location just off the High Street. This not only provided an ideal venue for events promoting women's suffrage, but between 1910 and 1912 this house became a centre of operations for organising meetings over a wider area, involving members of a variety of suffrage groups.

As her 1932 obituary makes clear, Mrs Hamilton was a determined and longstanding activist for equality and justice for women, whose involvement in the women's movement continued after the vote was won. She is described, by Muriel Matters, as, 'A bonny fighter for Women's Freedom.'[3]

In August 1910, 'two weeks of propaganda' was arranged in the district, in connection with Mrs Hamilton's cottage.[4] Miss Gertrude Eaton is named as a key speaker. Miss Eaton, a resident of Kensington, was apparently well-known at the time in London's music world and was also involved in prison reform.[5]

Miss Canning was also in the area, and may well have been the speaker for one of the two weeks. She was an active member of both the CLWS and the Conservative and Unionist Women's Franchise Association. With the encouragement of Millicent Fawcett from the NUWSS, the CUWFA had been formed in late 1908 as a single-issue organisation, designed to ensure the Conservative party was not politically out-flanked concerning women's suffrage. It became one of the largest suffragist organisations.[6]

---

[1] *VW*, 3rd September 1909, p. 1136.
[2] *Kelly's* - 1903, 1907.
[3] *The Vote*, 29th April 1932, p. 141, obit.
[4] *VW*, 19th August 1910, p. 771.
[5] *The Vote*, 5th August 1911.
[6] Crawford, - *WSM*, p. 139.

Miss Canning spoke at meetings in Aylesbury market square that Summer, and in Chesham in 1912. The 'well attended' meeting, held in support of the Conciliation Bill before Parliament, was in the Parish Room and was presided over by Dr Edwin Woollerton.[1] Woollerton lived in the High Street, and his wife, Elizabeth, was from a local landowning family who owned 'The Hale'. Mr C.T. Adams, given special mention, was a well-known figure associated with the Wendover's parish church, St Mary's. Miss Eaton was present, but the talks were given by Miss Canning and Miss Violet Marten of CUWFA. In his brief report, the *Advertiser* reporter chose to highlight, 'the good conduct of a number of lads present'.

The *Herald* reporter gave a full account of the meeting, which helps to explain the lack of disruption to the meeting. Miss Marten tried to reassure those concerned about the effect of the female vote in relation to national defence. She suggested that this limited franchise, based on the same qualifications that existed for men, was the best defence against adult suffrage. Her comments about the leaders of the Conservative Party, Lord Salisbury and Mr Balfour, having both spoken in favour of women's suffrage, coupled with the Chairman's concluding remarks criticising Asquith and Lloyd George, demonstrated the party political nature of this meeting. Miss Canning was herself less partisan, mentioning that the Conciliation Bill was cross-party and that all the women's suffrage societies were prepared to work for this limited measure.

This event, as well as others in the county, shows that to some extent the movement remained fragmented along party lines. Due to pre-existing loyalties, some women found it hard or impossible to unite under the non-party banner of the NUWSS. And the later religious suffrage societies served to perpetuate this divide, with the CLWS being effectively pro-Tory, and the FCLWS supporting the Liberal Government. It is not surprising, given the need for unity among the women that many suffragists in Buckinghamshire, most notably Miss Dove of High Wycombe, made a point of trying to rise above party politics in the earlier years of their campaigning.

Later that year, in *Votes for Women*, Miss Katherine Raleigh is reported as staying for a fortnight with Mrs Hamilton at Chestnut Cottage, Wendover.[2] In the short article, she invites readers to come and help 'in informal village meetings at places off the railway line and also at Amersham and Missenden'. The campaign was also highlighted by the WFL. Their short appeal read:

---

[1] *BAAN*, 20th August 1910, p. 11 and *BH*, 20th August 1910, p. 7.

[2] *VW*, 2nd September 1910.

'Amersham-Aylesbury. Informal village meetings will be held in this district of Bucks, 1st - 13th September. Most of these places are away from the railway, therefore cycles are useful. It is hoped to hold meetings in Amersham and Aylesbury. Anyone willing to help or desirous of help in their own plans, write: Miss K. Raleigh, Chestnut Cottage, Wendover'. [1]

Miss Katherine Raleigh was from Uxbridge and, as well as writing a number of pamphlets on women's suffrage, was instrumental in establishing an early suffrage society there.[2] Katherine was a Greek scholar and expert in classical history. Having been among the first women to join the WTRL, she seems to have been appointed by this group as a Local Organizer.[3] When publicising a lecture Katherine was due to give at Caxton Hall in November 1913 on 'The Worship of Athene', it was revealed that she had already resisted paying her taxes for six years.[4] Like some determined suffragists, she may have continued to resist paying taxes during the First World War. Katherine went on to become the first female candidate for Uxbridge Council.[5]

From her temporary base in Wendover, Miss Raleigh organised what appears to be the first open-air meeting on this subject in Great Missenden, which was supported by various women's suffrage societies .[6] It is likely there were other meetings in the area during the month, although they were seemingly unreported in the local newspapers.

The next event followed soon after, but seems to have been arranged independently of Mrs Hamilton or the Mid-Bucks suffrage society. The parish Debating Society hosted a debate on 9th November, on the topic of 'Are Women Citizens?' Speaking in favour was Miss Winifred Smith of the London Graduates' Union for Women's Suffrage.[7] Her resolution, seconded by Mr C.T. Adams, was: 'That this meeting call upon the Government to grant facilities for the passing of the People (Women) Bill this session'. Mr Molineux moved an amendment which replaced 'this session' with the term, 'at the earliest convenient opportunity'. The vote on the amendment was tied at eight for and eight against. The chair, Rev. A. C. Webber declined to give a

---

[1] *The Vote*, 3rd September 1910, p. 223.
[2] Hayes People's History blogspot - January, 2012.
[3] WTRL Committee Minute Book, 1909-13, 19th April 1912.
[4] *The Vote*, 31st October 1913, p. 449.
[5] *Uxbridge Gazette*, 22nd January 1922, obit.
[6] *VW*, 16th September 1910.
[7] *BAAN*, 19th November 1910.

casting vote on 'so important a matter'. When Miss Smith's original resolution was put to the meeting it was passed with a majority of six.

The first reported annual general meeting of the Mid-Bucks NUWSS occurred on 23rd March, 1911.[1] The branch boasted no less a figure than Mrs Bertrand Russell as President. Living in or around Oxford at this time, Mrs Russell was clearly willing to travel and speak at meetings for a cause close to her heart. She later spoke at a Liberal meeting in Great Missenden. Mrs Russell and her husband were increasingly estranged, but they shared a common passion for women's suffrage.

Another development in this local branch was the rapid turn-over of officers. The woman who appeared to be the original secretary of the branch, Miss Mackenzie, is not mentioned. Mrs Sichel as the previous Secretary was presented with a farewell gift following her marriage. This wedding gift serves to give a helpful, although not conclusive, insight into the size of the branch at this time, as 28 of the members subscribed to the gift. Mrs Sichel thanked her fellow suffragists for the gift and finished by saying that 'she and her husband took great interest in the work and would do anything in their power to further the cause.' Following Mrs Russell's speech, resolutions were passed by the branch to be sent to Prime Minister Asquith and the local MP, Mr Lionel de Rothschild.

Mrs Sichel's replacement was Miss Catherine Courtauld of Great Missenden. Catherine was niece to silk manufacturer Samuel Courtauld, whose wife Ellen signed the first women's suffrage petition in 1866.[2] Catherine herself joined the Central Society for Women's Suffrage in 1906. She is described as 'sculptor (artist)' in the 1911 census. By 1911 Miss Courtauld was already in the process of painting a banner for the branch, which had been made by the Suffrage Atelier. There are no further details of the appearance of the banner, and little in the way of a report on the branch's activities.

However, 1911 proves to be a significant year for the suffrage movement in Wendover. While the census passed off without much incident throughout the county, some women were willing to risk being fined for refusing to divulge their details in the census. While searches of the Wendover documents have ultimately proved inconclusive, one Wendover resident makes no appearance in the 1911 statistics. Mrs Florence Hamilton, a member of both WFL and WTRL, does not appear to have submitted to being counted that day. What lends extra weight to Mrs Hamilton's possible

[1] *BH*, 25th March 1911.
[2] Crawford - *WSM*, pp. 142-3.

census evasion is the important role in the census boycott taken on by her close suffragist friend, Katherine Raleigh. A brief report from Miss Raleigh earlier that year shows that she was active in recruiting other women to act as census agents in their own localities.[1]

The census was taken on Sunday 2nd April, only four days before Mrs Hamilton had some of her goods distrained, as a result of her refusing to pay her House Duty. It is quite likely that Mrs Hamilton decided on these two forms of protest as a result of having met other members of the WTRL, like Miss Eaton and Miss Raleigh. The WTRL had been instrumental in encouraging both the WFL and the WSPU to adopt these two means of passive resistance protest.

According to the full account in the *Herald*, there was a 'good number' present, including Mrs Kineton Parkes, secretary of the WTRL.[2] The meeting was called for the purpose of selling a silver coffee pot, one of Mrs Hamilton's family heirlooms. Held at the Red Lion Hotel, local estate agent and tax collector, Mr F. J. Mead, opened the sale by explaining that the reason they were there that day was Mrs Hamilton's refusal to pay 5 shillings of her Imperial Tax. He said he believed that this was the first sale of its kind in the district and he hoped it would be the last. He added that, 'He wished to thank Mrs Hamilton for the very kind way she had met him when he distrained. His experience had been very different from that of some of his colleagues in London'.

Following the sale of the coffee pot, which was sold to Mrs Norman for 15 shillings, Mrs Kineton Parkes stepped forward. She declared that Mrs Hamilton's protest had been done 'as a matter of principle, for many women now recognised that taxation without representation was tyranny'. And she posed the rhetorical question: 'Was it right that they should go on contributing year after year, without knowing in the slightest how that money was going to be spent?' In another account of this protest meeting, Mrs Parkes mentions the example of local hero, John Hampden, in his original 'defence of liberty' and urged other women to make a similar stand and for the men to understand the reason for these tax protests.[3] No other local women heeded this particular challenge.

---

[1] *The Vote*, 25th February 1911, p. 210.

[2] *BH*, 8th April 1911. Others listed as present were: Mrs Mead, Mrs Norman, Miss Clarke and Messrs Molineux, F. Sharp, C. T. Adams, G. Brackley, Eldridge, F. W. Blake, T. Dancer, J. Pearce, A. Proctor, Gillam, F. Thorne, P. J. Clark and C. G. Pickop.

[3] *The Vote*, 15th April 1911, p. 304.

Although the WFL's account is undoubtedly biased, it does not seem to be exaggerating when it claims that 'Mrs Parkes received a sympathetic hearing with not a single objection being raised'. An anonymous Wendover resident was reported to have subsequently commented: 'If there was ever a rebellion in the quiet village of Buckinghamshire, it was that day'.[1]

After Mrs Parkes offered a vote of thanks, Mr Mead commented that, 'all of them in that room liked to give ladies the opportunity of advancing their views at any time.' Mr Mead's sympathy for the cause was ultimately confirmed at a meeting in Aylesbury later that year.[2]

Mrs Hamilton followed up the sale with a letter in the *Herald* the following week:

'SIR - As a passive resister in Bucks, and a member of the Women's Tax Resistance League, will you kindly grant me space in your paper to explain the principle underlying our action. It is to be found in Clause No. 40 in King John's Charter in the great Magna Charta of England's liberties: "We will sell to no man, we will not deny to any man justice or right". Personal rights have become to be defined and enlarged and the constitutional right of representation for taxation is one of the foremost. The present Government denies this right to householders who are women, and as householders we are defending our personal rights, and are demanding redress by a protest of passive resistance. In John Hampden's county we are fortunate in possessing the best precedent in England for resisting unjust taxation. The success and growth of the League shews that the demand of women householders for representation appeal to the sense of justice of English men and women'.
Yours faithfully,
FLORENCE G. HAMILTON Wendover, Bucks, April 8th 1911[3]

The summer of 1911, which was a particularly hot one, saw the arrival of a women's suffrage caravan to the area.[4] This was the first introduction of the celebrated suffragette, Miss Muriel Matters, to Buckinghamshire, who had returned to Britain following a sell-out tour of her native Australia the previous year.[5]

---

[1] *The Vote*, April 29th 1932, p. 141.
[2] *BH*, 11th November 1911
[3] *BH*, 15th April 1911.
[4] Nicolson, Juliet - *The Perfect Summer: Dancing into Shadow in 1911.*
[5] Doughan, David - *DNB*, 2004-13; *Why Muriel Matters*. I am indebted to Frances Bedford and her infectious passion for Muriel's story.

Muriel Matters addressing a crowd in north Wales, probably 1909 or 1910. Courtesy of the Slusarczyk family and the Muriel Matters Society

Miss Matters started her working life as an actress and later an elecutionist. Initially coming to England in 1906, she found it difficult to get work in public recitals, so she took up writing as a journalist. This led her to an interview in London with the exiled Russian anarchist, Prince Peter Kropotkin. Muriel subsequently spoke of the meeting as a turning point in her life, as the anarchist challenged this gifted actress and speaker to use her art for the furtherance of important political causes.

Miss Matters became a member of the WSPU, but joined the WFL split in 1907. She embarked on a prolonged tour of the south east of England in the WFL caravan the following summer and autumn. This led to her first meeting the Quaker and fellow suffragist, Miss Violet Tillard, in Tunbridge Wells. Later in 1908, Muriel gained her initial notoriety as a result of her adventurous attitude to campaigning for the vote. With the help of Violet, Miss Matters and Miss Helen Fox chained themselves to the grille of the Ladies' Gallery in the House of Commons, as part of a wider suffragette protest on 28th October. As it took authorities some time to remove the two women, Muriel became the first woman to give a speech to the chamber of the House of Commons. She and Violet were later arrested the same day for 'obstruction'. They were imprisoned together in Holloway. Muriel's protest provoked a critical editorial in one of the local newspapers, which called the protest 'foolish and... wicked.'[1]

The following year, Miss Matters became the first woman to hire an airship. The purpose of the flight was to drop leaflets on the royal procession of King Edward VII to re-open Parliament on 16th February. Over this 80 foot long dirigible was displayed a huge message which read 'Votes for Women' and 'WFL'. Accompanied by the pilot, Captain Henry Spencer, Miss Matters took off from the Welsh Harp at Hendon, clutching a megaphone and equipped with 56 pounds of leaflets. Powered by a six horse-power engine, the airship had a top speed of 8mph and during the flight reached an altitude of 3,500 feet. However, due to a contrary wind, the airship never reached its intended destination and touched down in Coulsdon an hour and a half later.

Miss Matters commented in a subsequent BBC interview that due to 'winning her spurs' in the previous grille protest, 'I was entrusted with the aerial demonstration on the day of the opening of Parliament'.[2]

Described two days later in the *New York Times* as 'the Balloonist Agitator', Miss Matters took part in another protest surrounding the government minister and Buckinghamshire landowner, Lord Carrington. Dismissing the suffragette bomb threats circulated by the government, Miss Matters was reported to have made a derisive speech, saying, 'We women do not intend to make martyrs of the members of the Cabinet, we are simply going to make them look like a set of drivelling idiots'.[3]

It was this controversial and combative figure who toured 'the John Hampden county' with Violet Tillard in the WTRL caravan from 5th-19th July, 1911.[4] The two women started out from Missenden and finished at a garden meeting in Chesham. During the fortnight, they held one meeting in Wendover, two in Aylesbury, two in Stoke Mandeville, three in Chesham and four in Great Missenden. Due to the fact that the 1911 issues of the *Examiner* and the *Advertiser* no longer survive, there are no extant reports of these meetings. From their experiences in 1908 and from stories of other such meetings in Buckinghamshire, it is likely Muriel and Violet would have seen some large crowds and possibly also some disturbances.

Around this time Miss Matters came to live in Buckinghamshire, in a house called 'St John's Orchard', along Manor Road in Hazlemere.

---

[1] *BH*, 31st October 1908.
[2] www.bbc.co.uk/archive/suffragettes/8315.shtml, May 2012.
[3] *New York Times*, 19th February 1909, online archive.
[4] WTRL Committee Minute Book, 1909-13: entries for 9th June – 18th July 1911.

November 1911 saw her undertaking another two week mission in Buckinghamshire, this time centred on Aylesbury and without the caravan or her friend, Violet. Miss Matters stayed at Mrs Hamilton's cottage in Wendover during this CLWS mission, and developed another life-long friendship with this fellow campaigner. Like Muriel, Mrs Hamilton continued to work for women's rights after the First World War and after the vote was won in 1928. However, at times in 1911, the prospect of gaining the vote must have seemed a distant one for these friends united in the women's suffrage cause. And the following year saw an increased resistance to the message of women's emancipation in this normally quiet corner of Buckinghamshire.

The year started brightly enough for the women's movement in the area. The Annual General Meeting of the Mid-Bucks NUWSS branch at St Teresa's, Wendover, had a more up-beat tone than the previous year.[1] Meeting on Thursday 21st March, the branch now boasted a new President, in the form of NUWSS Executive member, Lady Francis Balfour, and no less than four Vice-Presidents: Mrs Luff, Mrs Lauriston Shaw, Mrs Sikes and Mrs Savory. Mrs Savory, occasionally referred to as Mrs Arthur Savory, may have been related to Miss Mary Savory by marriage. However, because no initial was recorded, and because it seems she was already widowed before the 1911 census, further details have been difficult to uncover. Mrs Savory does not appear to have lived in Wendover. There was a Mrs Savory recorded as living in Newport Pagnall.[2] But from her own brief account at a meeting later that year in Missenden, it seems Mrs Savory was interested in nursing and played some role in an earlier campaign for the Registration of Midwives legislation in 1902. [3]

At the annual meeting, Mrs Katie Sichel, having previously been Secretary (but stepped back from this post the previous year), was appointed Chairman of the group. There is a note of mystery too. Mrs Hamilton was reported to have resigned from the group and apparently, 'left the district'. It appears there may have been a disagreement, probably over the use of militant tactics, most likely prompted by the window-smashing raids on the West End, earlier that month. Until this point, Mrs Hamilton, as a member of the more moderate 'militant' WFL, had tried to hold the two wings of the local movement together.

---

[1] *BE*, 29th March 1912.
[2] *Kelly's* 1907, 1911.
[3] *BE*, 5th July 1912.

It is equally likely that the members of this local society may have disagreed with the anticipated plans of the WTRL to join forces with the WSPU in a week of protests across the county, starting with a march to Aylesbury prison. The march was to be followed by two tax resistance sales, one in Wendover, the other in Marlow. This co-ordinated plan was mentioned at a meeting of the WTRL Committee as early as 29th March, over a week before the suffragette prisoners were transferred to Aylesbury Prison. At this Mid-Bucks NUWSS meeting however, the new Secretary, Catherine Courtauld, makes a point of registering the society's 'strong disapproval of militant methods'. She herself moderates her comments by adding, 'they must remember to be charitable, and not to condemn the women who acted (however mistakenly) from a sense of duty at great cost to themselves'.

The reports of Mrs Hamilton having left the district were however either premature or completely unfounded, as she went on to make a second tax resistance protest in Wendover the following month. One of the extra burdens of taking a more militant approach in the struggle for the vote was that it ran the risk of losing former friends within the movement.

At the 1912 annual meeting there are members of the suffrage society not previously mentioned as being associated with the group, from Great Missenden and other villages: Mrs F. J. Mead, the wife of the local tax collector, along with Mrs Carvalho, Mrs Davies, Miss Wilkie and Miss Wright. It is impossible to know for certain, but Miss Wright is probably the young woman from the nearby village of Ballinger, who is mentioned in the list of women joining the NUWSS pilgrimage the following year. The *Examiner* article summarises the annual report:

'...the year 1911 had been one of satisfactory growth. Twenty-nine meetings had been held in Chesham, Aylesbury, Wendover, Missenden and Stoke Mandeville, and Miss Matters had also made a tour of the district. The membership of the society had trebled during the year and now stood at over 100. Mr Lionel de Rothschild had courteously received a deputation from the society, though he had pronounced himself opposed to women's suffrage, and had paired against the Conciliation Bill before receiving them.'

The next year's annual general meeting was not nearly so complimentary about the local MP. This report demonstrates there was much more going on in the district than revealed by the limited newspaper coverage, in 1911 particularly. Perhaps some of these events amounted to small, 'drawing-room meetings', but the low-key approach of the constitutional suffragists was clearly beginning to see some results in the trebling of their membership.

Miss Ruth Young, an NUWSS speaker from London, concluded the 1912 annual meeting with a hopeful speech, in anticipation of the Parliamentary vote over the Conciliation Bill that was due to take place the following Thursday, which if passed would enfranchise over one million women householders. Miss Young encouraged the campaigners 'not to let (MPs) make the recent deplorable events, for which the militant sections were responsible, an excuse for not voting for the Bill'. The speaker denied the common accusation that the Bill was just for the wealthy, and quoted the figure based on recent research, that 82 per cent of those due to get the vote would be working women. She finished by speaking of the benefits having the vote would bring for the 'industrial position of women workers'.

The next Wendover meetings the following month were organised by Miss Raleigh, from Mrs Hamilton's Chestnut Cottage, as part of a co-ordinated propaganda offensive coinciding with the Aylesbury prison protests on Saturday 13th April. A letter which appeared in the *Advertiser,* probably written by Miss Raleigh, invited people from the area both to come and see the prison protest in Aylesbury that day and the tax resistance sale in Wendover the next week. This correspondence which raised wider controversial issues stated that: 'Women's money is used to pay Members of Parliament who trifle with or ignore their just claims and also who wage wars which would be unnecessary if women had a voice in the Council of the Nations'.[1]

The second sale of Mrs Hamilton's distrained goods was held at the Red Lion Hotel on Tuesday 16th April. This was well attended by supporters and 'antis' alike, including Lady Louisa Smith. However, it seems notable that not many of the members of the Mid-Bucks NUWSS branch were mentioned as being present, with the exception of Mr and Mrs CT. Adams, Dr Woollerton and Miss Mackenzie. However, the opponents of women's suffrage had clearly drawn up their own plans, so that the speakers for tax resistance did not go unchallenged, like the previous year.

The *Herald* reporter remarked on the 'curious coincidence that the sale followed so closely after the incidents at Aylesbury', and concluded that the local interest in the sale had increased as a result.[2] Indeed, people had travelled to witness the sale from a wide area, including Amersham, Tring, Aylesbury and the villages surrounding Wendover.

---

[1] *BAAN*, 13th April 1912, p. 9.
[2] *BH*, 20th April 1912.

Mrs Hamilton had again refused to pay her five shillings House Duty. She told the meeting that this was the only tax she could resist, as her income was taxed at its source. The items for sale on this occasion, which needed this time to raise nineteen shillings, to cover the cost of the sale, were a pair of silver-plated spoons in a case, a silver-plated tea caddy and a solid silver sugar basin. Mr Gurney from Amersham commented that 'he had come out of South Bucks to see what sort of fun they were going to have'. Describing himself as a 'Jack of both sides in this matter', he bought the basin for 15 shillings.[1] This is probably Mr William Gurney, previously a farmer and Conservative Alderman on Bucks County Council, as well as being a member of Amersham District Council.[2] He appealed to both sides for fair play and 'fair language' in dealing with such a 'burning question'.

There was plenty of humour on this occasion, some of it introduced by the local estate, Mr Mead. Having alluded to the window-smashing of the suffragettes in London, Mr Mead commented that, '...if the ladies did get the vote in the dim and distant future, which they probably might do, these articles would be worth a fabulous sum'.[3] At the conclusion of the sale of the three items and the offering of thanks to Mr Mead, the Wendover tax resister invited Mrs Parkes from the WTRL to address the meeting.

Mrs Parkes opened by saying what an honour it was to be present at this protest and mentioned in passing that this was one of five she would be attending that week alone. She commented, 'They were proud of their John Hampden, and she wished them to be equally proud of their Mrs Hamilton'.[4] She went on to argue that, 'the Government, to be logical, must do one of two things - they must remove the burden of taxation from women, or they must give them the vote'. Having remarked that this was the first time this year she had attended the sale of goods of a repeat tax resister, she concluded with a rousing assertion. She declared, to some applause, that, '...they would not leave off agitating until they got the vote, because they thought it was only justice'.

Miss Raleigh followed the speech and said that she herself had also resisted paying taxes on two occasions. She delivered a reasoned argument against the 'physical force' argument of the 'antis'. She said that as the army represented only 2 per cent of the male population, the belief that only those who defended their country should be able to vote, would result in a tiny

---

[1] *BAAN*, 20th April 1912.
[2] *BE*, 29th May 1914.
[3] *BAAN*, 20th April 1912.
[4] Ibid.

electorate. Mrs Juson Kerr, another member of the WTRL, then commented that 'They were beginning to be ashamed of being English women, for all over the world smaller countries were giving women freedom'.

Mr Mead then mentioned that he had received, 'an application from a lady who wanted to speak to the other side'. According to the *Advertiser* account, despite an objection by Mrs Parkes, Miss Mabel Smith of the NLOWS stepped forward 'amidst cheers'. She thanked Mrs Hamilton for allowing her to speak and said that as she was going to put the other side of the case, she would be happy to oppose a resolution put by Mrs Parkes. However, Mr Mead ruled that he would not allow a resolution to be submitted to the meeting.

Miss Smith then proceeded to say that voting and taxation were not connected and that the reason for women to pay taxes was for the protection of their own lives and property. She repeated the often quoted claim of the 'antis' that there was not a majority of people wanting votes for women nationally, among the men or even the women. Someone in the audience loudly disagreed with this statement. But Miss Smith re-iterated the claim and said that it would be both 'disastrous' and an 'injustice' to grant women the vote under these circumstances. She then accused the WTRL of 'fraud' in bringing taxation and representation together in this way to support their demand for the vote.

As was often the case with active opponents of women's suffrage, Miss Smith had to present women as being already powerful, while drawing an apparently arbitrary line as to their natural limitations regarding political involvement. From the viewpoint of most of those in the audience, Miss Smith succeeded in humorously presenting a positive vision of women's role in social reform, while at the same time arguing against immediate political reform. She commented:

> '...in the present day women were able to bring an immense power to bear on public opinion, for most of them were able to talk. (Laughter). They were represented in Parliament by their husbands, their sons, and their brothers, and if a woman had no male relatives, surely she had some male friends.'[1]

Miss Smith also took to some unfounded scaremongering, with the claim that granting the vote to women would, 'injure our commercial confidence,

---

[1] *BAAN*, 20th April 1912, p. 12.

upon which our whole prosperity as an empire depended'.[1] She descended from the platform amidst loud applause and 'great enthusiasm' and the meeting ended. A large crowd had assembled in the High Street, but there were no disturbances. The *Herald* writer concluded his report with these words: 'There was little or no excitement afterwards, but later, in the evening a procession was formed bearing a banner, "No Vote for Women", and altogether the Anti-Suffragists were victorious all along the line'. This is how the *Advertiser* described the scenes: 'Later the same evening some Wendover worthies attired themselves as suffragists and addressed several meetings a great deal of fun'.[2]

Despite this setback, the local suffragists held two other unusual events in the town shortly afterwards, only reported by the *Advertiser*. These involved several new characters in the local campaign. The presence of Mr Nicholas Lee helps to give some insight into how the women's suffrage movement grew and developed. Mr Lee moved out of Shepherd's Bush to Wendover, following his marriage to a Cornish woman called Erva, three years previously.[3] They moved in to the High Street, next door to the Meads, who were supportive of the women's cause. Setting up business as a draper in town, Mr Lee would probably also have known the 'dress goods merchant', Alfred Sichel, and they shared a common bond of being Londoners and outsiders in this rural Buckinghamshire town. These new friendships with people from a similar business background probably helped to cement a further common bond: a commitment to a more progressive understanding of gender relations, perhaps not generally shared by the majority of the local population.

During the week after Mrs Hamilton's second sale of goods, two informal discussion meetings were held as part of the opening of Mr Lee's new drapers show-room on the High Street. The afternoon gathering was for women, over a cup of tea, while the evening one was for men, when a cigar was offered to everyone attending, courtesy of Mr Mead, who was himself unable to attend due to business. Those hosting both meetings were: Miss Raleigh, Miss Weir and the Misses Lees, presumably sisters to Mr Lee.

The 'communicated' article featuring these two meetings listed the nine points presented for discussion:

'1) The present position of men as regards the vote;

---

[1] *BH*, 20th April 1912.
[2] *BAAN*, 20th April 1912.
[3] 1911 England and Wales Census.

2) The claim of women to share this position exactly...;

3) The injustice of bringing on adult suffrage before women get a say;

4) The necessity that responsible women who pay rates and taxes should help to elect M.P.s;

5) Some offences for which women are punished and men get off scot-free;

6) The under-selling of men by "sweated" women;

7) The inadequate moral protection afforded to girls by law...;

8) The traffic in women's souls and purses;

9) The necessity for men and women to work together to make the world better'.

The influence of the WFL on this agenda can be clearly seen, especially from the fifth point. The WFL's newspaper, *The Vote*, had a regular column which kept a record of legal cases where there was a manifest inequality between the sentences given to men, compared to punishments delivered to women. This list also reveals the growing strength of feeling in the suffrage movement in its later years, over issues to do with prostitution and women's employment.

As Chairman for both meetings, Mr Lee made some remarks on the women's movement being a sign of progress. Lively discussions followed. The article concludes by thanking Mrs Hamilton of Chestnut Cottage for her hospitality, which apparently, 'made everything easy and pleasant for those organising this week's meetings'.[1]

There is one further mention of the events of that week, in the subsequent issue of the *Herald*. It seems Mrs Hamilton was upset by the hi-jacking of her sale of goods by the 'antis', so she wrote to the *Herald* and the *Examiner*. Her letter included the following comments:

'The Commissioners give permission to all passive resisters to make a protest... The Anti-Suffragists had no such claim. Until Miss Mabel Smith came forward to the rostrum I was unaware of her presence in the room, or that the local Anti-Suffrage branch had arranged that she would come down from town to speak. Twenty public meetings have been held in the neighbourhood of Wendover during the past year, but Anti-Suffragists have not availed themselves of these opportunities. Suffragists never refuse a challenge, but on the occasion of my sale - which was neither a debate nor a meeting - both sides were heard at the expense of one'.

Yours faithfully

---

[1] *BAAN*, 20th April 1912.

FLORENCE G. HAMILTON
Wendover, Bucks, April 23, 1912"[1]

There are a number of interesting points from this letter, including the claim of 20 meetings in the last year. This does not tally with the NUWSS annual report, but is still a larger number than picked up by the local press. Mrs Hamilton's letter also points towards a willingness on behalf of the suffragists to take on the 'antis' in set public debates, an approach which the Mid-Bucks, Wycombe and Beaconsfield branches of the NUWSS adopted from 1912 onwards.

This letter is the last time Mrs Hamilton's name appears in the local papers regarding women's suffrage. So it is possible that Mrs Hamilton left Wendover after this 1912 campaign in the town. There are certainly no further reports of meetings at Chestnut Cottage, or of campaigns conducted from there. However, Mrs Hamilton did take part in a quiet WTRL demonstration in Aylesbury later that year.

From this point on it seems that the centre of gravity for the Mid-Bucks branch campaigns shifts from Wendover to Great Missenden. This was probably not an attempt by the NUWSS branch to evade the attentions of Wendover's well-organised anti-suffrage group. Suffragists tended to welcome the attentions of 'antis'. This was certainly true of the Beaconsfield suffragist, Miss Olave Snow, who welcomed a new anti-suffrage branch to her town in a 1913 letter. She commented their presence would 'no doubt help to make the question a living one'.[2]

This geographical shift of focus was an inevitable consequence of the appointment of a new Secretary, Miss Catherine Courtauld, who lived just outside Great Missenden. The next annual meeting, for example, was held at Miss Courtauld's house, instead of at St Teresa's. And the multiplication of meetings in this area rather than in Wendover would suggest that a change in personnel led also to a change in geographical focus. This was coupled with much more public criticism of the militant WSPU by these constitutional suffragists, which made any informal alliance with the WFL or the WTRL less tenable.

Many of the early campaigners from Wendover continued their involvement with events in Great Missenden. But with the later development of a sub-committee centred on Kingshill, just beyond Missenden, the local

---

[1] *BH*, 27th April 1912; *BE*, 26th April 1912.
[2] *SBS*, 13th February 1913: 'Woman Suffrage at Beaconsfield'; Burgin, p. 51.

campaign centre not only shifted its location, but it also subtly changed its approach.

Chapter 5: Aylesbury and the Prison Protests

'What were a few broken windows (compared) to the vote? ... Although they had commenced by breaking windows, they would continue by breaking heads'.
- Anonymous suffragette protester in Aylesbury, *BH*, 20th April 1912.

UNLIKE the story of High Wycombe, there is no local figure that stands out in the twentieth century history of the women's suffrage movement in Aylesbury. No-one seems to have taken up the political challenge of Dr John Lee of Hartwell House. His convincing defeat at the 1852 elections seems to have relegated the issue of women's suffrage well down the local political agenda. However, this did not prevent leading suffragists holding a meeting in the town to raise a women's suffrage petition in 1874, as they also did in High Wycombe and also Buckingham that same year. But Aylesbury may not have been quite so responsive in the 1890s, when there seems to have been a stirring of interest in the question in the High Wycombe area, for example.

Throughout the period and especially in the 1890s with the formation of the Independent Labour Party, there was a strong labour movement in the town. This was sufficient to attract some high-profile speakers, notably the man who went on to become leader of the Labour Party and the first Labour Prime Minister. The Co-operative movement seems to have been well-supported, including an active Women's Co-operative Guild in the town. This may, perversely, have contributed to the women's suffrage movement struggling to make headway there. The earliest meetings recorded in the newspapers were inspired by the call, from the local labour movement, for nothing less than 'Adult Suffrage'.

Ramsay Macdonald visited Aylesbury in March 1907. He and his wife, Margaret, spoke on a number of issues, including women's suffrage to a 'fairly large audience', at the Aylesbury Co-operative Hall on the High Street. This appearance in Buckinghamshire was only a few weeks after the historic Belfast Conference, when Keir Hardie had warned that if the Independent Labour Party did not support women's suffrage more readily, they were in danger of losing some of their best women campaigners. Ramsay appeared alongside his wife. Margaret Macdonald followed her husband's speech with an address of her own, in which she advocated votes for women. Her speech is not recorded. Ramsay in his speech had been keen to publicly distance himself from the Pankhursts. He is reported to have said that, 'He was not in sympathy with a certain section of women who were carrying out a campaign in the country, but at the same time he thought that justice should be done'.[1]

This is symptomatic of the wider labour movement's ambivalence and even hostility towards the Pankhursts and the wider women's suffrage cause. Not many working men were prepared to see propertied women gain the vote ahead of them. Mr J. Fox of The Mount, Aston Clinton, who chaired this meeting, was clearly an ardent ILP supporter, along with men at the meeting like Mr H. Bentley, Mr T. Burgess and Mr W.J. Atkins. However, none of these names appear in the accounts of meetings which were supporting women's suffrage in subsequent years. The apparent lack of enthusiasm for 'votes for women' amongst the local labour supporters, may well have caused the women's movement to struggle here initially. It was only later, when the ILP and the NUWSS united, that the campaign began to gain some momentum in the town.

However, there was not much that would deter the thick-skinned suffragettes from attempting to reach Aylesbury and places like it. In the summer of 1909, the first suffragette open-air meeting took place in Aylesbury. Although an impromptu affair, only advertised shortly before, it still managed to attract a crowd of over 200 people. The crowd were cordial, if not enthusiastic. A local newsagent offered to display a poster and sell copies of 'Votes for Women' on a trial basis, which suggests either a degree of sympathy in the town, or that here was someone with a keen eye for business, willing to make the most of the latest sensation.

The photo of the butcher's shop in Cambridge Street, with a display board showing a suffragette protester, demonstrates impact of the suffragettes in the popular imagination. This advert may have been put up in response to the first visit of suffragettes in 1909, or perhaps in 1912 at the time of the prison protests.

Being able to publicise meetings well in advance was not always an advantage. This gave opponents of votes for women, as well as those simply out to cause trouble, a chance to gather in numbers to disrupt proceedings. On Saturday 30th November, 1909, a more prominent suffragist received a much less friendly welcome, compared to the welcome afforded to the suffragettes earlier that year. This was the year of the formation of the CLWS, which may have been the inspiration for what was probably one in a series of meetings across the country. There is no mention of this in the local

---

[1] *BH*, 16th March 1907.

newspaper article, but the *Advertiser* reporter did estimate the staggering number of 1,000 people present.[1] Lady Frances Balfour came to speak to a meeting in the Town Hall. Lady Balfour had been on the executive of the NUWSS since its launch in 1897, as well as being President of the London Society for Women's Suffrage.

The meeting was chaired by Mr H. T. Shawcross of the Men's League for Women's Suffrage. This was the male equivalent of the non-militant NUWSS. The Rev. Hugh Chapman, Chaplain of the Royal Chapel, Savoy was also due to speak, along with Miss Helgo Gill of Norway. Miss Gill was due to talk about 'How the women won the vote in Norway', as the women there had gained the vote earlier that year. (Those listed as present include a number from Wendover, current and later members of the Mid-Bucks NUWSS: Miss Solomon, Miss Sichel, Mrs Hamilton and Mrs Mead, Mrs Adams, Mrs Sikes, Miss Mullett, Miss Mackenzie and Mrs Bedford. Lady Battersea again wired an expression of her support. Canon Scott Holland, Mr F. W. Mallam, and Mr Moseley sent their apologies). Earlier that year, Hugh Chapman had written an article for *Votes for Women*, describing his 'First Impressions' of a WSPU meeting on 8th July in St James' Hall.[2] He wrote of how the 'atmosphere of sternness and fearlessness... had for me the same sort of charm as must have moved a recruit in the early Crusades'. He went on to suggest in the same article that the lack of resounding support for the suffrage cause among the churches was probably due to 'the old Biblical idea of women's position'.

An indication of how the meeting in Aylesbury was going to end came at the beginning of the evening, when a man stood up before Lady Balfour could speak and loudly demanded to ask a question. The question was more of a statement: 'It's a woman's place at home to cook a man's dinner or breakfast. We don't want women in Parliament. We want men who can speak and do justice to the working man'.

Lady Balfour did not allow this to put her off her stride. She fought fire with fire and countered by saying that '... if every woman in the country refused for three weeks to cook any dinner, they would get the vote immediately'. As Norman Maclean, a family friend had once observed, Lady Balfour was 'A mistress of invective,...(who) wielded the dagger of sarcastic wit with the same zest as her ancestors had wielded the broadsword'.[3] More significantly, she responded by detailing ways that women had already been

---

[1] *BAAN*, 4th December 1909, p. 6.

[2] *VW*, 23rd July 1909, p. 968.

[3] Huffman, Joan B. - *DNB*, 2004-13.

involved in politics, via the Temperance movement, the Primrose League and the Liberal Federation. She pointed to the millions of homes where women had to work to get food for their children. Her conclusion that '...it seemed unfair, and quite impossible, to tell them to stay at home and cook dinners when they had to go out and earn materials for their dinner', received polite applause. But directly after this the meeting descended into chaos, with a huge commotion being made by the men at the rear of the hall.

The mob ignored appeals by Rev. Hugh Chapman. Miss Gill went, 'in a most plucky manner' to try to reason with the men, accompanied by Mrs Bedford and Miss Mackenzie and 'Mr Wright of Aylesbury', possibly Percy Wright, the Town Clerk. But no progress was made and some gentlemen from the platform had to create a way for the ladies to return, who were jostled as they did so.

After over an hour of almost non-stop disruption, the speakers abandoned the platform and retreated across the Market Square to the George Hotel, guarded by a detachment of policemen. The rowdy element in the crowd gleefully swarmed onto the platform, but the police soon cleared the hall. One of their favourite means of disruption had been to sing 'Three Cheers for the Red, White and Blue'.

It is interesting to speculate about those who disrupted this meeting. Were these mostly unenfranchised men, unwilling to see women gain the vote ahead of them? Or were they simply prejudiced voters? Their choice of a patriotic song may suggest that they were incensed by a 'foreigner' telling them what to do. In keeping with much anti-suffragist sentiment, these men may have considered it their patriotic duty to defend the status quo and the Empire against such revolutionary changes to the British way of life. Indeed, there were often close links between the National Service League and the anti-suffrage movement.[1] The Rev. Chapman and the Church League for Women's Suffrage seem to have taken this incident as a specific challenge to target Aylesbury with more suffragist speakers and propaganda. The CLWS and another suffrage organisation arranged visits to the town the following summer and autumn.

Before this, however, the movement for adult suffrage also brought its views before the local population. In May 1910, the Co-operative Hall hosted Miss Ward, from London, a member of the Executive Committee of the People's Suffrage Federation. This new organisation which had only been in existence a few months. Formed in October 1909, the People's Suffrage

---

[1] Harrison, Brian - *Separate Spheres: The Opposition to Women's Suffrage in Britain*, p. 76.

Federation was led by Miss Margaret Bondfield, who went on to become the first female government minister.

There were a large number of ladies present, including Miss Pescod, the secretary of the local branch. Mr W.A. Hutchins presided. The meeting opened by expressing sympathy for the Queen Mother at the loss of her husband, King Edward VII. Miss Ward went on to argue that 'Those who lived under the laws and suffered by the laws ought to take a share in saying what those laws should be'. She also claimed that '...every sane person of age should have a vote' and that '...the responsibility of a vote tended towards the education and enlightenment of the people'.[1] It is notable that there seems to have been no disruption or any attempt to disrupt this meeting. Perhaps those who felt their blood boil at the mention of 'women's suffrage' could not stir so much opposition when the object was votes for all. It is also possible that there was more local sympathy for working class speakers. The men of Aylesbury, in keeping with its Nonconformist history, seem to have had little time for wealthy aristocrats like Lady Balfour and well-connected clergymen like the Rev. Hugh Chapman.

The CLWS was not deterred, however. This organisation had been launched in 1909 and seen rapid initial growth in the numbers of branches being formed. Many churchwomen and men, from both the established church and the free churches, saw their mission as an extension of the mission of Christ, to bring wider emancipation to the whole world. A Baptist minister who supported the WSPU's efforts from the beginning, the Rev. J. Ivory Cripps, wrote, '... the Women's Movement and the Free Church ideal spring from the same spiritual principle of soul liberty....'[2]

Some of the residents of Aylesbury readily agreed with this thinking. The high profile of the CLWS locally may well have been encouraged by one of the leading churchwomen of the town, Mrs Elizabeth Allen Horwood. A Mrs Horwood is mentioned in association with suffrage meetings in Aylesbury and Wendover. Married to the prominent figure of Lieutenant Colonel Thomas Horwood, she had an extensive network of influential friends in the town, through her philanthropic church work, which included being appointed one of the first women Poor Law Guardians in Aylesbury. Coupled with her campaigning work for the Temperance League, this gave her experiences in common with many early suffragists. Mrs Horwood was

---

[1] *BAAN*, 21st May 1910, p. 8.
[2] *Free Church Suffrage Times*, March 1914.

perhaps hoping to establish a local branch of the CLWS in Aylesbury, although she was already in her early 70s at this stage.[1]

Miss Canning, one of the CLWS's regular speakers, held a series of meetings in the Market Square in the summer of 1910. Little seems to have been reported about these events. It seems the visiting women's suffrage campaigners were based in Wendover for two weeks in August. Miss Canning and Miss Gertrude Eaton stayed with Mrs Hamilton at Chestnut Cottage.[2] The CLWS was joined the following year by the Free Church League, which had only just been launched in 1910.

The 1910 campaigning in Aylesbury finished with two contrasting events in the same week of September: one an open-air meeting with speakers arriving in a caravan, the other an event organised by the local Co-operative movement. These meetings followed attempts by the cross-party Conciliation Committee to pressure the government to include the Women's Enfranchisement Bill early on in the next session of Parliament.

The WFL's caravan tour for this year spent most of August and September travelling from Bedfordshire to places in Hertfordshire. The tour was concluded in Berkhamsted, but not before the caravan visited Buckingham and Aylesbury. The meetings in Buckingham Market Square apparently attracted between 500 and 1,000 people. In her report in the WFL newspaper, Miss Marguerite Sidley makes no mention about numbers present at the meetings held at Aylesbury.[3]

Miss Sidley was clearly an experienced and engaging speaker. The crowds in Buckingham apparently listened to her 'stirring address' with 'rapt interest'. Of the Aylesbury visit she wrote: 'At the end of our first meeting we were told by many of our sympathisers that this was the best meeting ever held in the Market Square. Next day we were informed that chalking was prohibited, so we advertised other meetings by "town crying".'

Miss Sidley was accompanied at this stage of the tour by Miss Henderson of Lewisham. The short article in the *Herald*, entitled 'Suffragettes at Aylesbury' records some of Miss Sidley's remarks.[4] She employed humour by stating that '...99 men out of 100 were of the opinion that woman was an unsolvable puzzle. They could not understand woman, they said, and therefore could not legislate for her'. Miss Sidley also appealed to the recent history of the labour movement: 'Forty years ago men were sweated and

---

[1] *BAAN*, 25th November 1925, obit.
[2] *VW*, 19th August 1910, p. 771.
[3] *The Vote*, 1st October 1910, p. 266.
[4] *BH*, 24th September 1910.

exploited, and it was only through the power of the vote that they were able to alter this. The women of today used the same argument, maintaining that it applied to them equally as it did to the men'. People asked questions at the end of the meeting, but it appears there was no attempt to disrupt Miss Sidley's speech.[1]

During the same week there was another meeting in the Co-operative Hall. There was a significant development since previous similar meetings. The 'good company of women' present were addressed by Miss Ashford of the People's Suffrage Federation.[2] Opening the meeting, the Chairman, Mr T. Burgess confessed that previously he had 'strongly objected' to giving women the vote. He did not mention how he was convinced otherwise, or how long this process took. But his experience is evidence of the ability of the women's suffrage movement to change the minds of some resolutely opposed to this dramatic but long-awaited reform.

Miss Ashford argued for a widening and deepening of the practice of democracy, through the principle of rights for all citizens born in any country. She declared that 'It was the right and duty of every person to take an interest in the matter of government.' Married women should have as much of a right as those who were single, she felt. This was still a debatable issue for some, but the heat had largely gone from the divisive debates of previous decades. She refused to condemn the militant actions of the suffragettes, because to do so would hinder their cause. Miss Ashford then concluded by declaring that where other nations had given women the vote '... it had in no way been detrimental to the well-being of those countries'.

This may have been the last public meeting in Aylesbury to advocate adult suffrage on a separate platform to the wider women's suffrage movement. Whether this is because these two political cousins decided to join forces locally, it is difficult to discern. The somewhat lack-lustre meetings of 1911, coupled with the disturbances of 1912, may have helped convince both sides of the need to work together. And the decision of the leaders of the NUWSS to support the Independent Labour Party later in 1913 could have been decisive. This is certainly confirmed by the different nature of the last women's suffrage meetings which subsequently took place in the town.

The next time 'votes for women' featured in the local newspapers does not appear to be until July 1911. Some anonymous 'suffragettes' who were also described as 'non-militant' held a meeting in the market square, attended

---

[1] *BH,* 24th September 1910.
[2] *BAAN,* 24th September 1910.

by a 'fairly large audience'.[1] This was possibly the Australian suffragette, Muriel Matters, with the WTRL caravan. She started her fortnight's tour of the area on 5th July at Great Missenden and reported having taken two meetings at Aylesbury.[2]

In November 1911, the CLWS was back again. This time they were more ambitious, planning a two-week mission both in and around Aylesbury. The short introductory article in the *Herald* which was probably submitted by the CLWS, announced that the Rev. Claude Hinscliff, founder and secretary of the League, was devoting himself to forming branches throughout the country. Although 'hundreds of new members,' had just been enrolled at the recent Church Congress in Stoke-on-Trent, it does not appear that the desired formation of a branch in Aylesbury was ultimately achieved. This was despite the giving out of a reported 5,000 leaflets in the town during the fortnight. The article mentioned that the Parliamentary Chairman of the Conciliation Committee, Lord Lytton, was a CLWS member. It also quoted CLWS President, the Bishop of Lincoln, who declared: 'To my mind, St Paul's declaration of the equality of men and women in Christ (Colossians 3:11) stands as a principle of the Church's Gospel'. A member of the local FCLWS, Mr T. Rogers, was named in *The Vote* as 'organising secretary pro-tem' for a CLWS branch in formation in the district.[3] The fact that the vicar of St Mary's Parish Church, Rev. Canon C.O. Phipps, was himself an anti-suffragist may well have proved decisive in frustrating this determined effort to launch a local CLWS branch in the town.

Principle speakers for the fortnight were Miss Canning again and Miss Matters. Muriel Matters is described as 'local organiser' and her address is given as St Teresa's, Wendover

One Monday afternoon the inaugural service for the fortnight was held at the Literary Institute, Temple Street. Miss Matters and Miss Canning both spoke, introduced by Rev. Claude Hinscliff. It was possibly a provocative opening as the Rothschild family were closely associated with the Institute from its foundation and Lord Lionel de Rothschild, the local MP, was a prominent anti-suffragist. However, there was only a 'small attendance'[4]. One apology for absence was received from Mrs Horwood, who expressed sympathy with the movement.

---

[1] *BH*, 22nd July 1911, p. 5.
[2] WTRL Committee Minute Book, 1909-13: entries for 9th June – 18th July 1911.
[3] *BH*, 21st October 1911.
[4] *BH*, 4th November 1911

If this re-construction of events is correct, this meeting was shortly followed by a united meeting made up of representatives of the CLWS and the FCLWS at the Council Schools, Stoke Mandeville. An open-air meeting was held in the Aylesbury Market Square on the Saturday, addressed by Miss Matters, who '... met opposition in a tactful and humorous way'.[1] Another meeting was held at the Council Schools that evening, when Miss Canning and Miss Matters both spoke. Miss Matters commented,

'... they had already discovered that the Church League was badly needed in Aylesbury. She had been told by a clergyman in Aylesbury that day that they were taking on a tremendous thing, and he looked with surprise at their audacity. She told him they had faith, which simply meant they were going forward into darkness, knowing that the light was beyond somewhere'.

The local vicar, Rev. F. J. Winterton, presided. He told the meeting he had for years been, '... very much in favour of women having votes'. The reason he gave for this was the knowledge he had gained of the social conditions the women of the East End lived in, through his elder sister who was a worker there.

There was also a men's meeting organised one Monday at Mr Cecil's in Wendover. This was coupled with a mother's meeting at Mrs Mead's the following Wednesday in Wendover.

On the last weekend of the fortnight there were two meetings. One held in the Co-operative Hall in Aylesbury on the Friday evening.[2] Dr Rose presided, but it was poorly attended and received little comment. The final Saturday saw a meeting in Wendover at the home of Mr and Mrs Mead, Bosworth House, at no. 27 the High Street. Described as, 'an informal conference', Miss Matters gave details of the aims of the CLWS. Sketching a brief history of 19th century voting reform, she asserted that as merchants, the middle classes and most recently agricultural labourers had joined the aristocracy in being represented in Parliament, it was time that the women were too. She supported this with the often repeated argument that '... in the face of the domestic legislation that was constantly being brought forward which affected the home life of the nation, that women should have an opportunity through their votes of expressing an opinion.'

At the conclusion of the meeting, Mr Mead publicly stated his opinion that women who currently were able to vote in local elections should also be

---

[1] *BH*, 4th November 1911.
[2] *BH*, 11th November 1911.

able to vote in general elections. It is interesting to speculate whether he had recently arrived at this opinion, through being present at other women's suffrage meetings in the town, or whether he had already been persuaded by his wife.

In the process of thanking Mr and Mrs Mead, Miss Matters, who was never one to miss an opportunity, also expressed the hope that some of the men present would have the courage to ask the local MP for his views on women's suffrage the next time he visited the town. It is unclear whether anyone took up this particular challenge.

1912 provided a big spike in the profile of the women's suffrage movement in Aylesbury. The events of one particular weekend were important enough in the suffragette campaign to even attract a visit from Sylvia Pankhurst. Sylvia may have been the only one of the Pankhurst family to come to Buckinghamshire to speak. To really understand her visit to Aylesbury means having to place it in the wider context.

In the years 1910 and 1911 it began to seem just possible that the women's demands might finally be met. Despite the Prime Minister, Asquith, veering between ambivalence and outright hostility, and despite the Liberal government still being deeply divided on the issue, it seemed that some women had begun to hope that lasting change might be just around the corner. The Conciliation Bill, fully debated in Parliament in 1911, would have enfranchised over 1 million women householders. But this was shelved later in the year, in preference to a 1912 Manhood Suffrage Bill, supposedly open for amendment. After the high point of the Coronation Procession in the summer of 1911, the tide seemed to turn against those pressing for the vote. Things started to get uglier.

Early in 1912, feeling that police were deliberately arresting fewer protesters and using greater brutality against them, the WSPU made a surprise change of tactics. In March 1912, instead of targeting the Houses of Parliament, groups of suffragettes mounted attacks on shop windows in the West End and other less defended targets.

Many were arrested and summarily tried. Due to Holloway being over-crowded, 28 of these suffragette window-smashers were transferred from Holloway to Aylesbury Prison.[1] Built in 1847, this prison had been made a women's prison in 1890. It held 200 women serving sentences of three years to life.[2]

---

[1] Crawford - *WSM*, pp. 567-574, 'Prison'.
[2] Cook, Pat - *HMYOI Aylesbury*, May 1997.

Aylesbury Prison, c. 1910. From Wickipedia, April 2013

The suffragettes were sentenced to terms ranging from a few weeks to six months inside. Here are the names of some of the prisoners held in Aylesbury, including the sources of where they have been identified as having been inmates of Aylesbury Prison:

Dr Frances Ede (PRO, CBS)
Oomah Caillaigh (PRO, CBS)
Grace Branson (PRO, CBS)
Margaret Haley (PRO, CBS)
Annie Humphrey (PRO, CBS)
Olive Walton (Crawford - *WSM*, pp. 699-700)
Ada Cecile Wright (Crawford - *WSM*, pp. 759-761)
Violet Ann Bland (Crawford - *WSM*, p. 62-3)

Miss Wyley (Walker, Michael - http://our history-hayes.blogspot.co.uk,
'Pinner Prisoners' - June 2012) – possibly Miss Wylie ?
Brita Gurney (CBS)
Amy Hicks (PRO, Crawford - *WSM*, pp. 284-5)
Charlotte Marsh (CBS, Crawford - *WSM*, pp. 381-2)

These last two were considered ringleaders by the prison authorities, and
they considered moving them to Manchester Prison to stop them stirring up
their fellow prisoners.[1] Charlotte Marsh had previously been involved in
harrassing the Prime Minister at Bletchley Park. On this occasion, she had
been sentenced to six months imprisonment.

Fairly soon after their transfer to Aylesbury, on Good Friday, 5th April,
most if not all of these suffragettes were able to secretly start a hunger strike.
The women managed to smuggle food out of their cells, hidden in their
clothes, and disposed of it in the toilets. They adopted this protest, in
common with other suffragettes, because their petition to the Home
Secretary to be treated as political prisoners had not been answered. Mrs
Pankhurst described how word got around and the protests quickly spread to
a number of prisons at this time, so that very soon there were over 80
suffragettes on hunger strike in different prisons.[2]

The secret hunger-strike at Aylesbury Prison went undiscovered it seems
for three or four days. On discovery, forcible feeding was immediately
introduced, apparently on the evening of Tuesday 9th April. Nine of them
were force fed by cup, twelve by nasal tube and two by a tube down the
throat. This first incident of force feeding apparently took nearly 4 hours to
complete. The next day, however, the prison contacted Dr Smalley, a
Medical Inspector of Prisons, to check the health of the prisoners. Having
come from London on the 3.20pm train, he pronounced that four of the
prisoners were in no fit condition to be forcibly fed, due to underlying health
problems, and another one was later added to this list: Dr Frances Ede,
Oomah Caillaigh, Grace Branson, Margaret Haley and Annie Humphrey.
Due to health problems including 'aortic disease', 'cardiac weakness' and
asthma, these five were granted an early release from prison.[3] Dr Smalley
concluded his report by stating that he saw no reason not to continue force-
feeding the other prisoners.

---

[1] PRO archives.
[2] Pankhurst, Emmeline - *My Own Story*, p. 251.
[3] The Prisoners Remission Warrants, signed on 11th April by King George V.

This incidence of early release from Aylesbury prison, probably contributed to the Government's decision to introduce the infamous 'Cat and Mouse Act' the following year. This was legislation hurried through Parliament, which enabled prisons to release hunger-striking suffragettes for a time, until they regained their strength, when they were subsequently re-arrested and immediately taken back into custody. Another battle of hunger-strike and forcible feeding usually followed.

After her early release, Dr Ede claimed in a letter to the *Times*, that following the Health Inspector's visit, water was taken away from the cells and milk was put in its place.[1] However, this attempt to break the hunger strike was abandoned after the women threw the milk away. Dr Ede commented '...by far the more terrible experience than my personal suffering was to hear the agonising cries from the other cells as the prisoners in turn were subjected to the painful treatment.'[2]

Dr Ede was 60 years old when subjected to this treatment. She was described by Dr Smalley as being 'very persistent in her resistance' to force feeding.[3] Her experiences in Aylesbury Prison obviously stiffened her own resolve in the militant struggle. The following year she accompanied Mrs Pankhurst on a visit to Christabel in Paris.[4] She also continued, with Dr Sheppard, the partner in her medical practice, to resist paying her taxes.[5]

Most of the remaining suffragette hunger-strikers continued to be forcibly fed. Ada Cecile Wright had been sentenced to six months because of previous offences. Miss Wright had been featured in a newspaper photo of the 'Black Friday' protests in London in November 1910. She appears a tiny figure, lying, cowering on the ground.[6] The photograph was apparently suppressed by the government, but not before there had been a short-lived outburst of sympathy for the suffragettes, in the face of police and public intimidation and violence.

Miss Wright's subsequent letter shows how traumatic force feeding was for the suffragettes, and to a lesser extent, for the wardens and doctors:

'The door of my cell was flung open and 4-6 or seven officers entered and seized me. There was a deep, breathless struggle as I clung to my iron

---

[1] *Times*, 13th April 1912, p. 11.
[2] Ibid.
[3] PRO archives.
[4] Crawford - *WSM*, p. 510.
[5] *The Vote*, 3rd April 1914, p. 389.
[6] Crawford - *WSM*, pp. 759-60.

bedstead... I was tied down into a chair, hands and arms held firmly by the wardresses either side. The two doctors began their objectionable work. They forced open my jaws and a steel gag was inserted between my teeth and my mouth was then prized open and kept so by the doctor behind. The doctor in front rammed the stomach tube down my throat (unspeakable instrument of disgust and torture)... We rub our eyes and ask if this is Christian England in the 20th century?'[1]

A protest march was hastily organised for Saturday 13th April. The MP for Bow, George Lansbury, raised a question in Parliament about the plight of these women.[2] Home Secretary McKenna simply replied with a factual statement, giving a break-down of the type of feeding employed with those remaining.

A party of suffragettes from London, preparing to march from Aylesbury market square to the Prison. From the Buckinghamshire County Museum Collections

---

[1] *VW*, 12th July 1912, p. 665.
[2] *VW*, 20th April 1912, p. 4.

Around 100 protesters arrived in Aylesbury on the train from London, and assembled in the market square. The protesters came from a number of different suffrage organisations, but were led by the WTRL. The tax resisters sported their black, yellow and white colours, while the members of the WSPU their trademark purple, green and white. Other organisations represented were the WFL and the CLWS, the Men's Political Union and the Men's Society for Women's Rights. Curiosity in the town was clearly at a high level. Some seemed to be expecting the suffragettes to attempt to break their fellow campaigners out of the prison.

Headed by the London Prize Band, the marchers moved off along Cambridge Street, in the direction of the prison. One of the marchers was Elizabeth Wilks of Clapton. Mrs Wilks and her husband, Mark, went on to gain some national notoriety. Mark Wilks was imprisoned later that year for refusing to pay his wife's taxes, a case which was also raised in the Commons.

The day after the protest in Aylesbury, Mrs Wilks wrote a letter from 47 Upper Clapton Road, to her sister, Nelly Taylor, a fellow suffragette. She described the scene in Aylesbury: 'We met at the Market Place and marched in procession around the gaol, with the band playing the Women's March and all the inhabitants of the town following, as they understood we had come to rescue our friends'.[1]

The protesters carried banners, including one with a portrait of John Hampden, which bore the slogan, 'Taxation without representation is tyranny'.[2] The band played the 'Women's March' and at the prison they all sang the Marseillaise, with words adapted for the campaign:

'To Freedom's cause 'til death,
We swear our fealty.
March on! March on! Face to the dawn,
The dawn of Liberty !'[3]

A line in one of the verses was: 'Our comrades, bravely daring, through prison bars have led the way'. At the rear of the prison, the marchers made so much commotion that a herd of cattle wildly rushed up and down a neighbouring field. The prisoners acknowledged the salute of the marchers by hanging towels from their cell windows and waving their handkerchiefs.

---

[1] Wilks, Elizabeth - *Taylor Letter Collection*.
[2] *BAAN*, 20th April 1912, p. 11.
[3] Cockroft, V. Irene and Susan Croft - *Art, Theatre and Women's Suffrage*, pp. 112-13.

On returning to the market square, the carnival atmosphere quickly changed. The account in the *Advertiser* managed to record something of the speeches given by two of the speakers in the market square that day. Here is a summary of Mrs Cobden Sanderson's remarks:

'(The Women's Tax Resistance League) said they would no longer continue to pay Imperial Taxes, if they were not allowed to say how that money was to be spent... The women were therefore constitutional in refusing to pay taxes. Just as John Hampden had fought and whose memory the town of Aylesbury intended to honour... They saw the misery and starvation in our big towns and cities, the sweating of men and women, the white slave traffic, and they... could no longer sit at home in quietness... They had marched to Aylesbury, where 23 women were suffering as John Hampden suffered, going to prison for the same principles.' [1]

Miss Georgina Brackenbury's remarks were also recorded. They are summarised here:

'Why did the working men get the vote in 1867? Because they marched 50,000 strong to Hyde Park and broke down the gates closed against them, with the result that Mr Disraeli said in the House, "We cannot withstand this demand any longer because the people have shown they are in earnest"... British women were not cowards, they were in earnest... They were fighting for the true principle of the British Constitution, which was government by consent... Although in the last two years women had broken windows, men in the House of Commons had broken pledges made to the women... She appealed to her audience as fair-minded men... to say that the women were entitled to recognition.'[2]

In contrast, the *Herald* reporter focussed on the increasingly disruptive and violent behaviour of the crowds. Here is a summary of this lengthy account:

'Three sections of the crowd were addressed by Mrs Sanderson, Miss Brackenbury and Mr Victor Duval, and at first they made considerable headway... Miss Edith Bell and Miss Taylor, representing the WSPU, took their stand near the lions, and for a time got a fair hearing, 'til the crowd surging round the Clock Tower became aware of the progress of another meeting. Then there were some ugly rushes and the male section of the

---

[1] *BAAN*, 20th April 1912, p. 11.
[2] *BH*, 20th April 1912.

party had their work cut out to protect the temporary platform. ... Very soon the speakers were in the midst of a fusillade of tomatoes, potatoes, rice and other vegetables... At least this was the fate of the lady speakers. More drastic methods were meted out to a male speaker... he was thrown violently to the ground and the platform and chair smashed out of all recognition. From this point on there was no holding the crowd in check, despite all the efforts of the police, under D.C.C. Pitson, who were assisted by P.S. Faithfull on horseback. ... The other two meetings came to a dramatic termination and the speakers and their supporters were hustled here and there.... Several of (the protesters) took refuge in the neighbouring houses... To the credit of Aylesbury... only in a few isolated incidents were the ladies attacked viciously in any way... It was now nearly 9 o'clock and at intervals the visitors made their way, still greatly harassed in the direction of the Joint Railway Station... Every now and then there would be a wild shout, and a stampede in the direction of someone or other whom the crowd thought were members of the Suffragette party... The appearance of a man with the banner of the League was the signal for a determined effort to wrest it from his possession. He however... was forcibly assisted onto the platform... Interviewed at the station by our representative, several of the party expressed their astonishment that the crowd should have assumed such hostility... our representative replied, "Yes... but do you not think the supporters of the movement have made a mistake in tactics?" "Oh no", one lady replied. "Certainly not; if we cannot get what we want peacably, we cannot be blamed for attracting attention to our desires in another way". Several of them spoke highly of the part played by the police, and were convinced that had they not acted in the way they did, some of them might have been really injured...'.[1]

Mr and Mrs Wilks were also caught up in the market square disturbances. In her letter she describes how her husband only managed to escape being ducked in the horse trough by climbing onto a high wall, from where he was rescued by the police. Mrs Wilks herself had an anxious time in the melee, but more out of concern for someone else caught up in it. She wrote:

'I had with me a young woman who had never seen a suffragist except me. She had lost her parents. She was going into the country with them for the afternoon. I felt so anxious for her lest she should get hurt. It was alright

---

[1] *BH*, 20th April 1912.

however. She was only shaken and horrified and repented I think that she had ever signed an 'Anti' petition'.[1]

The young woman's reference to signing an 'Anti' petition is revealing. However, there is no way of knowing whether this was at a recent, local event or elsewhere. Mrs Wilks' final comment was that 'The women of the town were quite roused to indignation at the way the men behaved and quite a number of the men told us they were not Aylesbury people'.[2]

An Aylesbury butchers shop along Cambridge Street, with advertising board featuring a stereotypical suffragette. From the Buckinghamshire County Museum Collections

It is difficult to understand the level of hostility directed towards this march. However, there was much in the national newspapers about the 'hysterical' behaviour of the suffragettes, combined with either blatant or

---

[1] Elizabeth Wilks' letter to Nelly Taylor, 14th April 1912.
[2] Ibid.

subtle justifications of violence towards them. The popular perception of the WSPU, if not the whole of the women's suffrage movement, was extremely negative. The women involved were routinely held up for ridicule. Furthermore, suffragettes were often seen, understandably, as anti-Liberal and therefore came to be seen as pro-Tory in popular thinking. Coupled with the way militant tactics had estranged much support, this may have resulted in a lack of enthusiasm or even hostility among Aylesbury's labour movement.

Despite local's attempts to point the finger elsewhere, as also happened with a similar incident in High Wycombe the following year, it was surely difficult to blame all the 'rowdyism' entirely upon outsiders. The 'County Towners' resume' in the *Examiner* certainly displays no sympathy for the hunger-strikers or the protesters.[1] This is despite his assessment that the crowd he estimated at several thousand 'kept the place in uproar for hours'.

The events in Aylesbury must have been widely commented upon in the rest of the county. At a meeting in Bourne End on April 15th, organised by the NCSWS, a resolution was proposed by Mrs Constance Davies concerning the forcible feeding of suffragettes at Aylesbury Prison.[2] However, it seems that this was the only suffrage meeting in the county to specifically protest against the treatment of these women. The more common suffragist response was to distance themselves from the militancy of the WSPU. Florence Balgarnie, at a Women's Liberal Association meeting in Missenden, not long after these events, commented in reference to window-smashing that 'They did not go with hammers because they thought it was foolish'.[3]

In the battle for hearts and minds, the subsequent discussion of the councillors at the annual meeting of the Aylesbury Urban District Council on 16th April is revealing. They called the scenes 'disgraceful' and the suffragette speeches 'inflammatory'.[4] Most of the councillors seemed to blame the organisers of the demonstration for the trouble. At a later meeting, Councillor Elliston arguing that by splitting into four meetings, they had divided the strength of the local police force.[5] At the earlier meeting, the councillors were in no mood to respond positively to the request from Mrs Drummond of the WSPU to hold a ticketed meeting in the Town Hall that

---

[1] *BE*, 19th April 1912.

[2] Crawford, Elizabeth - *Campaigning for the Vote, Kate Parry Frye's Suffrage Diary*, p.101

[3] *BAAN*, 22nd June 1912.

[4] *BAAN*, 20th April 1912.

[5] *BAAN*, 18th May 1912.

week or the next. Councillor Cook suggested they should meet on the Wendover Hills, while someone else darkly suggested the sewage works. The decision was taken not to grant permission to the WSPU for use of council buildings at the present time, on the proviso that this decision did not bind the council on future occasions.

Before this discussion of the Council, there had been a separate development. On Sunday evening, the day after the disturbances in the market square, Sylvia Pankhurst came to Aylesbury, just back from a visit to her sister, Christabel, in Paris.[1] Sylvia had not long returned from a visit to the United States and, after a period of soul-searching, was keen to throw herself back into campaigning for the vote. Accompanied by two fellow campaigners, she was told that the town authority would not allow a meeting in the market square. As an expectant crowd had already gathered by the clock tower, they initially refused to comply with the order, but were eventually escorted by the police to the railway station.

Two mounted constables kept the crowd back from the station, while Sylvia and her companions waited for the train to take them back to London. Sylvia tried to address the distant crowd from the platform, speaking on the importance of free speech. Before the train departed at 9.40pm, Sylvia's male companion spoke from a window of the train, with the residents of California, an area of housing beyond the railway tracks.

A crowd also gathered in the square the following evening, in anticipation of another visit by suffragettes, but this did not materialise. That same day, a London housekeeper, Elizabeth Annie Bell, was brought to the County Court, on the charge of breaking a window at the prison, on the day of the march. Giving her address as the address of the WSPU offices in St Clements Inn, she explained that she only threw the stone once she saw that the blind behind the window was pulled down, so she '...knew that the stone or glass would not hurt anyone'.[2] Miss Bell also expressed the wish that she might have 'put out all the windows of Aylesbury'. As she had previous convictions, she was sentenced to two months in prison.[3]

Several letters were written to local papers following these events. One from an anonymous correspondent complained about, 'the disgraceful proceedings in the Market Place'. For this woman at least, the crowd's behaviour was not related to anti-suffragism but was 'hooliganism pure and simple', carried out by groups of youths. She put this down to them having,

[1] Pankhurst, Sylvia - *The Suffragette Movement*, pp. 383-5.
[2] Ibid.
[3] *BAAN*, 28th April 1912.

'a neglected childhood in a bad home' and reported the comment of one bandsmen: 'uncivilised cannibals I call them'. Her perception was that, 'Many of the processionists... were astonished to learn that constitutional societies had been working in the area for the last three years'.[1]

Miss Elizabeth Annie Bell before Aylesbury County Court. From the Buckinghamshire County Museum Collections

Another letter on the same issue, took the opportunity of explaining the principles of tax resistance and invited people to hear Mrs Kineton Parkes of the WTRL speaking at Wendover about the distraint of goods. A third letter is a remarkable defence of suffragette militancy, written under the pen name of 'Juvenis'. (See Appendix 8).

Miss Helen Gordon Liddle, temporarily appointed a local WSPU organiser in the town, also wrote a letter about the prison protest weekend. She was protesting specifically about the Council's decision to prevent the WSPU from holding meetings in the Town Hall. The suffragettes were clearly continuing to campaign in the town. Liddle wrote:

'We understand this refusal only applies to the present and we are undertaking a house to house canvas, to enable the inhabitants of Aylesbury to express, by means of a petition, their wish that the Council should re-

---

[1] *BAAN*, 28th April 1912.

consider their decision... We have ascertained that there is a decided expression of condemnation amongst the townspeople against the disgraceful proceedings of Saturday April 13th... The WSPU should be allowed a fair hearing... in this matter of refusal of free speech, Aylesbury stands alone.'[1]

This 'numerously signed' petition for the Council to re-consider its position was presented to the Council at its meeting on 13th May.[2] The account in the *Advertiser* gives the number of signatures on the petition as 254, which the WSPU claimed were 'principally ratepayers or their wives'.[3] However, a number of the councillors cast doubt upon this assertion, saying that the shop in the High Street identified as 'the promoters' of the petition, had apparently secured a signature from a 16 year old 'tradesman's daughter'. Equally, Councillor Sherriff was outraged that the campaigners had called at his house and requested his niece to sign the petition.

After further discussion, the Council rejected the later appeal against its initial ruling. Chairman H. L. Nippin felt that while the prisoners were still being held, 'the feeling in the town' meant that he did not think the application should be granted. However, Councillor East felt that they should not be 'dominated by the hooligan element', so an attempt was made to amend the original decision to make the Town Hall available, on condition that the organisers agreed to pay for any damages. Councillor Burgess commented that 'There are women incarcerated in Maidstone, Birmingham and London and there is no disturbance there'. His amendment, supported by Councillors Buckingham, East and Smith, was defeated by 13 votes to four.

A number of other threads can be pursued from this notable weekend in the history of Aylesbury. One of the speakers at the market square protest had been Miss Georgina Brackenbury. She was a former a student at the Slade School of Art in London. With her mother, Hilda, she turned their London home into a refuge for suffragettes released from prison. This house in Camden Hill Square was dubbed 'Mouse Castle'.[4]

The Duchess of Bedford, Mrs Adeline Mary Russell, was another figure who became associated with the suffragettes held in Aylesbury prison. A devout churchwoman, she had been heavily involved in the temperance

---

[1] *BAAN*, 4th May 1912, p. 5.
[2] Aylesbury Urban District Council Minute Book, 1911-1913, p. 219-220.
[3] *BAAN*, 18th May 1912, p. 9.
[4] Crawford - *WSM*, p. 75-6; Cockroft, V. Irene- *New Dawn Women*, p. 29.

movement and consequently developed a keen interest in prison work. In 1900 the duchess became the first President of the National Lady Visitor's Association, having become a regular visitor to Aylesbury Prison, alongside Lady Battersea. As well as visiting the State Inebriate Reformatory there, Adeline was also involved with founding the borstal wing, opened in 1908.

After having visited the suffragettes in April 1912, the Duchess of Bedford reportedly wrote a letter in a national newspaper, urging the prisoners to give up their hunger strike, as she believed they were committing a sin in threatening suicide.[1] However, not long after this, Adeline joined the ranks of the suffragists. Perhaps she had been influenced by her conversations with the suffragettes in Aylesbury, as well as by long friendship with her fellow prison-visitor and suffragist, Lady Battersea.

In June 1912, Adeline was listed as a supporter of a meeting in the Queen's Hall to 'consider the religious aspect of the women's movement'.[2] The Duchess of Bedford joined the WTRL and became a tax resister for women's suffrage, having some of her goods distrained in April 1913.[3] This was despite the fact that in 1910, when approached by the anti-suffragist, Lord Curzon, she had declined to sign a public appeal for the NLOWS, explaining that she did not wish to weaken her 'slight influence' by, 'taking part in matters of controversy'.[4] The Duchess of Bedford's country home was Woodside House, Chenies in Buckinghamshire. She was buried here in the Bedford family vault, at St Michael's Church.

Mrs Florence Hamilton of Wendover followed up the letter-writing campaign to Aylesbury Council with another letter which detailed 'the behaviour of the crowd at the recent women's suffrage demonstration and stating that the WTRL with which she was connected was a non-militant body'.[5] No action was taken, although the letter may have ultimately helped her and her fellow suffragists to gain permission, for the next more low-key action they took in Aylesbury.

At the end of the month, on 27th June, the John Hampden statue was unveiled in the Market Square. Members of the WTRL, including Mrs

---

[1] Forsythe, Bill - *DNB*, 2004-11.

[2] *Times*, 8th June 1912, p. 6.

[3] *The Vote*, 25th April 1913, p. 439.

[4] Jalland, Pat - *Women, Marriage and Politics, 1860-1914*, Clarendon Press, 1986, p. 211.

[5] A.U.D. Council Minute Book, 1911-13, 10th June 1912, pp. 242-3.

Hamilton, 'immediately after the unveiling... pressed forward and placed wreaths on the pedestal steps'.[1]

Unveiling ceremony of the John Hampden statue, Aylesbury market square. From the Buckinghamshire County Museum collections

At the very last moment they had been grudgingly allowed to present this commemorative wreath, in honour of the four women who joined John Hampden in his original protest against the Ship Money tax. The names of the four local women were highlighted in gold ribbon: Mrs Westall, and widows Bampton, Goodchild and Temple. Mrs Hamilton was to later write about her hope that 'At some future date Aylesbury may find some way of honouring them'.[2] 'In the course of that day, the women were able to distribute 2,000 leaflets and sell 200 booklets on the life of John Hampden, produced by the WTRL.[3]

Around this time, some of the remaining suffragette prisoners went on hunger strike again. Their forced feeding appears to have provoked no further protests. Charlotte Marsh and Brita Gurney, both serving a six

---

[1] *BAAN*, 29 June 1912.
[2] *BAAN*, 13th July 1912, p. 9.
[3] WTRL Minute Book, 1909-13, 4th July 1912.

month imprisonment, were both released early on 6th July.[1] There appears to be no mention of their release in the local newspapers. So, the part Aylesbury played in the suffragette prison protests came to a muted close.

However, the struggle for gender equality rumbled on in another way, below the surface. In October 1912, the vicar of St Mary's, Canon C.O. Phipps, was speaking to a quarterly meeting of the local Church of England Men's Society branch about the White Slave Traffic question, which had been raised the previous week at the Church of England Men's Society Reading conference. He reported that 'some women who were very enthusiastic in this matter' were planning to arrange a meeting on the subject in the Town Hall that November.[2] These women had been hoping, not only that both the Earl of Buckinghamshire and the Archdeacon of Buckingham might be persuaded to come, but that Canon Phipps would agree to chair the meeting.

Phipps declared that he had consented to be in the chair that evening on two conditions: 'that the meeting would be non-party, non-sectarian and non-suffrage... and that any circulars or bills ... were first submitted to him for his approval'. His stance is not surprising, given that he had expressed support for the establishment of the county's first anti-suffrage branch in Wendover in 1909. The vicar went out to point out that he knew, 'the Urban District Council would not let the hall for the meeting if they thought the women's suffrage question was going to be discussed.'[3]

However, at the very same meeting, Phipps went on to say that he was now planning to hold a men's meeting on the same subject. He had written to the women concerned, saying that, 'he did not want any competition in the matter as it was too important'.[4] However, despite the importance of this question, no meeting on the White Slave Traffic seems to have been reported in Aylesbury towards the end of 1912.

Aylesbury was the scene of some remarkable battles in the fight over women's emancipation. And there are two other remarkable links between the women's suffrage movement and Aylesbury Prison in particular. Britain's first woman elected to Parliament was imprisoned here. Countess Constance Markievicz, who took part in the 1916 Easter uprising in Dublin, was also a passionate suffragette. She was given a lengthy sentence, but following an 'epiphany', in prison, her sentence was commuted. She was released from

---

[1] Aylesbury Prison Remission Warrants.
[2] *BAAN*, 2nd November 1912.
[3] *BAAN*, 2nd November 1912. p. 5, 'C.E.M.S. Aylesbury Branch'.
[4] Ibid.

Aylesbury Prison on 18th June, 1917 and went on to stand successfully as a candidate in the 1918 General Election. However, as a member of Sinn Fein, she never took up her seat in Parliament. At the time of the elections, she had been interned in Holloway, where it was a week before she found out about her triumph at the ballot box.[1]

The second story of subsequent imprisonment of suffragettes at Aylesbury also occurred during the war. This was the case of Alice Wheeldon, a suffragette and pacifist from Derby, who provided a refuge for men fleeing conscription. In a bizarre case of entrapment, allegedly by the security services, Alice was accused, with some of her family members and friends, of plotting to poison Prime Minister Lloyd George. Sentenced to ten years penal servitude, Alice went on hunger strike once imprisoned at Aylesbury. She was later moved to Holloway and released on 31st December, 1917. Alice died in 1919 in the influenza epidemic.[2]

Finally, the story of Aylesbury Prison itself marks the growing influence of the movement for gender equality. In July 1914 it was the first prison to appoint a woman as a Deputy Medical Officer and subsequently Governor there. Dr Selina Fox, who qualified from the London School of Medicine in 1890, briefly became a missionary and went on to found the Bermondsey Mission Hospital.[3]

There were further meetings in Aylesbury, particularly in 1913, to try to win support for 'votes for women'. A meeting was organised by Mid-Bucks NUWSS in January of 1913 at the Co-operative Hall. This coincided with the anticipated attempt to introduce a female franchise amendment to the legislation then before Parliament, proposing to extend the vote to all men over 21. However, even here, the local NUWSS organiser, Miss Dora Mason, did not realistically hold out much hope of this amendment being passed. Miss Frances Dove of High Wycombe was the main speaker. She remarked that 'She regretted to hear that the disturbances which occurred in Aylesbury last year had affected the growth of the Society in the town.'[4] She may have been referring here to the likely plans of the Mid-Bucks NUWSS to set up a separate branch in the town.

Miss Dove, now over two years into her retirement, was increasingly looking towards the role of future generations. She expressed the hope that mothers might instil in the minds of their children the importance of women

---

[1] Cook, Pat - *HMYOI Aylesbury*; McGuffin, J - *Internment*, 1973, chapter 6.
[2] Wikipedia, *Alice Wheeldon*, September, 2012.
[3] *The Vote*, 14th July 1914, p. 197.
[4] *BH*, 25th January 1913.

working in the world, as well as in the home. Thus, 'They would find that when those children grew up they would realise that the female sex had their public duties to perform as well as the men'.[1] She ended by moving the following resolution, which was later unanimously agreed: 'That this meeting urges the member for Mid-Bucks, Mr Lionel de Rothschild, to abstain from voting against the inclusion of women householders in the Franchise Bill.' Similarly, she said that, although the member for South Bucks was currently intending to abstain, she hoped he would be persuaded to vote in their favour instead.

That there was a 'large attendance' at this meeting which, despite the events of the previous year, indicated a renewed interest in the issue in the town. A series of meetings later in 1913 also suggests a groundswell of interest and some significant developments, as a direct result of the NUWSS deciding to support the Labour Party that autumn.

Miss Dora Mason headed the campaign, assisted by Miss Elias. Miss Mason first addressed a meeting of the National Union of Railwaymen at the White Hart Hotel on October 17th.[2] The Secretary of the branch, Mr Lightfoot, proposed a resolution in favour of women's suffrage and only one person present voted against. There was a social meeting on 20th October, when posters decorated the walls of the Co-operative Hall and Miss Mason spoke. The following day Miss Elias talked to the Women's Co-operative Guild on the subject of 'Citizenship'.

The campaign was completed with a public meeting on 22nd, also at the Co-operative Hall, when the venue was described as, 'quite full' and the audience, 'markedly sympathetic'.[3] Dr Rose again presided and Mrs Helena Swanwick spoke. Swanwick was from the Sickert family, who formed part of the literary and artistic circle in London which included William Morris and later, Oscar Wilde. Helena became a journalist and wrote regularly for the Manchester Guardian. She joined the women's suffrage movement in 1905 and was editor of the NUWSS newspaper, the *Common Cause*, from 1909-14.[4]

A powerful and persuasive speaker, Helena appealed to the men to show some understanding of the women's situation: 'How would they like it if their minds, politically considered, were upon marriage put into a state of suspended animation, as long as their wives lived?' She ended on a high note by declaring that '...every single organised body of women in the Kingdom,

---

[1] *BH*, 25th January 1913.
[2] *BE*, 24th October 1913.
[3] Ibid.
[4] Harris, Jose - *DNB*, 2004-13.

with the sole exception of the elementary teachers, had declared in favour of women's suffrage: the last to come into line being the National Union of Women Workers, which at their conference in Hull this summer pronounced for the vote by a great majority, though Mrs Humphrey Ward fought hard against it'. The resolution for women's suffrage, seconded by Miss Catherine Courtauld, again attracted only 'a single dissentient'.

At the end of the 1913 campaign, 50 people from Aylesbury had been enrolled as 'Friends of Women's Suffrage' and three people had become members of the local branch.

The 1914 caravan tour, organised by the Kingshill sub-committee of the Mid-Bucks NUWSS branch demonstrates the increasing reach and ambition of the Buckinghamshire suffragists.[1] The tour was designed to win over the agricultural villages around Aylesbury, previously largely untouched by the campaign. The caravan started at Weston Turville and visited Wing, Oving, Quainton, Waddesdon and Cuddington. Aston Clinton and the Kimbles had to be omitted from the planned tour, but Stoke Mandeville was visited. Several speakers, mostly from outside of the county, were employed on the caravan tour. Miss Wright (of Ballinger?), Miss Dering Curtois (a member of the Lyceum Debating Club and President of the Conservative and Unionist Debating Society), Miss Stirling from London, Miss Farnell, an Oxford Extension lecturer, and Mrs Savory, the most active Vice-President of the Mid-Bucks NUWSS. Special mention was made of the assistance of 'Miss Neill of Aylesbury'. She also displayed some photographs at the women's suffrage art exhibition in Great Missenden that summer.

The 1913-14 Annual NUWSS Federation report highlighted the dramatic development of trade union support for women's suffrage across the region. Five union branches and Labour organisations in Aylesbury passed resolutions in favour: the Amalgamated Society of Engineers, the Trades and Labour Council, the Associated Society of Locomotive Engineers and Firemen, the National Union of Railwaymen and the British Amalgamated Union of Basketmakers.[2] The Basketmakers were represented at the Albert Hall women's suffrage demonstration on 14th February that year.

It is possible to argue that the disturbances surrounding the prison protests in April 1912 were, ultimately, the reason why the NUWSS Pilgrimage the following year did not visit Aylesbury at all. These marchers seemed to go out of their way to avoid the town, as their chosen route went

---

[1] *BH*, 1st August 1914.
[2] *Third Annual Report*, NUWSS Federation, 1913-14.

from Oxford, through Thame, on to Princes Risborough and down to West and High Wycombe.

Aylesbury may not have played such a sustained and numerically significant role as High Wycombe in the women's suffrage movement in central Buckinghamshire. And for all the previous campaigning, the 1914 local elections for the Urban District Council provide an interesting glimpse into women's continuing lack of political engagement in the area. No women were nominated to be councillors and only a small proportion of women seem to have played any part in nominating male councillors. One of the candidates for the West Ward, Mr H.J. Joscelyne listed those who nominated him in the *Herald*.[1] Out of 28 proposers and seconders, only four were women: Miss F. Kingham, Mrs Marshall, Mrs Wilson-ffrance and Miss Rebecca Bates. This demonstrates again Miss Dove's remarkable, pioneering example. At the time of her death 1942, Miss Dove remained the only woman to have been elected to local government in High Wycombe.[2] It also demonstrates how it continued to be very difficult for women to develop political careers even after they had won the vote.

Aylesbury did play a unique role in the story of 'votes for women', both in the nineteenth century and the early twentieth century. And, in the final year or so before the war, the campaign in Aylesbury began to gain considerable momentum and broke new ground by campaigning in the local villages. The Mid-Bucks suffragists moved towards a wider popular support, especially with the later promotion of women's suffrage by the local trade union branches. And the 1914 annual report mentioned that of the 218 'Friends of Women's Suffrage', a high proportion were from Aylesbury.[3] Many people in the area rose to the challenge of highlighting the vital issue of 'votes for women' and took an active part in the varied and dramatic unfolding of this campaign across Buckinghamshire.

---

[1] *BH*, 4th April 1914.
[2] Kidd-Hewitt, David – Buckinghamshire Heroes, p. 109.
[3] *BE*, 12th June 1914.

Chapter 6: Great Missenden: Liberals, Ladies, Artists and Motorists

'(Liberals) were not quite clear and logical in their explanations why the vote should not be given to women'
- Mrs Bertrand Russell, speaking at a Liberal meeting in Missenden. *BAAN*, 3rd September 1910.

THERE is little mention in the local newspapers of women's suffrage events in Great Missenden before 1910, although there may have been meetings in the town arranged by a band of itinerant suffragettes, as early as the summer of 1908. Missenden is certainly mentioned in the appeal the WSPU made to local supporters immediately before the Buckinghamshire campaign in the summer of 1909. The appeal to 'members and sympathisers', specifically mentions 'Aylesbury, Amersham, Chesham, Thame, High Wycombe, Wendover, Great Missenden, Princes Risborough...'.[1]

However, nothing seems to have appeared in the local newspapers that year, regarding events in Missenden. But then, in 1910, the town bursts onto the scene of the local women's suffrage movement, with a magnificently classical period set-piece: the political garden party. Held in the grounds of The Old House, Church Street, and hosted by Sir Denham and Lady Alice Warmington, this meeting attracted the great and the good of the Liberal Party from across the Mid-Bucks constituency. The Thursday afternoon meeting had representatives from Aylesbury, Chesham, Kingshill, Wendover and Weston Turville, as well as Missenden.[2] This was described, during Sir Denham's welcoming speech, as the first meeting of its kind in Missenden. The Chesham and District Women's Liberal Association had only been formed towards the end of the previous year, with Mrs J.S. Henry of Missenden as its President, and Lady Warmington as its Secretary.[3]

Both the main speech and the responses given that day, highlight the struggle that was going on within the Liberal Party at a crucial moment for the women's suffrage movement nationally. This and subsequent events in the town also revealed, not surprisingly, the potential for disagreements

---

[1] *VW*, 13th August 1909, p. 1066.
[2] *BAAN*, 3rd September 1910.
[3] *BE*, 19th November and 17th December 1909.

between husbands and wives on this issue. It seemed that while Sir Denham Warmington's much younger wife, Lady Alice was in favour of votes for women, he remained unconvinced. But he was gracious enough to bow to his wife's wishes and allow the meeting to go ahead at his house. The main speaker was Mrs Alys Russell, who was living near Oxford and was the estranged wife of Bertrand Russell, the mathematician and philosopher. It seems likely that Alys Russell may have only just also agreed to be President for the newly formed Mid-Bucks branch of the NUWSS. She was warmly introduced to the gathering by Sir Denham Warmington.

Mrs Russell began by outlining the current political situation facing the Liberals nationally and in that region of Buckinghamshire. Going by her eyewitness account of the previous general election, earlier that year in Aylesbury, the Mid-Bucks Liberals had struggled to launch a significant election campaign in the district. However, she encouraged her audience by reminding them of the progress the Party had made at the 1906 elections, and with the 'flourishing' condition of the local Women's Liberal Association. She echoed the Liberal rallying cry of this period by raising the prospect of a constitutional crisis, being precipitated by a belligerent and unrepresentative House of Lords vetoing potential Liberal reforms and which included the proposed introduction of national insurance and state pensions. Mrs Russell raised the possibility of the Liberal Party having to call another general election on the matter, which they duly did at the end of the year. However, the Mid-Bucks Liberals chose not contend this particular election battle.

Using this wider context of the need for the people to have a more fully representative Parliament to challenge the power of the landowning minority, Mrs Russell then launched into a justification for extending the vote to women. Appealing to the principles of liberalism as the main reason for advocating this further electoral reform, she said 'If men would now imply the principle that it was not possible for one class to legislate for another class, then they must conclude that it was not possible for the working men to legislate for the women'.[1]

Commenting that she herself in the past 'did not seek to enter the field' of political campaigning, now that she and other women were involved, she concluded that it was not, 'a dignified position to get women to work for the Liberal party during an election, and for them to turn round and say that women were not fitted for the vote'.[2] Having mentioned issues particularly

---

[1] *BAAN*, 3rd September 1910.
[2] Ibid.

relevant to women, such as education, housing and temperance, she argued that women should not be told to wait until they were educated before they were granted the vote, as she believed that 'the vote was the great engine of education'.

Her speech was greeted with applause and by qualified support from the influential local Liberal, Sir John Thomas. He had made a fortune from paper manufacturing and was knighted in 1907. He and his wife, Ada, lived at Brook House, Wooburn. They spoke on a number of occasions at meetings in the county in favour of votes for women, for example at a similar meeting of the South Bucks Liberal Association at High Wycombe Town Hall in March 1911.

Other Liberals who responded to Mrs Russell's speech showed more ambivalence on the question. Mr R. Wallace Atkins, who had been the unsuccessful Liberal Parliamentary candidate for Mid-Bucks in the January 1910 elections, displayed a certain hesitancy on the issue. In common with other Liberals, he was probably fearful that most of the women householders who might be enfranchised by the current Conciliation Bill, were more likely to vote Conservative.

The next event in the town, which followed soon after, was of a very different nature. An open-air meeting was held on Saturday 10th September. This was variously described as being near the Schools or on the village green.[1] The three suffrage societies which took part indicates the way the groups were able to collaborate in more remote areas when necessary. The militant WSPU and non-militant NUWSS were represented, along with the New Constitutional Society for Women's Suffrage, which attempted to hold a mediating position between the two wings of the movement. The fact that the WSPU were currently observing a truce from militant actions, while Parliament considered the Conciliation Bill, surely facilitated this collaboration.

The meeting was part of the fortnight of events in the district, organised by Miss Katherine Raleigh, in the role of regional organiser for the NCSWS. She was staying temporarily in Wendover with Mrs Hamilton.[2] Although the *Examiner* reporter described the meeting as 'poorly attended', he commented on how attentive the audience were and that the meeting was 'orderly'. The fuller account given by the *Advertiser* mentions that alongside Miss Raleigh there was a Miss Lees of the WSPU and Miss (Geraldine?) Cooke and Miss Herford of the NUWSS. The short account in *Votes for Women* makes a point

---

[1] *BAAN*, 17th September 1910; *BE*, 16th September 1910.
[2] *The Vote*, 3rd September 1910, p. 223.

of highlighting local sympathisers who, through a door in a wall behind the speakers, offered some boxes for the speakers to stand on.[1]

Miss Lees was invited by Miss Raleigh to speak to the meeting. She denied the common idea that 'suffragettes were against men' and pointed to what she called 'an army of men who were working to help them'.[2] Referring to the Conciliation Bill which had been before Parliament earlier in the year, she pointed out that in its second reading the Bill had achieved a majority of 110, more than that achieved by the Government for its budget. However, the Government had still refused to give facilities to get the Bill passed. Listing five reasons why women should have the vote, Miss Lees declared her confidence that they could get the legislation passed that autumn and issued an appeal to everyone present to help in the campaign.

The meeting was opened to questions and there followed a lively exchange between the women and one elderly questioner, who concluded by saying 'Your Bill does not give the working classes the same opportunities as the wealthy, and for that reason I would support a Bill for the enfranchising of all the women'.[3]

Others in the audience raised more common objections, about women needing to fight for their country if they wanted a vote and the well-worn observation that 'A woman's place is at home'. Both of these, Miss Raleigh dealt with in short order. Miss Herford concluded the meeting by stating that if the Conciliation Bill was passed by the Commons, around one million women would be enfranchised, over 80 per cent of whom would be working women. A final appeal for help from the local population was followed by literature being distributed among the crowd. The *Votes for Women* report made the claim that several men 'promised to study' these leaflets about the Conciliation Bill.

The following year, 1911, saw the emergence of new suffragists in the area. Miss Catherine Courtauld, along with her elder sister Renee Sydney, moved into a house named 'Bocken', on Frith Hill overlooking Great Missenden. Catherine drew many suffragist propaganda pictures while she was living in Buckinghamshire.[4] Several of these were turned into popular post-cards. Catherine soon became an influential figure in the local movement and took up the post of secretary of the Mid-Bucks NUWSS

---

[1] *VW*, 23rd September 1910, p. 831.
[2] *BAAN*, 17th September 1910.
[3] Ibid.
[4] Tickner, Lisa - *The Spectacle of Women*.

branch. These two gifted women appear to have joined forces with Lady Warmington to raise the profile of the movement locally.

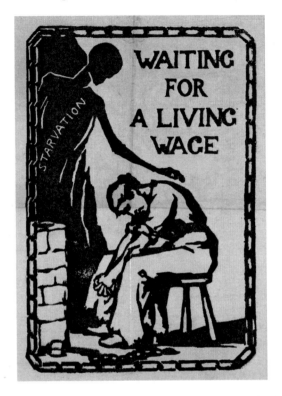

A poster designed by Catherine Courtauld, highlighting the low wages and poor working conditions of the women chain makers of Cradley Heath. From the Women's Library/Mary Evans Picture Library

With the Conciliation Bill still being considered by Parliament again that year, it is likely that there were several meetings in Missenden in 1911. However, due to the paucity of the newspaper record for that year, the District Liberal Association meeting, held in the School on Thursday 14th December is to be the only one reported. Both Courtauld sisters were present, along with the President of the Association, Sir Denham Warmington. He addressed the meeting with his usual candour, confessing that he was currently opposed to giving women the vote as he felt there were 'many difficulties in the way'.[1] With some foresight, he said that he personally did not want to see women clergy or judges and finished by saying that only about two-thirds of the present Liberal Government were in favour of the measure.

Mrs Rackem of the NUWSS declared her life-long commitment to the Liberal Party. She repeated Mrs Russell's view that it was inconsistent to allow women to campaign politically without granting them the vote. Quoting the opinion of the Chancellor, Lloyd George, that it would be impossible for the Government to pay women factory workers such low wages if they were enfranchised, Mrs Rackem referred to the example of the improved wages of the newly enfranchised women of Norway.

She went on '...much of the opposition to giving women the vote arose from fear - fear because there were more women than men'.[2] Mentioning the 40 year history of the attempts at women suffrage reform, Mrs Rackem felt hopeful about the current situation now that the Conciliation Bill had achieved a majority of 167 in the House of Commons. She for one was clearly confident that the generous allowances Prime Minister Asquith had made for amendments to his proposed legislation of a Manhood Suffrage Bill the next year would secure the necessary change. The WSPU, in contrast, had returned to its former militant tactics in response to the Prime Minister's proposal. The meeting closed with the local Baptist minister, Rev. Thomas Rowson, seconding the vote of thanks given by Miss Courtauld.

The New Year saw another meeting at the Missenden Schools, organised by the Mid-Bucks NUWSS. Advertised for Thursday 25th January, it featured the speakers Lady Aberconway and Miss Muriel Matters.[3]

A similar 'well attended' meeting in March, at the same venue, was more widely reported in the local papers.[4] Mr and Mrs Carvalho were among the crowd. Rafe Carvalho was a stockbroker born in Highbury who had moved to Buckinghamshire with his wife and two sons. They were living at 'The Chilterns', Grimms Hill in Missenden at the time of the 1911 census. Mrs Lucy Carvalho came originally from Liverpool. The week following the March meeting in Missenden, it was reported that Mrs Carvalho had joined

---

[1] *SBFP*, 22nd December 1911.

[2] Ibid.

[3] *BE*, 12th January 1912.

[4] *BE* and *SBFP*, 22nd March 1912. Those listed as attending and representing both sides of the question were: Sir Denham and Lady Warmington, Capt. Bruce-Dresser, Mrs Magrath, Miss Gomm, Mrs A. Kimber, Mrs Russell Smith.

the Mid-Bucks NUWSS committee.[1] It is possible that Lucy had already joined the women's suffrage movement when she lived on Merseyside, or even during the early years of her marriage when living in Kensington and Regents Park. However, there is also the possibility that she may have been convinced to become personally involved in the movement by attending this March 1912 NUWSS meeting in Missenden, or previous meetings arranged by the Mid-Bucks suffragists.

Dr Drysdale, Miss Muriel Matters and Mrs Davies shared the platform. Mrs Davies lived at 'Hillside', Ballinger and was married to John Davies, a local doctor and JP.[2] The main speakers were introduced by Miss Catherine Courtauld, who deplored the recent incidents of window-smashing carried out by the suffragettes in London. She even went as far as to say that, 'The militant suffragists had nothing to do with them whatever', a position not entirely shared by either of the main speakers.[3]

Dr Charles Vickery Drysdale was already a controversial figure at the time.[4] He helped to found the Men's League for Women's Suffrage in 1907. But he was probably better known for continuing the work of his father and uncle, of campaigning in favour of contraception and birth control. He did this on the grounds of the need to eradicate deformity and to encourage progress through improving the genetic make-up of the British people.

Dr Drysdale opened his talk by proposing to answer three simple questions: 'Did women want the vote; ought they to have it; and was it good for the country as a whole?'[5] By side-stepping the first question, he avoided one of the main objections of the anti-suffragists, that they had not established that a majority of women wanted the vote. Instead, Drysdale answered the first question by including it within the second question. The two reasons he highlighted for giving women the vote were firstly the taxes women paid, and secondly the sacrifices women made for the nation. His unusual argument is worth quoting more fully:

'He often heard the physical force argument urged against votes for women, and it was sometimes said that as women could not fight, they should not vote. He considered that a disgraceful argument. More than a million

---

[1] *BE*, 29th March 1912.
[2] 1911 England and Wales Census; *Kelly's* 1911, 1915.
[3] *BE*, 22nd March 1912.
[4] Benn, Miriam J. - *DNB*, 2004-10.
[5] *SBFP*, 22nd March 1912.

women went down into the maternity battle every year, and more than 4,000 lost their lives in this battle'. [1]

When the Doctor answered his third question, he once again appealed to his own familiar field of procreation and genetics, which at this time was a significant matter of national concern.

'Was (votes for women) to the advantage of the nation? ...Most of his hearers would be aware that thoughtful men and women were experiencing grave fears through the undoubted physical deterioration of the nation as a whole... He was perfectly certain that there was no chance for any race in this world which refused to allow its women a place in its national life...'.[2]

Drysdale turned the argument of the 'antis' on its head by proclaiming that 'The way to get the finest out of a woman was to enfranchise her'. He concluded by pointing to the growth of the movement internationally and by warning that unless the nation heeded this call, England would fall behind. Referring to the recent outrages, he said that considering the nature of unrest surrounding previous reform movements of men, he did not wish to judge the women militants for their actions. They had been waiting 50 years for this reform, so he finished by expressing the hope that 'his fellow men would do all in their power to forward this great reform'. [3]

The second speaker, Miss Matters, is introduced by the reporter with the observation that she was, in appearance, 'the very antithesis of the modern conception of a suffragette'. [4] This demonstrates the common demonising of the suffragette in the popular press, which often presented these women as hysterical and unsexed harridans.

Muriel Matters began by saying that she was not there to discuss militant tactics, but nevertheless goes on at some length to defend them. Having referred to the practice of 'sweating' or underpaying employees, Miss Matters then asserted that 'There were far worse crimes being enacted every day, far worse crimes than smashing windows'.

Appealing repeatedly to the principle of justice, Miss Matters refers to the experience of her own country, Australia, where the vote had brought about significant change. She went on: 'Women who formerly took no

[1] *BE*, 22nd March 1912.
[2] Ibid.
[3] Ibid.
[4] Ibid.

interest in national affairs now openly discussed with their brothers and husbands questions of national importance'.[1] Matters added that she felt that giving women the vote would break up the unhelpful approach of party spirit in politics. She argued trenchantly that:

'It was absurd that these great important matters were made party matters. If they believed in Home Rule they were obliged to accept the Budget, the Licensing Bill, the Land Taxes, Mr Winston Churchill and Mr Lloyd George. If on the other hand they were opposed to Home Rule, they must accept Tariff Reform, no Licensing Bill, no land taxes, a big navy, and Mr F. E. Smith'.[2]

Miss Matters concluded by arguing that the women's suffrage movement could be seen as a religious movement, which sought to positively address matters of national importance by bringing the work of men and women together. At the end of the meeting, there were objections to some of the speakers' statements from both Captain Bruce-Dresser and also from Sir Denham Warmington. The resolution was passed, although, 'a large portion of the audience voted against'.[3]

A meeting the following month, also organised by the Mid-Bucks NUWSS, only received a brief paragraph in the *Free Press*. This was held at the Methodist Chapel on 11th April and was addressed by Miss M. Martineau.[4]

Lady Warmington hosted a Women's Liberal Association meeting at her home in June 1912. This meeting was addressed by veteran suffragist, temperance campaigner and Liberal Party activist, Miss Florence Balgarnie, and also by London County Councillor for Hackney South, Mr William Augustus Casson.[5]

As well as addressing other political matters of the day, both speakers mentioned their support for women's suffrage, a view clearly supported by their host. Apologising for the absence of her husband on this occasion, Lady Alice took this opportunity to express her personal pleasure that women were getting involved in politics. The vote of thanks was given by the Secretary of that branch of the WLA, Mrs Denton Samuel, who was

---

[1] *BE*, 22nd March 1912.
[2] Ibid.
[3] Ibid.
[4] *SBFP*, 19th April 1912.
[5] *BAAN*, 22nd June 1912.

already, or was shortly to become, corresponding secretary for the NUWSS in Chesham.

The next two meetings in the town, reported later that year within a week of each other by the *Examiner*, show the growth of the suffrage movement locally, but equally show the 'antis' developing a strong counter campaign.

A 'successful garden party' was held at the Courtaulds' on Thursday 27th June. After the sixty members and friends of the NUWSS Mid-Bucks society had taken tea, they listened to a talk by Mrs Savory. Mrs Savory began by addressing the fifteen objections to women's suffrage published by prominent anti-suffragist Lord Curzon.

Mrs Savory followed this defence of the arguments for women's suffrage by describing her own part in the battle to get the Midwives Registration Bill through Parliament. This had eventually been passed without enthusiasm by the House in 1902. Mrs Savory referred to the current debates on the White Slave Traffic Bill, which had already been long delayed and was now in danger of being weakened by amendments, before going on to detail other legislation which was 'unfair to women'. She concluded with an appeal '...to all women to combat these evils by supporting women's suffrage, which is the only certain way of bringing the women's point of view to bear on legislation'.[1] The article reports that several new members joined the society that day.

The numbers recorded at this meeting, coupled with the response to Mrs Savory's appeal, certainly indicate that the women's suffrage movement in Missenden and the surrounding areas was making significant progress. However, this was coupled with an awareness that anti-suffragist propaganda had to be addressed. The next meetings in the area confirm the suffragists' assessment that they were fighting an uphill battle for the hearts and minds of the local population.

Two meetings were held in Missenden on Wednesday 3rd July, organised by the Wendover branch of the NLOWS with the evening one having been previously advertised.[2] The first afternoon meeting was held in the home of Mr and Mrs Ker, leading local anti-suffragists. They lived at Frith Hill House and were close neighbours of the Courtauld sisters[3].

---

[1] *BE*, 5th July 1912.
[2] *BAAN*, 29th June 1912, p. 6.
[3] *Kellys*, 1911.

Later a 'large company gathered' for the evening meeting in the Infant Schoolroom.[1] The talks, given by representatives from the NLOWS, were characterised throughout by both enthusiastic applause and laughter, coupled also with some dissent and hissing. Some of those in audience, like Mrs Carvalho, Mrs Savory and Miss Sichel, were committed suffragists.

A resolution was put to the meeting by Mrs Norris: 'that to grant women the vote was contrary to the best interests of women and ought not to be passed into law without being put clearly before the country and voted upon by the country'.[2] Following the resolution being carried by a large majority, those present witnessed, 'a spirited interchange' of questions and answers. The *Advertiser* reported that 'the suffragists were not subdued' and were busy after the meeting, handing out leaflets on why women should have the vote.[3]

It may have been this lively meeting which encouraged those on both sides of the argument to organise a public debate on 31st October. Great Missenden's Public Hall was described as being 'uncomfortably full'.[4] This evening was extensively reported in both the *Examiner* and the *Free Press*. Present at what was described as 'one of the best attended meetings' on the subject in Great Missenden, were the Earl and Countess of Buckinghamshire.[5] Lady Frances Balfour and Miss Muriel Matters spoke in favour and Miss Gladys Pott against. Miss Pott was a member of the North Berkshire NLOWS branch, a persuasive speaker and also a significant figure in the anti-suffrage movement.

The meeting was chaired by the Earl of Buckinghamshire who clarified that the NLOWS had agreed to be represented by only one speaker. He commented to applause that 'There were a very large number of people in the country who make up their minds after only hearing one side of a subject, but that would not be the case of those who were present that evening. (Applause)'.[6]

Lady Balfour fired the opening volleys for the suffragists. She started by reminding her audience of previous campaigns by the men against electoral injustice. She highlighted political under-representation in the past, when large manufacturing towns had no MPs, while some smaller places had two MPs. This imbalance had been justified at the time because the uneducated

---

[1] *BE*, 5th July 1912.
[2] *BE*, 5th July 1912.
[3] *BAAN*, 6th July 1912.
[4] *BE*, 1st November 1912.
[5] *SBFP*, 8th November 1912.
[6] Ibid.

were claimed to be unfit to vote. But the 'male citizens' of the country had indulged in, 'a good deal of fuss and violence before they persuaded Parliament that they should have a vote'.[1] Now that women were educated as well as men, she went on, there was now no justification for withholding the parliamentary vote from the women.

Lady Balfour used the image commonly portrayed in suffragist literature of the insult to the women of being classed as unfit to vote, alongside 'the pauper, the felon and the lunatic'. But seeing as women were allowed to be involved with local government and other 'local bodies', she argued it made sense to allow the financially astute 'home-makers and home-keepers of the country' to have their say in parliamentary elections, especially now that the Commons was increasingly passing legislation which had a bearing upon domestic matters. In a rare reference to her personal experience, Lady Balfour commented that she hoped that the men always considered the women in the making of legislation but that 'she knew of instances where the presence of women on a local authority made men look at questions from a women's point of view...'.

Concluding by challenging the frequently used 'physical force' argument of the 'antis', Lady Balfour pointed out the inconsistencies of this way of thinking. She highlighted the fact that the majority of men in the audience were themselves not fit or too old for military service. Not only that, she pointed out the irony that those in the armed services themselves were usually excluded from voting, as they did not fulfil the residence criteria. The *Free Press* reporter records these as Lady Balfour's closing words that evening: 'The physical force argument ought to be excluded until we had universal service in this country, and until we refused to give a vote to a man until he served his country. (Applause).'[2]

Miss Gladys Pott, in response, did not once refer to the 'physical force' argument. However, she twice attempted to trump the suffragists with reference to the British Empire. By exalting and idealising the imperial nature of the duties of Parliament, she was implying that the important issues surrounding the defence of the Empire were beyond the experience and understanding of women. She appealed to the commonly held notion of the progress of world civilisation through the means of the British Empire.

Miss Pott refuted Lady Balfour's assertion that women's views and needs were overlooked, citing instances of legislation improving the position of women, for example in the labour market. While 'She did say for a moment

---

[1] *SBFP*, 8th November 1912.
[2] Ibid.

that women could not understand politics', she argued that there was a big difference between governing municipal matters, which she felt women were more suited to compared with affairs of state and empire.[1]

Miss Matters then responded by comparing the loss of 25,000 soldiers in the Boer War with a similar loss of life each year due to poor social conditions at home. She then referred to the progress Australia had made in tackling social problems, she argued, as a direct result of women being given the vote there.

With a thinly-veiled example of anti-colonial snobbery, Miss Pott stated that, 'there was no comparison between the duties of a great State and those of a great Empire (Applause)'.[2] She added that, just because Australia had given the vote to women, did that also mean Britain had to adopt this and other policies of the Australian government, including Home Rule (for Ireland) and Tariff Reform (protectionism), questions unpopular to various political persuasions in Britain ?

A number of questions were asked at the end of the meeting, including two probably by Mrs Savory, concerning the White Slave Traffic Bill currently before Parliament, and about the previous difficulties of getting the House of Commons to agree about the registration of midwives. No vote was taken at the end of the meeting, probably by prior agreement. But judging from the laughter and applause which more commonly greeted Miss Pott's comments, it seems unlikely that the suffragists would have won if a vote had been taken that evening.

The next meetings reported in the Missenden area, were in the summer of 1913. The first is the third annual general meeting of the Mid-Bucks NUWSS branch.[3] For the first time this was held at the Courtauld's home in Missenden, instead of Wendover, on Friday 27th June. Mrs Sichel from Wendover chaired the meeting. The financial report was seen as being 'satisfactory', with a £6 surplus in hand, following receipts of nearly £40. This compared to a surplus of over £2, from receipts of £35 the previous year. Over a third of the receipts for 1912-13 came from subscriptions to the branch, and over a quarter from a rummage sale held in Great Missenden. Printing and advertising costs amounted to nearly £7, while the greatest expense at just over £7 was spent on speaker's expenses and fees.

In response to the annual report presented by the committee, it was felt that 'the society had made satisfactory progress in spite of the difficulties of

---

[1] *BE,* 1st November 1912.
[2] *SBFP,* 8th November 1912.
[3] *BE,* 4th July 1913.

the political situation'.[1] It appears that some people had resigned their membership of the branch during that year, in response to militant 'excesses'. This perhaps refers specifically to the local arson attacks against Saunderton Station and Penn Church. Perhaps some of these resignations had been fairly prominent supporters as there were some changes to personnel compared to the previous year. The President and Vice-Presidents remained the same, but those no longer mentioned as on the committee were: Mrs F. J. Mead from Wendover, as well as Mrs Adams and Miss Wilkie. Mrs Greaves on the other hand, had clearly not been deflected from campaigning for the vote and was the one new name on the committee.

The report also mentioned another deputation made to Mid-Bucks' MP, Lionel de Rothschild. The unsatisfactory result of the meeting was summarised: 'He did not swerve from his anti-suffrage attitude, but promised to support any amendment improving the local government qualifications for women'.[2]

Miss Courtauld then spoke to the meeting and referred to some remarks Mr Rothschild had made recently in Aylesbury, where he had claimed that the constitutional suffragists were 'showing no life'. She said that reading his comments had made her 'very angry'. She herself had 'written to him on the question several times and forwarded resolutions'.[3] Miss Courtauld went on 'That was a direct challenge to them all to be up and prove they were very much alive, and very keen on obtaining their object'.[4] She gave a rallying call to those present to join the national NUWSS pilgrimage later that month.

The meeting was then addressed by the NUWSS regional organiser, Miss Dora Mason from Bedford. Despite reverses in Parliament and public reaction to suffragette militancy, she denied that their cause had suffered significant setbacks. Asserting that the cause was still advancing, she quoted the figure of 1,000 new members being added to the NUWSS each month. She argued that the movement's momentum was unstoppable, only adding a warning that, 'If they were to sit down and say they were going to do nothing until militancy stopped, the whole cause would be identified with militancy, and a greater disaster than that she could not conceive'. She finished by highlighting the needs of the working women:

---

[1] *BE*, 4th July 1913
[2] Ibid.
[3] S*BFP*, 4th July 1913.
[4] *BE*, 4th July 1913.

'There were thousands of women working day in and day out for 7 shillings a week, and yet men said they had no grievances. They had many, and they would only be remedied by the gift of the vote'.[1]

According to the account in the *Free Press*, eight new members of the society were enrolled that day. And the impression of growth and gathering momentum is impossible to ignore in the next development in the area. A sub-committee of the Mid-Bucks branch has been formed to arrange a 'rummage sale' at 'Sonamarg', the home of Mrs Alice Pilley in Kingshill, on July 10th. This appears a very mundane form of advance for the movement. But according to the *Herald* report, the sub-committee was formed specifically with the wider purpose of 'carrying on the propaganda work among the women of Little Missenden, Holmer Green and Kingshill'.[2] This marks a strategic extension to the work of the Mid-Bucks branch, which had been clearly bolstered by steadily growing numbers across a wider area.

The meeting was due to be a garden party, but due to the rain, this was held instead in Mrs Pilley's 'commodious motor-house'. Mrs Pilley, originally from Boston in Lincolnshire, was the widow of Samuel Pilley, a solicitor. They had previously lived in Ealing, where it seems Mrs Pilley had been a Poor Law Guardian. She was one of several local wealthy women, who made their properties, and in Mrs Pilley's case, her motor car and garage, available for use in the name of women's suffrage.

Around 50 people attended the sale and tea, at which Mrs P. Leach from Aylesbury spoke about 'women's suffrage from a working woman's point of view'. Miss Courtauld concluded the meeting by outlining the aims of the NUWSS and by appealing for people to join up with the NUWSS pilgrimage at Princes Risborough on 22nd July. No doubt Miss Courtauld and her fellow campaigners were pleased that thirteen people enrolled as sympathisers to the women's suffrage cause that afternoon.

After being cheered by witnessing and taking part in the NUWSS pilgrimage that summer, the local suffragists suffered a blow that autumn, following the sudden death of Lady Alice Warmington. Perhaps she had not been able to play much of a part in the local campaign due to ill health in 1913. She had travelled with her sister to Lake Como to undergo medical treatment, but died on the journey back on 29th October at Boulogne.[3] Under her well-known signature, 'L.M.P.', Mrs Louisa Matilda Page, a fellow

---

[1] *BE*, 4th July 1913.
[2] *BH*, 19th July 1913.
[3] *BE*, 31st October 1913, p. 6.

suffragist from Chesham, sent a tribute to the *Examiner*, praising her role in campaigning work, both for the local Liberal Party and against the White Slave Traffic.[1]

The campaigning continued the following year with meetings organised by both sides of the debate in the first two months. A meeting in the 'Public Hall' organised by the 'antis' on 27th January was chaired by Mr G. Carrington, who was supported on the platform by Lady Susan Trueman from Chesham, along with Mrs C. Hodginkson Smith, Mr and Mrs Lawson, Mr Alfred Ker and Major-General Swann.[2] Two weeks later, many of the same people came to a meeting at the same venue, this time organised by the Mid-Bucks Suffrage Society.[3]

A fuller account of this evening was recorded by the *Herald*.[4] This event was a significant statement of the branch's confidence and sense of identity, with the hall being 'tastefully decorated' in the NUWSS colours of red and white (and green). A banner depicting John Hampden was prominently displayed, which also bore the slogan 'He serves all, who dares be free'. However, the 'large attendance' was clearly bolstered by the 'anti-suffragists' who turned out in force.

From behind a large bowl of red and white tulips, Mrs Savory chaired the meeting and made some introductory remarks about the history of the movement. Mentioning the membership of the NUWSS as having passed 50,000, she highlighted the fact that of the forty suffrage societies, only two employed militant tactics. She went on to challenge some of the comments made at the previous 'anti' meeting in that same hall, where the Chairman of that meeting had remarked that before women were given the vote, it would be necessary for everyone to be 'practically unanimous' about this reform. Mrs Savory responded, to some laughter, that this would mean they would be close to the Millennium.

Addressing the fear of 'petticoat government' raised by Mr Carrington, Mrs Savory denied that gaining the vote automatically meant being able to sit in Parliament. She also denied that admitting women to Parliament would mean that, 'they would see some funny things'.[5] Furthermore, she countered the claim of Mrs Solomon, speaker at the previous anti-suffrage meeting, that if the armed services and commerce needed 'expert' representatives,

---

[1] *BE*, 14th November 1913.
[2] *BE*, 30th January 1914.
[3] *BE*, 13th February 1914.
[4] *BH*, 21st February 1914.
[5] Ibid.

then surely it was equally true that some expertise was needed regarding more domestic legislation discussed by Parliament.

Miss Geraldine Cooke then spoke in general terms about votes for women resulting in the 'uplifting of the race'. She moved a resolution in favour of the Parliamentary enfranchisement of women, which was seconded by Mrs Garrett Jones. Mrs Hodgkinson Smith then entered into a debate with Miss Cooke and Miss Hatch on the subject of the wages of women teachers in elementary schools. Women were entitled to sit on the boards of these schools, but still their wages were less than their male colleagues. Her point seems to have been one often made by 'antis', that even if women were represented, it would not necessarily lead to the significant changes the suffragists claimed would come once they had the vote. Mr Freeman, from Amersham, also raised some similar points.

The *Herald* reporter concludes his account with these words: 'the resolution was put to the meeting and defeated, amidst loud applause by the opponents of the movement'.[1] In the same issue of the newspaper there appeared three letters, contesting comments made in the paper about the previous anti-suffrage meeting in the town. Two of the letters were from speakers that day, Mrs Helen Page, Assistant Secretary of the NLOWS and Mrs Gladys Gladstone Solomon from Hendon. The third was written by local suffragist, Mrs Alice Pilley. In this letter, written the day after the 10th February suffrage meeting, Mrs Pilley addressed the question about elementary school teacher's salaries still being less than those of their male counterparts. Drawing on her experience as a Poor Law Guardian in London, she described how she along with her three fellow female Guardians, had successfully managed to persuade the thirty men of the committee to award a newly appointed female Dispenser equal pay with the previous male incumbent. It was clear to Mrs Pilley that, wherever they were poorly represented, it was always going to be an uphill struggle to gain justice and equality for women.

The Mid-Bucks suffragists repeated the successful approach of the previous year by arranging another rummage sale, on 3rd June, this time in Holmer Green. Held in the 'motor garage' of the Bat and Ball pub, close to the village green, those who came to the sale were afterwards treated to a speech on the suffrage question. Mrs Coales was the speaker, presumably the leading suffragist in the village. Speaking from her own experience, she

---

[1] *BH*, 21st February 1914, p. 139.

delivered a stirring challenge, urging her audience to 'help on this truly Christian movement...'.[1] She went on to stress:

'... how much real happiness is gained from this work, which gives those who take part in it a keener and wider interest in matters of importance, strengthening the feeling of sisterhood amongst women and when the time comes, as come it must, that they have the vote, they will indeed feel they are fellow citizens with men of the finest Empire the world has ever seen'.[2]

The ninety people who were present apparently listened with great interest, some signing up as 'Friends of Women's Suffrage' and others asking for literature.

The suffragists followed this success with their annual meeting, which was held the following day at the Courtauld sisters' house, when 40 members of the local society were present. The most detailed of all the annual reports, this one boasted of a growth in membership from 109 to 177. This was a significant increase, despite a loss of 28 members, reportedly mostly made up of those who had left the area. The report told of 'a steady advance in almost all parts of our constituency' and compared this with the 'standstill in the House of Commons'.[3] And those who considered themselves 'Friends of Women's Suffrage' now numbered over 200. Many of these were from Aylesbury, Amersham and Little Kingshill, although these areas were well represented because other districts had yet to launch the 'Friends' scheme.

The President and Vice-Presidents of the NUWSS branch remained unchanged. However, numbers on the committee, which was still chaired by Mrs Katie Sichel from Wendover, had been boosted by the addition of Miss Neill from Aylesbury, Mrs Denton Samuel from Chesham, Miss C. Jevons from Little Kingshill (also named Press Secretary), as well as Miss C. C. Lyon of 'Ashcroft', Prestwood. Miss Lyon, who is only mentioned in later accounts of the Mid-Bucks Society meetings, was also Secretary of the NUWSS Oxon, Beds, Bucks Federation. Mrs Davies of Ballinger had relieved Catherine Courtauld of the role of Treasurer. One committee member from the previous year was not mentioned: Mrs Carvalho from Missenden.

It is not hard to see, given the numerical growth of the society and the appointments to the committee from various parts of Mid-Bucks, that the

---

[1] *BE*, 12th June 1914.
[2] Ibid.
[3] Ibid.

society was already planning to launch new branches within the area, just as in South Bucks. There were already seven sub-committees (Little Kingshill, Prestwood, Wendover, Aylesbury, Great Missenden, Chesham and Chesham Bois). Three of these had started financing their own work, and Little Kingshill had enough of a surplus to contribute to NUWSS national funds. However, the Chesham Bois sub-committee had clearly suffered a serious setback, with the death of Mrs Hopkins, correspondent for Chesham Bois. So far, they had been unable to find someone to replace her.

The original written report gave 'a detailed review of the meetings at various centres'. But the details given in the *Examiner* just give the basic statistics. In 1913-14 the Mid-Bucks suffragists had held a total of 25 indoor meetings, including seven lectures on subjects related to the welfare of women and children. This was ten more than the previous year, and many more than were reported in the local press.

Other details are revealing, including the noticeable increase in male members of the society. The suffragists also seemed to have welcomed the 'antis' forming local branches, despite the intimidation experienced by some suffragists and the difficulties they sometimes encountered in securing venues for their meetings.

Buckinghamshire suffragists were clearly pleased by the growing support of the Trade Unions. A whole paragraph is devoted here to naming the local Unions which sent resolutions in favour of a government measure for women's suffrage to their MP, as well as those who sent delegates to the NUWSS London demonstration in February. These developments were also trumpeted by the Wycombe suffragists. More details are revealed by this Mid-Bucks report, which stated that women delegates to this demonstration also attended from the Chesham Women's Liberal Association, the Chesham branch of the British Women's Temperance Association and the Aylesbury Women's Co-operative Guild.

The NUWSS national pilgrimage gets a brief reference, specifically to the 18 local suffragists who joined in from Princes Risborough and the three who then walked all the way into London. The Lending Library is mentioned as having recently received a number of new books for the education of the members 'on various subjects of interest to Suffragists'.[1] The report concludes by expressing gratitude to the local newspapers for reporting on their meetings and inserting news on women's suffrage more generally,

---

[1] *BE*, 12th June 1914.

which was probably a specific reference to the policy of the *Examiner*, which of including regular 'Women's Suffrage Notes'.

The annual Federation report for 1913-14, published in the autumn of 1914, revealed extra details. This showed that the income of the Mid-Bucks suffragists that year was £54, roughly half of the income of the Wycombe suffragists.[1]

In their arguably unequal battle with the 'antis' in set-piece debates and formal meetings, the Mid-Bucks suffragists continued to look for alternative and creative ways to appeal to the local population. The art exhibition organised in July, as well as a caravan tour of some outlying villages, certainly must have served to gain the society a wider audience. However, a cycling tour planned for August by local NUWSS organiser, Miss Dora Mason and Miss C.C. Lyon, had to be abandoned due to the outbreak of the war.

The art exhibition, held at the Courtauld's house outside Missenden on Friday 17th and Saturday 18th July, was described briefly in the *Examiner* and in greater detail in the *Herald*. According to the *Examiner*, the exhibition was broken up into six sections: needlework, art, photography, cookery, literature and horticulture.[2] The *Herald* reporter commented, 'The people who hold the view that "suffragettes" are but a useless and disappointed class of the community... would have found that idea effectively dispelled...'[3]

As well as paintings produced by Miss Courtauld and Mrs Pilley, many other names of gifted women associated with the society are mentioned: Miss Neill of Aylesbury for her photographs; Miss Pratley for her Maltese lace work; Mrs England for her silk pictures; Miss Rio Winterton of Stoke Mandeville for her silver and metal work; Miss Curtois for her river scene painting in oils and her calendars; Miss Taylor of Aylesbury for her carved chair; Dr Scuby for his brass rubbings; Mrs Lowndes of Chesham for her patchwork quilt; Miss Hatch for her educational designs; Mrs J. Sharpe for her painted calendar cards; and Miss Agar of Chesham Bois for her model of a garden she designed in Cairo the previous year[4]. There were several books written by members which formed a literature display. These authors were listed as: Miss Herford, Miss Bluett, Miss Wilnersdoeffer, Miss W. Jevons and finally Miss Eckinstein, the medieval historian who had a property in Little Hampden.

---

[1] *Third Annual Report*, 1913-14, NUWSS Federation.
[2] *BE*, 24th July 1914.
[3] *BH*, 25th July 1914.
[4] 'Miss Agar' may be a mis-spelling: *Kelly's* 1911 & 1915 records a Mr Frederick John Algar at 'Briars', Chesham Bois.

There was some humour amongst all the earnest endeavour. Anti-suffragists were warned against entering one particular room. Here Catherine Courtauld had collected her widely reproduced posters, which ridiculed various anti-suffrage arguments. Finally, there was on display a collection of the badges of 19 suffrage societies. The *Examiner* reporter finished his account of the exhibition by noting that, as well as the interest provoked by the two days, eight new members joined the Mid-Bucks branch.

One of Catherine Courtauld's cartoons, lampooning the anti-suffragists. From the Women's Library/Mary Evans Picture Library

Organised by the Little Kingshill Mid-Bucks sub-committee, a caravan tour took place on 20th July, led by Miss Wright and Miss Dering Curtois, assisted by Miss Lily Wooster.[1] Miss Curtois was both a member of the

---

[1] *BH*, 1st August 1914.

Lyceum Debating Club and President of the Conservative and Unionist Women's Franchise Debating Society. The tour was arranged with the specific aim of breaking new ground for women's suffrage in some of the outlying agricultural villages in the Mid-Bucks constituency. The campaign began at Weston Turville green on Monday 25th July, and was addressed by Miss Curtois. She gave a short history of the women's movement and took on the mantle of the anti-suffragists by claiming justice for the women who paid for and contributed so much to the 'upkeep of the Empire'.

The following day the caravan visited Wing, where a hundred attended the meeting. Miss Stirling from London spoke about the inability of the women employees of the Post Office to obtain redress for their grievances, due to their lack of representation in Parliament. The following morning several men asked to sign up as 'Friends' of the movement and asked to be able to wear the NUWSS colours of red, white and green.

On Wednesday, Oving was visited. Here, Miss Stirling and Miss Curtois spoke and then invited a debate on the green. The next day, Mrs Savory was the speaker at Quainton and Waddesdon. The latter meeting, under the nose of the Rothschilds at Waddesdon Manor, was described as 'particularly large and encouraging'. A resolution was passed, calling on Mr Rothschild to, 'do the utmost to get a Government measure for the enfranchisement of women passed with as little delay as possible'.[1]

Friday saw Miss Farnell, an extension lecturer from Oxford join the tour at Cuddington and Stone. The evening meeting at Stone was described as 'large'. One detail of Miss Farnell's talk was particularly remembered, as it involved the 'pathetic' story of a book-keeper's wife, who was forced to accept half pay on the death of her husband, even though she did exactly the same work as he had done.

The caravan tour ended prematurely at Stoke Mandeville on Saturday 25th July. Miss Wright had originally planned to include Aston Clinton and Little and Great Kimble, but the tour had to be curtailed for some unmentioned reason. However, the article remarked upon the way the working men of the places visited had readily grasped the justice of the women's campaign. Two examples were given in the report. One was of a proud father, who pointed to the baby in his arms and said, 'I wish her to have the vote, as I know what it has done for me'. Another elderly man, who was lying in bed and apparently close to death said: 'I'm past it all but you've my best wishes if you're a follower of Mrs Henry Fawcett; she's a good

---

[1] *BH*, 1st August 1914.

woman'. As a result of the caravan tour, 59 people signed 'Friends' cards and three people became members of the Mid-Bucks NUWSS.

The NUWSS Federation report for 1913-14 lends weight to this impression of the expanding size and vision of the Mid-Bucks and other NUWSS branches in Buckinghamshire. It also reveals, intriguingly, that Mrs Leopold de Rothschild donated one pound to the cause during that year, which might indicate either that she did not entirely share the anti-suffrage views of some of the rest of her family, or that at least she was beginning to have some sympathy with the women's suffrage movement. Such small hints of dissension perhaps point to the beginning of significant fissures in the anti-suffrage edifice. It may be an exaggeration to say this long-standing edifice came crashing down at the end of the war, but over a longer period it was quietly subverted and ultimately undermined.

The eventual granting of votes to women, without fanfare in 1918, had as much to do with the persistent and less spectacular campaigning of the women of Mid-Bucks, like Miss Courtauld, Lady Warmington, Mrs Savory and Mrs Pilley, than with the dramatic deeds of the suffragettes. While the suffragettes ensured the issue could not be ignored before the war, the suffragists with their respected leaders, growing numbers and ability to organise events like a national pilgrimage, ensured that the question of 'votes for women' could not be completely ignored during and after the war.

Chapter 7: The Anti-Suffragists in Buckinghamshire

'We do not pretend, of course, to estimate the exact majority against Woman Suffrage, but it is certain that it is very large, and it is probable that it is enormous'
- *The Anti-Suffrage Review*, January 1911.

THE Women's National Anti-Suffrage League was launched in London on 20th July 1908, at an overflowing meeting in the Westminster Palace Hotel. The men's anti-suffrage league was later amalgamated with the women's, in December 1910, to form the National League for Opposing Women's Suffrage.[1]

From the beginning, the anti-suffrage movement saw dramatic growth, provoked by the strong popular reaction initially against the suffragette 'rushes' on the Houses of Parliament towards the end of 1908. These protests certainly proved a significant watershed for one of the Buckinghamshire newspapers, provoking as it did a very critical editorial, with which most anti-suffragists would have agreed. The editor of the *Herald* wondered '...in what sort of fashion public affairs would probably be conducted if such women as these received the suffrage and were admitted to Parliament'.[2]

A later editorial, reflecting on the debates in Parliament surrounding the Conciliation Bill, was written in a more measured tone. Its more balanced view was probably due to the support for women's enfranchisement, voiced by the leader of the Conservative opposition, Mr Balfour. Not surprisingly, the piece concluded by echoing the words of both Asquith and Balfour, who warned the suffragettes not to resort to '"methods of menace" in the future'.[3]

The first edition of the WNASL newspaper, *The Anti-Suffrage Review*, appeared in December 1908. The front page of this first issue laid out the basis of the anti-suffrage campaign:

---

[1] *The Anti-Suffrage Review*, October 1912, p. 242.
[2] *BH*, 31st October 1908.
[3] *BH*, 16th July 1910.

'We protest against the Parliamentary franchise for women, because it involves a kind of activity and responsibility for woman which is not compatible with her nature, and with her proper tasks in the world... Women are citizens of the State no less than men, but in a more ideal and spiritual sense'.[1]

This same opening article also mentions Miss Dove of High Wycombe and refers to her rejection as Mayor for the town as a sign that people across the country were awakening to the threat of the suffrage movement. The article, signed 'M.A.W.', was written by Mrs Mary Augusta Ward, better known at the time as Mrs Humphry Ward, the celebrated novelist and philanthropist.[2]

Mrs Ward was the most prominent woman in the anti-suffrage movement and was heavily involved in campaigning work, including supporting the candidacy for Parliament of her son, Arnold Ward, who became the Conservative MP for Watford in 1910. This apparent inconsistency with her own principles meant that she was probably the most lampooned anti-suffragist. Mrs Ward once famously pronounced that 'the political ignorance of women is irreparable and is imposed by nature'. The suffragist, Mrs Ethel Snowden, singled out Mrs Ward's behaviour and this comment for particular criticism in one of her books.[3]

As well as featuring on suffragist post-cards, plays were written and performed which satirised Mrs Ward and other anti-suffragists. One such play, called *The Master of Mrs Chilvers,* was written by Marlow resident and author of *Three Men in a Boat,* Jerome K. Jerome, who was himself a suffragist.[4] Three similar dramas, called *A Chat with Mrs Chicky, The Anti-Suffragist* and *An Englishman's Home,* were performed one night by members of the Actresses' Franchise League at the Beaconsfield Town Hall in January 1913.[5]

Mrs Ward lived briefly in Buckinghamshire, at Hampden House, in 1889. Her stay here provided some of the inspiration for her novel, 'Marcella'. That same year, Mrs Ward was also at the forefront of the earliest anti-suffrage protest, when, along with many other prominent women, she put

---

[1] *ASR*, December 1908.
[2] Sutherland, John - *DNB*, 2004-13.
[3] Snowdon, Ethel - *The Feminist Movement*, p. 161, London 1913.
[4] *SBFP*, 19th May 1911.
[5] *SBFP*, 17th January 1913.

her signature on a letter in the *'Nineteenth Century Magazine'*.[1] Mrs Ward eventually settled in the Chilterns, living just over the Hertfordshire border, at 'Stocks' in the village of Aldbury. Here she entertained the Asquiths and other leading figures of the day. She sometimes visited her near neighbours, the Rothschilds.[2] It was probably on the railings of Mrs Ward's Aldbury home that one suffragist protester put a WFL poster, protesting against the 'Cat and Mouse Act'.[3] A similar poster attached to the local police noticeboard the same day which was signed by 'G. Ballam', caused 'a disturbance' in the quiet village.

Her daughter, Miss Dorothy Mary Ward, supported her mother's anti-suffragist stance and her brother's political career. Dorothy spoke at the annual meeting of the Tring branch of the Federation of the West Herts. Womens' Conservative and Unionist Association, in June 1910.[4] Commenting that certain military and international matters were beyond the experience of women, she went on to argue that 'women's opinions should be especially valuable' in regard to other issues. This, coupled with her comment about women not having the vote 'at present', indicates she was not a practised anti-suffragist speaker.

When Mrs Humphry Ward herself spoke at a Conservative meeting in Tring in December 1910 to support the election of her son, Arnold Ward, she started by saying that this was 'the first political meeting she had addressed in her life'.[5] The organisers anticipated disruption by suffragettes, which did not materialise, even though some women identified as 'suffragettes' were in the hall. Instead, one lady came to the front of the meeting to ask whether he considered it true democracy when half of the population were not represented Arnold said that he opposed women's suffrage, but was open to 'the question being submitted to the direct judgement of the people'.

While emphasising the defensive nature of their movement, anti-suffragists did not hesitate to go on the offensive. One of the key planks of their argument, that suffragists represented a minority view, was sometimes conceded by suffragists, including one of the earliest historians of the women's suffrage movement.[6] This was the very first point made in the first

---

[1] Strachey, Ray - *The Cause*, p. 285.
[2] Ward, Mrs Humphry - *A Writer's Recollections*, p. 305, London, 1918.
[3] *The Vote*, 26th September 1913, p. 359.
[4] *BH*, 25th June 1910.
[5] *BH*, 10th December 1910.
[6] Strachey, Ray - *The Cause*, p. 285.

article of *The Anti-Suffrage Review*: '...the Executive Committee of the League... believe that the large majority of their sex do not want the vote, and that to force it on them would be a great injustice'.[1]

During the course of 1910, when the Conciliation Bill was before Parliament, the NLOWS conducted a postal canvass of women municipal voters in many different constituencies. This canvass was the brain-child of Miss Gladys Pott, who was at this time living in north Berkshire, and often paid visits into Buckinghamshire.

One of the polls was conducted in Mid-Bucks. The results showed only a slim majority opposed, which did not fully support the anti-suffragists' exaggerated assertions.[2] Out of nearly 1,400 women canvassed, less than 500 replied, 222 in favour and 248 against. The small number of women who declared they were undecided on the issue could have tipped the balance in the suffragists favour. The vast majority appeared apathetic to the issue, which was why those on both sides of the debate devoted so much of their energies to trying to persuade the undecided.

From the beginning of the anti-suffrage movement, six Branch Organising Secretaries were appointed. By 1912, the NLOWS boasted over 260 branches across the country, which including a newly formed one in Haddenham, as well as the more established one in Wendover, which by 1912 had formed a sub-group in the village of St Leonards. Other branches appeared that year, just over the borders of Buckinghamshire, in Thame, Henley and Uxbridge. Further Buckinghamshire branches followed the next year: Amersham, Beaconsfield and Marlow respectively.[3] The Wendover and Beaconsfield branches were both represented at the 1913 NLOWS annual meeting.[4] A 'Chalfonts' and Gerrards Cross branch was formed later.[5] There was also a branch being formed in High Wycombe in 1914.[6]

However, according to Ann Caulfield, who visited some branches in 1909 to gain signatories for the anti-suffrage petition, this activity was often deceptive. She observed that only the branch officials were active in campaigning and that it was only the presence of 'a great lady presiding' which drew the crowds to the spectacle.[7]

---

[1] *ASR*, December 1908.
[2] *ASR*, January 1911, p. 11.
[3] *ASR*, September 1912 - April 1913 issues.
[4] *ASR*, July 1913, p. 142.
[5] *SBFP*, 17th April, advert, 24th April 1914.
[6] *SBFP*, 13th February 1914.
[7] Harrison, Brian - *Separate Spheres*, p. 147.

The first of the anti-suffrage branches in Buckinghamshire, Wendover, was formally constituted in the Spring of 1909. While its first public meeting was on 24th May, there must have been earlier meetings to organise this. From the start, the Wendover group of anti-suffragists seemed to enjoy significant support, some of which included the more influential families of landed gentry in the county, combined with some leading local churchmen. Many people from a wide area were listed as having sent their sympathy to the movement, along with their apologies.[1] The afternoon and evening meetings on Monday 24th May, were both held in the Parish Schoolroom, with the permission of the vicar, Rev. Albert Smith. The meetings were chaired by Mrs Moberly Bell, from the East Marylebone NLOWS Branch, with speakers Mrs Baynton and Miss Lilla B. Strong. Mrs Bell was married to the Managing Director of the *Times*, Charles Moberly Bell. Miss Strong was a local suffragist who lived at 'Hazeldean' in Wendover and was closely involved with the organisation of the NLOWS branch from the beginning, despite poor health. A teacher and head teacher with experience of schools in South Africa and India, she had also been Headmistress of the Church of England High School in Baker Street, London.[2]

The afternoon gathering was recorded by the *Advertiser*. In opening the meeting, Mrs Bell commented 'Some thoughtful women realised that what was at first regarded as a noisy outburst was actually becoming a menace to the empire and a danger to the womanhood of their land'.[3] This appeal to the sanctity of the British Empire was typical of the anti-suffragists. Those who organised these meetings, clearly felt it particularly appropriate to launch their new branch on Empire Day itself. The article in the *Advertiser* shares the page with a series of reports on county-wide Imperial celebrations, which also record the fact that over 4 million children from 17,000 schools were taking part in similar events nationwide. It is no wonder that the anti-suffragists found it so easy to raise support, by scare-mongering about the danger a female-dominated electorate posed to an Empire, commonly associated with marching and military songs.

Mrs Baynton, an Australian, started by paying homage to the 'Mother Country'. She then described her experience of life in New South Wales:

---

[1] Mrs Liberty (The Lee), Mrs Cave-Brown-Cave (Chesham), Miss Carrington (Missenden), Mrs Murray (Little Kimble), Rev. and Mrs Clarke (Ellesborough), Mr and Mrs Hedderwick (Weston Turville), Mrs Routh (Wendover) and Rev. C. O. Phipps (vicar of St Mary's, Aylesbury), *BAAN* and *BH*, 29th May 1909.

[2] *BAAN*, 29th June 1912, p. 6, advert; *BH*, 18th April 1914, p. 10, obit.

[3] *BAAN*, 29th May 1909.

'Her youth was spent in the Bush, where brave pioneer women had to do unnatural tasks. To hear some people speak they would think that Australia, with its women's suffrage, was a charming place, but she could assure them that it was not so. The Bill to enfranchise women in Australia came as a rude awakening to them, for it was passed at 3 o'clock one morning, and great was their surprise to find they had allowed what they regarded as a mere agitation to become an actual fact. The effect of the Parliamentary vote on the women was to produce Socialism of the worst kind'.[1]

Mrs Baynton then proposed the resolution which included the statement: 'This meeting binds itself to support the Anti-Suffrage League in every way within its power'.

Miss Strong added her support to the resolution with the assertion that, 'God made man and woman as two separate functions to perform two separate organizations'. This was the traditional 'separate spheres' argument so much favoured by the anti-suffragists. Miss Strong closed by urging her audience to 'give this important subject careful study before they changed the constitution of the country and brought about a great revolution, not only nationally but in creation'.

Just before the close of the afternoon meeting, Mrs E. D. Lee was recorded as having wittily observed that 'There are far too many "old women" in Parliament now without sending any in petticoats'.[2]

The reporter from the *Advertiser* commented that at both meetings, 'a fair membership was enrolled'. At the afternoon meeting a resolution opposing Parliamentary votes for women was passed with eight dissentients, with a similar 'few' at the evening meeting. At both meetings people were invited to add their signatures to a Parliamentary petition opposing women's enfranchisement, which already bore the names of a quarter of a million people.

Immediately following the afternoon meeting, a branch was formed with Lady Louisa Smith as President, while Miss Perrott and Miss Strong agreed to be Secretary and Treasurer respectively. Miss Strong was involved locally, along with Lady Smith, in the Deanery Women Church Workers' Association. Combining this observation with the evidence of the people involved in the later Amersham branch, it seems that the backbone of the Buckinghamshire anti-suffrage groups was often drawn from networks of churchwomen. Some leading Bishops and other churchmen and women

---

[1] *BAAN*, 29th May 1909.
[2] Ibid.

were publicly sympathetic towards 'votes for women'. However, leading local suffragist, Miss Dove, herself a committed Anglican, once commented on how slow the established church had been in supporting the movement.[1] Equally, Free Church suffrage campaigners also felt that their churches displayed a lack of enthusiasm towards the women's campaign. Baptist Minister of Swindon Tabernacle and sympathetic supporter of the WSPU, Rev. J. Ivory Cripps commented that he had 'never been able to understand why the Women's Movement, especially the part of it dealing with the demand for political equality, has had so little active response and sympathy from the Free Churches'.[2] Mrs Ward was herself very pleased to point to 'the equal representation of political parties, and of Church and dissent', at a meeting at a Bristol anti-suffrage meeting in 1909.[3]

The evening meeting at Wendover, reported by the *Herald*, included a talk by 'a barrister well-versed in the objects of the League', Mr A. H. Richardson.[4] He was, however, not so well-versed in the history of the women's suffrage movement as he started by making a mistaken observation about the suddenness of its appearance. He seems to have associated the women's suffrage movement with the advent of the Pankhursts and other suffragette leaders, who he decried for their 'obscurity' and the 'violence' of their propaganda. He then went on to challenge what he saw as the main thrust of the suffragette's case, that man-made laws were unjust to women, arguing to the contrary that 'Women had always been treated by man as a favoured creature. (Laughter).'

Regarding the patent injustice of wage inequality between men and women, Mr Richardson asked why the women did not form Trade Unions. He proposed that the only two possible answers to the question were either that they recognised their work could not justifiably receive higher wages, or that they were incapable of organising themselves. If the latter was true, he went on, then the women had 'conclusively demonstrated they were also unfit to be entrusted with the affairs of the nation'.[5]

Mr Richardson displayed the typical thinking of most anti-suffragists, who simultaneously sought to circumscribe women's capabilities, while also exalting the spiritual and moral superiority of the female sex. He was

---

[1] *SBFP*, 13th March 1914.

[2] *Free Church Suffrage Times*, March 1914: 'The Free Churches and the Women's Movement'.

[3] Harrison, Brian - *Separate Spheres*, p. 123.

[4] *BH*, 29th May 1909.

[5] Ibid.

obviously not being entirely honest about some of his fellow 'antis' when he said, 'No-one thought woman was inferior to man'. He continued that, '...in the highest points of character, (woman) was infinitely superior'. Mr Richardson's comments were naturally well-received by his audience, but, as was also the case with the suffragist speakers, he exaggerated his case to make a point. Some male anti-suffragists in particular were guilty of undermining the anti-suffrage cause with the bluntness of their arguments. In contrast, women speakers on both sides of the argument, tended to employ a more subtle approach.

Anti-suffragists, in the political landscape of Buckinghamshire at least, were largely preaching to the converted. From 1910, two out of three Buckinghamshire MPs at this time were both Unionist and 'staunchly anti': Lionel de Rothschild and Sir Alfred Cripps of Parmoor House, near High Wycombe, whose later elevation to the peerage precipitated the South Bucks by-election in 1914.

However, even the Liberal candidates who stood against them, in 1910 and then in the 1914 by-election, seemed un-persuaded of the desirability of this reform, even if convinced of the justice of the suffragist argument. The suffragist organiser from Bourne End, Kate Frye, refused to campaign for Mr Herbert, the Liberal candidate for South Bucks in 1910, commenting in her diary that he was 'so very "anti"'.[1] This was despite persuasive campaigns by the suffragists among the branches of the Buckinghamshire Liberal Women's Associations. In February 1912, five WLA meetings held in four days throughout the South Bucks constituency recorded either a unanimous vote or an overwhelming majority in favour of votes for women.[2] Addressed by Miss Florence Balgarnie and Mrs Holman, the meetings were held at Bourne End, Marlow, Wycombe, Slough and Beaconsfield. This was significant progress for the suffrage cause, continuing the work Miss Balgarnie and Countess Kearney had done among the county's Liberals in the 1890s. These five votes in favour must have been viewed as a personal triumph by Lady Ada Thomas, the suffragist President of the South Bucks WLA.

What must have been disheartening for suffragists everywhere over many years, was that public pledges made by MPs at the hustings were themselves no guarantee of how they would actually vote faced with a division in Parliament. At least the Mid-Bucks MP, Lord Lionel de Rothschild never held out to the suffragists a false hope of a change of heart.

---

[1] Crawford, Elizabeth - *Campaigning for the Vote*, p.30.
[2] *SBFP*, 1st March 1912.

Despite his well-known antagonism to the cause, a deputation to see Lionel de Rothschild was organised by the Mid-Bucks suffragists on 27th April, 1911, led by Miss Katherine Raleigh, Miss Frances Dove and Mrs Savory.[1] Miss Raleigh opened by using the example of the 16th Century Buckinghamshire woman, Dame Dorothy Pakington, to show that women had not always been excluded from voting. (However, she was wrongly named as Dame Dorothy Perkins in the newspaper account). She asked Rothschild that, if he could not vote for the Bill, perhaps he might abstain. Miss Dove then weighed in on the subject of women's education and asserted that 'equal advantages' for boys and girls from infancy would produce a 'higher quality of the race'. Mrs Savory pointed to the inequality of wages between the sexes and then, highlighting the progress of the movement, she mentioned the seventeen 'successful meetings' the society had held in the last year.

Having listened to the appeals of the three women, Rothschild replied that he could not support the Conciliation Bill. He said that he valued the work which ladies did in relation to municipal government, even going on to concede that '... I can quite see that women with property have a claim in the Government of the country also'. However, he then gives the reasons for his opposition to the women's requests:

> '...I cannot myself see if you once admit that women should have a Parliamentary vote, you could stop by only giving the franchise to those possessed of property. I believe that even ladies themselves realise that it would be impossible to give universal adult suffrage in this country...'.[2]

Rothschild argued that the alterations to the existing Bill proved that 'the present proposed franchise is not going to be the final one'. He then went on in a more conciliatory tone to say that:

> 'I shall be only too pleased to support any fair measures which the women of this country really demanded... but as regards Women's Suffrage itself, at the present time, at any rate, I fear I cannot support it, although I agree with Mr Winston Churchill in so far as I think that this is a question which might easily be placed before the people by the means of a Referendum'.[3]

---

[1] *BH*, 13th May 1911.

[2] Ibid

[3] Ibid.

As well as demonstrating how often the 'antis' appealed for a referendum on the subject, this exchange also shows that opposition to women's suffrage was bound up with a widespread fear that this concession would inevitably lead to a socialist revolution of adult suffrage.

Miss Dove then had an exchange with Rothschild where she not only talked of the injustice of women teachers receiving lower salaries than male teachers, she also went on to reveal her own experience of sexual discrimination during her time as a Headteacher. This was presumably at St Leonard's School in Scotland. Perhaps Lord Rothschild's attitude reminded Miss Dove of other men in the past who had treated her with the amused contempt common to some men in positions of power at the time. While charming, Rothschild certainly seemed to share a common ability, along with Prime Minister Asquith, of being able to effortlessly offend. It is not difficult to imagine how these three ladies probably felt about his closing observation at their meeting:

> '... he thought a great deal might be done if the organisers of the movement would state in which direction they principally required an amendment to the existing laws, and he considered that their cause would make greater headway if they could prove that they had done everything legitimate to further those objects, but that they were unsuccessful because they had not got the vote'.[1]

Shortly after this meeting, Rothschild contacted the *Herald*, which then published this brief statement:

> 'Mr Lionel de Rothschild wishes us to state that he has received a number of letters from Suffragettes and others regarding the present Conciliation Bill, but they are too numerous for him to answer personally. Will those correspondents who have written to Mr Rothschild on the subject please accept this as a reply to their communications'.[2]

Rothschild re-emphasised his opposition to women's suffrage when he appeared on the platform of the great Anti-Suffrage Demonstration at the Royal Albert Hall on 28th February 1912.[3] His antipathy to granting parliamentary votes for women, was further demonstrated by his public

---

[1] *BH*, 13th May 1911.
[2] *BH*, 6th May 1911.
[3] *ASR*, February 1912, pp. 34-5.

criticism against the suffragists for their inactivity, reportedly made in Aylesbury in 1913.

That same year, the wider Rothschild family was exposed by an anonymous suffragist correspondent, as one of the principal contributors to NLOWS funds.[1] Mr Nathanial Mayer de Rothschild, Lionel's uncle, gave the largest sum of £3,000 to aid the 'antis' campaigns. This figure was nearly twice as much as the total contributed by all the anti-suffragist women.

There was, however, one exception to this unrelenting anti-suffrage political landscape in Buckinghamshire. Frederick William Verney, Liberal MP for North Bucks between 1906 and 1910, was sympathetic, possibly as a result of the family connections with Florence Nightingale. At his adoption as Liberal candidate for North Bucks, it was reported that he 'expressed himself in favour of Adult Suffrage, and said that in spite of all that had happened he adhered to the justice of the principle that women should have the vote'.[2] However, his nephew, Sir Harry Verney, who took over the seat from the end of 1910, was not sympathetic to the women's campaign, instead calling on the women at one election rally to '...use their influence, which was considerable'.[3]

It is difficult to identify much in the way of development in the trench-warfare in the county between the two sides of this question. There were those who did alter their views, like Mrs Macdonald, who described herself as having once been Headmistress of a High School.[4] Mrs Macdonald was courageous enough to take up the challenge of giving an impromptu presentation of the anti-suffrage position at a debate organised by the Wycombe suffragists in February 1913. Although ultimately defeated in the vote taken at the end of the meeting, Mrs Macdonald described how she had been an unenthusiastic subscriber to a suffrage society until 1908, but had since changed her views.

There was also Mrs Gladstone Solomon, who described her gradual change of heart against the suffragists' position at an anti-suffrage meeting at Claremont House, Amersham Hill in High Wycombe in February 1914.[5] What is not clear from her account was when, or how, she came to swap sides.

---

[1] *SBFP*, 11th April 1913.
[2] *BAAN*, 1st January 1910.
[3] *BAAN*, 3rd December 1910.
[4] *SBFP*, 28th February 1913.
[5] *SBFP*, 21st February 1914.

Despite these two exceptions, it seems generally true that once battle had really commenced between these opposing forces, instances of people changing sides were relatively rare. Those on both sides had so much invested, psychologically in their own opinions, and also socially in the networks they had built up during their campaigning.

There were examples of some men, previously opposed, becoming sympathetic to the women's cause over time; notably Mr T. Burgess of Aylesbury and Mr Charles Raffety of High Wycombe. (see Appendix 3 for Charles Raffety's 1907 letter) There were of course those who became less enthusiastic and less active in either campaign, for all sorts of reasons. But it was usually the case that, once an 'anti' always an 'anti', or indeed, once a suffragist always a suffragist. This was the feeling expressed by Mr J. Pendlebury from High Wycombe, who went on to join the NUWSS women's suffrage pilgrimage later that year. John Pendlebury, Head of the Elementary School in Priory Road and near neighbour of Miss Dove, made a declaration which received much sympathy from the audience at the end of a public debate at High Wycombe Guildhall:

> 'He was one of those who could not be turned from the straight path by the acts of the militants. He had always been in favour of women having the vote, and he had seen no reason whatever to change his views. (Hear, hear)'.[1]

Of course, the anti-suffragists at their most forthright attempted to blur the distinction between constitutional and law-breaking suffragists, increasingly so as the militant actions of the suffragettes intensified. Miss Helen Page, Assistant Secretary for the NLOWS, made this charge at a meeting at Amersham Town Hall in February 1913. She said that non-militants and militants were 'hand in glove' and that 'there was really no difference between Miss Fawcett's societies and the militant organisations'.[2] Similarly, Nesta Forrest, writing from 'New Court', Marlow, denounced the suffragists' protestations: 'By their too frequent sympathy with the militants in the past, the 'Constitutional Suffragists' must bear the moral responsibility for this disgraceful violence and it is too late for condemnatory resolutions'.[3]

A polarising of opinions was noticeable much earlier, some time before the first suffragette arson attacks in Buckinghamshire itself. A shocking

---

[1] *SBFP,* 28th February 1913.
[2] *BE,* 7th March 1913.
[3] *SBFP,* 26th June 1914.

comment piece was published in the *Standard*, under the initials 'TJN'.[1] This was likely to have been Thomas John Northy, who was listed as a 'journalist and author' in the 1911 census and was then living in Peterborough Avenue, High Wycombe. The writer not only suggested that these suffragette 'fiends in human shape' should be transferred to mental hospitals like Broadmoor, but justified 'the public (beginning) to take matters in their own hands'. He even commented darkly '... though it would be a deplorable thing to witness the advent of "Judge Lynch" in a country like ours, the militants will have only themselves to blame'. The following year, Mr Northy was appointed Managing Editor of one part of the newly amalgamated newspaper, the *South Bucks Herald and Standard*, after the *Standard* stopped being printed.[2]

Similarly, shortly after the attempt to burn down the church in Penn, Frances Anne Collins of 18 Roberts Road, High Wycombe called for suffragette prisoners to be privately flogged before starting their hunger-strikes.[3]

With this hostile background, many of the underlying arguments against women's suffrage, did not develop much during the years the battle raged between the two sides. Lord Curzon's leaflet, *15 Objections to Woman Suffrage*, provides a useful summary of the 'antis' position. These arguments, many of which were visited and re-visited in meetings across Buckinghamshire, were summarised in a leaflet probably written by Katherine Raleigh:

1) Political activity will tend to take away woman from her proper sphere and highest duty, which is maternity.

2) It will tend by the divisions which it will introduce to break up the harmony of the home.

3) The grant of votes for women cannot possibly stop at a restricted franchise on the basis of a property or other qualification. Married women being the women, if any, best qualified to exercise the vote, the suffrage could not be denied to them. Its extension to them would pave the way to Adult Suffrage. There is no permanent or practicable halting-stage before.

4) Women have not, as a sex, or a class, the calmness of temperament, or the balance of mind, nor have they the training, necessary to qualify them to exercise weighty judgement in political affairs.

5) The vote is not desired, so far as can be ascertained, by the large majority of women.

---

[1] *SBS*, 27th February 1913.

[2] *BH*, 4th July 1914.

[3] *SBFP*, 23rd May 1913.

6) Neither is the proposed change approved, so far as can be ascertained, by the large majority of men.

7) If the vote were granted, it is probable that a very large number of women would not use it at all. But in emergencies or on occasions of emotional excitement, a large, and, in the last resort, owing to the numerical majority of women, a preponderant force might suddenly be mobilised, the political effect of which would be wholly uncertain.

8) The presence of a large female factor in the Constituencies returning a British Government to power would tend to weaken Great Britain in the estimation of foreign powers.

9) It would be gravely misunderstood and would become a source of weakness in India.

10) The vote once given, it would be impossible to stop at this. Women would then demand the right of becoming M.P.s, Cabinet Ministers, Judges etc. Nor could the demand be logically refused.

11) Woman, if placed by the vote on an absolute equality with man, would forfeit much of that respect which the chivalry of man has voluntarily conceded to her.

12) The vote is not required for the removal of the hardships or disabilities from which woman is now known to suffer. Where any such exist they can equally well be removed or alleviated by a legislature elected by men.

13) Those persons ought not to make laws who cannot join in enforcing them. Women cannot become soldiers, sailors, or policemen, or take an active part in the maintenance of law and order. They are incapacitated from discharging the ultimate obligations of citizenship.

14) The intellectual emancipation of women is proceeding, and will continue to do so without the enjoyment of the political franchise. There is no necessary connection between the two.

15) No precedent exists for giving woman as a class an active share in the Government of a great country or Empire, and it is not for Great Britain whose stake is the greatest, and in whose case the results of failure would be most tremendous, to make the experiment. It would not, indeed, be an experiment, since if the suffrage were once granted it could never be cancelled or withdrawn.[1]

Formal debates in the county, which touched on many of the above points, were mostly won by the anti-suffragists. From the small Debating Society evening at The Lee in 1908, to the bigger formal discussions, like the one in Beaconsfield in October 1913, the 'antis' were usually able to muster a majority in opposition. Lady Hulse was another prominent local anti-suffragist who lived at Hall Barn in Beaconsfield. She not only took part in

---

[1] *15 Objections to Woman Suffrage, By Lord Curzon, Answered by K.R.*, 1913.

the debate, alongside G.K. Chesterton, but also engaged in a combative public correspondence with Mrs Helena Swanwick in the days following the meeting.[1]

What must have been even more galling for the suffragists was that the numbers which anti-suffragists could occasionally muster meant that some resolutions supporting votes for women were not carried. However, there was one debate in High Wycombe in February 1913, which proved a notable triumph for the suffragists: 70 voted for and 27 against.[2] But while this might seem to indicate the growing momentum of the longer-term campaign of the suffragists in High Wycombe, too much should not be read into this result. This hopeful result came only five months before the very hostile reception of the NUWSS Pilgrimage to the town.

Throughout this later period, a proliferating round of meetings was organised by the 'antis', in an increasing number of towns in the county, culminating in the formation of a third Buckinghamshire branch of anti-suffragists. Launched at a 'drawing room' meeting held at Amersham Grammar School on January 3rd 1913, this new branch drew on people from the area surrounding Chesham and Amersham. Lady Susan Trueman was elected President, and several 'antis' from the area were chosen as Vice-Presidents, including Lady Liberty, two JPs and a doctor. Also appointed Vice-President was the newly knighted, Sir Arthur Lasenby Liberty, who with his knowledge of textiles and the Orient, had opened the first 'Liberty's' shop in London in the 1880s.

Lady Susan Trueman, daughter of the 2nd Earl of Stafford, was married to Colonel Thomas Trueman. Living first at Bayman Manor, she later came to live at White Hill House. A worshipper at Christ Church, Waterside, Lady Trueman was heavily involved in the Chesham Cottage Hospital Committee and in overseeing the Mother's Union in the diocese. Clearly a hugely energetic, influential and formidable woman, she went on to sit as a JP for Buckinghamshire and to take part in the later campaign of the Women's Institute for the appointing of women police officers.[3]

The Amersham and District branch of the NLOWS very quickly organised their first meeting at the Amersham Town Hall on 27th February. Chaired by Mr G. H. Weller and supported on the platform by Lady Trueman, Miss Helen Page, Assistant Secretary of the NLOWS, addressed the crowded meeting. She remarked on how the branch had gained 200

---

[1] *SBS*, 16th October 1913.
[2] *SBFP*, 28th February 1913.
[3] *BE*, 14th February 1936, p. 5, obit.

members in its first 6 weeks. This was a rate of growth un-matched by any local suffrage society. Going on to attack the outrages of the militant suffragettes, she remarked that she was 'astonished that women could do such cold-blooded deeds'.[1] She concluded with the declaration that 'Now was the time to save the Empire from destruction'.

Mr A. Maconachie was the second speaker. He was publicly challenged when he was foolish enough to state that, 'women had traded on their sex'. When he went on to explain this statement by saying that women who broke the law had not 'taken their punishment like men', someone in the audience responded by saying: 'Women have had their hair torn out'.[2] Mr Maconachie then clarified what he meant by saying that he hadn't been talking about women's treatment at the hands of the mob. When the vote for the resolution was taken at the end, there were a dozen dissentients.

A similar meeting the following year, prior to the South Bucks by-election, was addressed by Mrs Gladstone Solomon from Hendon. Mrs Solomon had just written a letter in response to 'A Suffragist', as part of her extensive campaigning in the area. (See Appendix 10) On the same page as this letter, the *Herald* reported on the 'remarkable scenes' witnessed at the Amersham Town Hall that week.[3] According to the article, a long time before the anti-suffrage meeting was due to begin, a large crowd had gathered and 'hundreds clamoured for admission' to the ticketed meeting, many without success.

Colonel Trueman opened the meeting, referring to his 33 years of military service and appealing to the history of the Indian mutiny as the kind of courageous spirit women should exhibit. Mrs Solomon spoke and urged her audience 'not to let the suffragettes dupe them'. Mr Maconachie also spoke, asserting that, 'Women... did not realise the political results, the political importance, the political value of the vote'. His limited experience of the women's suffrage movement should have told him otherwise.

At the end of the meeting, his wife moved a resolution, which received only a few dissentients:

'That this meeting... protests against any extension of the franchise to women, and calls upon the successful candidate for the Parliamentary

---

[1] *BE*, 7th March 1913.
[2] Ibid.
[3] *BH*, 21st February 1914.

vacancy in South Bucks to vote against any proposal to give votes to women'.[1]

It is interesting to compare these two public meetings at Amersham Town Hall, organised by the local anti-suffragists, almost exactly a year apart. There was a notable growth in local awareness and support within 12 months. This was probably due to the branch being organised by some prominent and wealthy local residents. Mrs Sandford Freeman, who lived at 'High Wood', Chesham Bois had been appointed Secretary. Her husband was Treasurer of the branch, which asked for associates to pay an annual subscription of one shilling and for members to pay anything above this sum.[2] The 1914 event was ticketed and had a number of uniformed stewards, 'wearing the badge and colours of the Branch'.[3] The key figures involved, and the arguments employed, were the same as the first meeting in 1913, but the 1914 turn-out seems huge in comparison.

This NLOWS meeting was held just 10 days before the first meeting organised by the NUWSS in Amersham. It was also at the Town Hall and was also packed.[4] Those mentioned as leading the meeting were: the chairman Mrs Constance Davies, Mrs Whalley, the NUWSS organiser Miss Dora Mason, Mr Barrs Davies and Rev J. G. Scott. An opening exchange set the tone for the evening when someone in the audience shouted out at the start of the meeting, 'Are you connected with the suffragettes?' Mrs Constance Davies replied smartly by saying, 'No, we only suffer from them'.[5]

At times 'jollied' by a youthful element in the crowd, there had to be a second count before the resolution in favour of women's enfranchisement was announced as carried. Although there was an equal representation of suffragists and 'antis' at this meeting and a clear division of local opinion, it would seem that the anti-suffrage campaign had the greater public support.

By August that same year, all the excitement and furore surrounding this issue in Amersham and across Buckinghamshire, was quickly forgotten with the outbreak of the First World War. Mrs Pankhurst called an end to the militant campaign. And most of the women within the suffrage movement in Buckinghamshire joined the anti-suffragists in calling for women to support the war effort. Old animosities were largely forgotten. Ultimately, the terrible

---

[1] *BH*, 21st February 1914.
[2] *BE*, 24th January 1913.
[3] *BH*, 21st February 1914.
[4] *BE*, 6th February 1914.
[5] Ibid.

and unforgettable experience of the war contributed to a collective amnesia of the women's suffrage movement in Buckinghamshire and elsewhere.

It was without fanfare that Lionel de Rothschild announced his change of attitude. In a letter written from the House of Commons, Rothschild explained his change of heart, prompted by the overwhelming majority in the Commons in favour of the Speaker's recommendations on voting reform, including votes for women. He wrote: '... for various reasons I am convinced that some measure of women franchise is urgent just now'.[1] He was sure that his, 'constituents... do not wish their Member to be behind in any new reform which may come before the country'.

Subsequently, as Parliamentary candidate for a re-organised Mid-Bucks division, Major Lionel de Rothschild, addressed a meeting prior to the 1918 General Election at Beaconsfield. Talking of women's suffrage he joked that some might see him as, 'one of those who left a sinking ship'.[2] He went on that he 'voted for women's suffrage when it became law because he was absolutely convinced of their claim by the patriotic attitude they had taken in the war (Applause)'.[3]

At a later meeting in Chesham's Town Hall, at which women electors were well-represented, coalition candidate, Major Rothschild, received the hearty support of the local population. Miss G. M. Sutthery, active in the Mothers' Union under the presidency of Lady Trueman, was asked to support the resolution of support for Rothschild, 'as representing women's suffrage'. It seems however, from Miss Sutthery comments, she had herself been entirely unsympathetic towards the suffragists' cause. She said:

> '... her position with regard to it was very much like the position of the majority of women towards the suffrage: they did not expect it, they did not want it, and they did not know quite what to do with it now that they had it. But... women had shared to the full the burden and grief and work of these last four dreadful years... and they were resolved to do their share in helping to make this a better, healthier and happier world.'[4]

In a later letter to the *Examiner*, Miss Sutthery proposed a different type of war memorial for the town. She suggested a building 'for a Working Women's and Girl's Institute or Club', as a way of recognising the role the

---

[1] *BE*, 3rd April 1917.
[2] *SBFP*, 29th November 1918.
[3] Ibid.
[4] *BE*, 6th December 1918.

women played in the war.[1] She asked, 'Would it be helpful to Chesham working women and girls? I say, yes. Women now have larger responsibilities as citizens.'

Inevitably, Chesham plumped for a more traditional town centre memorial statue. But Miss Sutthery's letter is a final reminder that at the end of the war, Britain was indeed standing on the threshold of a new era; an era in which, despite the sometimes desperate efforts of the anti-suffragists, women were increasingly beginning to take a part in nearly all spheres of national life.

---

[1] *BE*, 3rd January 1919.

Chapter 8: Growth and Set-backs in Wycombe and South Buckinghamshire

'... a nation which was putting on one side one-half of humanity was like an individual trying to work with only one arm...'
- Miss Frances Dove at the launch of the Gerrards Cross NUWSS, reflecting on her experience of a broken arm. *SBS*, 22nd February 1912.

JUST as 1911 closed with the launch of a second NUWSS branch in South Bucks, 1912 opened with the establishment of a third, in Gerrards Cross. As before, some of the original campaigners from the 1904 meeting at Wycombe Abbey School, formed the backbone of the new group. Miss Stevenson of Hedgerley Park, Stoke Poges went on to be made President of the branch at its first public meeting at Gerrards Cross Town Hall in February. Miss Dove opened the meeting by congratulating the local suffragists on a 'splendid beginning', and mentioned their monthly 'drawing room' meetings which had meant 'the numbers of adherents had grown 'very sensibly'.[1] However, the 250 people estimated to be present were not entirely composed of supporters. When Mr Chancellor, MP for Haggerston, told the meeting he was a 'whole hogger' and in favour of women MPs, there was an outbreak of hissing from the audience.

This branch later went on to be bold enough to hold an open-air meeting at Austin Wood Common, near Chalfont St Peter, in July of that year, which was presided over by the ever-present Mrs Constance Davies. Their second annual meeting, in February 1913, also at the Town Hall, included 'lively scenes' and was addressed by Dr Barbara Tchaikovsky, Mrs Ada Nield Chew and Mr Henry Harben. The resolution was passed, but with many dissentients. The following year, the Gerrards Cross anti-suffragists arranged a NLOWS meeting at the Assembly Rooms, Oak End Waye, which was described as having a 'splendid attendance'.[2]

The Wycombe branch was also seeing growth. Two teachers who publicly joined the ranks of the Wycombe suffragists around this time were Mrs Edith Berney and Miss Mary Christie. Mrs Edith Berney, originally from Wakefield, was a Schoolmistress at Godstowe. Although not present at the

---

[1] *SBS*, 22nd February 1912.
[2] *SBFP*, 24th April 1914.

1904 meeting, she later became Secretary of the Wycombe NUWSS and turned one of the houses of Godstowe, 'Ulverscroft', where she lived, into the local branch office.[1] Her involvement in the movement was supported by her husband, Robert, who was a Schoolmaster at Godstowe.

Miss Mary Christie was Headmistress of what became High Wycombe High School. From Arbroath in Scotland, she distinguished herself when she was made Head Girl of the High School there and won a scholarship to St Andrews University in 1891. She went on to be the first woman to be awarded an MA by the university in 1896. Having then taught in Nelson, Lancashire, she was appointed first Headmistress of the County Day School for Girls in 1901.[2]

Painting of Miss Mary Christie, first Headmistress of Wycombe High School. Courtesy of Wycombe High School

[1] *SBFP*, 27th March 1914, p. 1 advert.
[2] Sutcliffe, Rachel (ed.) *Wycombe High School: The First 100 Years, 1901-2001*, p. 8.

In June 1912, Miss Christie announced her support for votes for women by seconding a motion at a suffrage meeting.[1] Prior to this, her involvement in the women's suffrage movement may have been hindered by the fact that Alderman Deacon, an influential and convinced anti-suffragist, was for some time the Chair of the High School Governors, probably until mid-1912, when Miss Dove took over from him.

Suffragist numbers grew more slowly than the anti-suffragists, whose branches were also multiplying. At times they witnessed spectacular growth. The NLOWS in the county were clearly boosted by public outrage at the suffragette attacks on property in different parts of the country after the summer of 1912.

While the Wycombe NUWSS had lost members to the development of new branches in Gerrards Cross and Beaconsfield, it seems that they steadily gained new members, and from across a wider social spectrum than before. Many of those within the committed core of the Wycombe society were either teachers, members of school staff or married to teachers. However, other professions as well as locals from the working classes, began to become more noticeable within the suffragist ranks. Frederick J. Chipps the carpenter was one example. Probably sympathetic to the ILP, Mr Chipps was involved with both the WEA and the local Co-operative Society. He also employed his carpentry skills at Godstowe School.[2] Married to Margaret, who was originally from Pennsylvania, his American wife may well have had an influence on his views.[3] Chipps was later mentioned as having played a part in helping the suffragist pilgrims during the disturbances of July 1913.[4] Another male recruit of relatively humble origins was Ronald Rice, son of Rev. George Rice, the minister of Union Baptist Church, Easton Street. Aged 21 and described as a student in the 1911 census, he was there to support local suffragists at meetings for workers outside the gates of two chair-making factories in 1913.[5]

The High Wycombe suffragists opened their 1912 campaign by re-launching the society as one now affiliated to the NUWSS for the first time. A well-attended meeting, on Tuesday 5th March, was held in the Large Room of Wycombe Abbey School. Those who had helped arrange the meeting, as part of a provisional committee alongside Miss Dove, Miss

---

[1] *SBS*, 13th June 1912; Burgin p. 11.
[2] *Godstowe School – An Informal Story of its Beginnings,* p. 3.
[3] 1911 England and Wales Census.
[4] *SBS*, 24th July 1913.
[5] *SBFP*, 14th March 1912.

Wheeler and Miss Berney, who had already agreed to act as officers, were listed as follows: Mrs Scott, Dr Meredith, Miss Dring, Miss Gilley (sic.), Miss Daniel and Mr Berney.[1] The meeting was timed in anticipation of the Conciliation Bill for women's suffrage, which was due to come before Parliament on 28th March.

Mrs Constance Davies opened the meeting with observations on the growth of the movement locally and the assertion that they were 'now at the door of success'.[2] Miss Maude Royden followed this by congratulating those present for coming that night despite the recent events in London, which was a reference to the new suffragette tactics of systematic window-smashing. Miss Royden, was a founder member of the CLWS and a member of the NUWSS Executive.[3]

Having effectively blamed the inactivity of too many suffragist sympathisers for the creation of militancy, Miss Royden invited the audience to send post-cards to their MP, Sir Alfred Cripps, to encourage him to at least abstain from voting against the Conciliation Bill. However, the MP for South Bucks had recently reiterated his opposition to this reform, without a referendum on the issue, at a Conservative Party meeting in Gerrards Cross.[4]

Towards the end of the meeting, after having asked a question about suffragette militancy, Mr Norton Fagge went on to second Mrs Scott's proposal to form a NUWSS branch in the town. He pronounced (to loud cheers) that he was 'totally opposed to militant tactics, but in agreement with the Suffrage movement'. According to the census, in 1911 Mr Fagge was living at 'The Nook' in Roberts Road, High Wycombe. It seems he was teaching at Wycombe Grammar School and also was a Captain in charge of the Officer Training Corps at the school. However, by 1st May that year, for whatever reason, he had, 'ceased to serve with the contingent'.[5] Mr Fagge's public declaration demonstrates the extent to which the women's suffrage movement was continuing to galvanise a wider section of the population, despite suffragette militancy.

However, in proposing a vote of thanks, Dr H. J. Wheeler stated that he had for a long time been 'a convinced supporter' of women's suffrage. The only argument he knew against giving women the vote was, 'the behaviour of some of the women'. He described the recent attacks as 'abominable' and

[1] *SBS*, 7th March 1912.
[2] *SBFP*, 8th March 1912.
[3] Fletcher, Sheila - *DNB*, 2004-10.
[4] *SBS*, 1st February 1912.
[5] *The London Gazette*, 9th July 1912, p. 4977.

feared they would do much harm to the movement. It seems that, for some, suffragette militancy could easily become a reason for distancing themselves from the campaign. And certainly, the WSPU window-smashing raids on the West End were seen by some as the reason why the Parliamentary vote for the Women's Suffrage Bill was narrowly defeated later that month.

The progress of the movement at this time had been emphasised by a series of South Bucks Liberal Association meetings that February, which consistently voted in favour of women's suffrage.[1] The meetings were held within four days in five places: Bourne End, Marlow, High Wycombe, Slough and Beaconsfield. However, only a few weeks later, at a meeting in the Wycombe Guildhall, when the South Bucks Women's Liberal Association tried to ensure the next Liberal candidate for South Bucks would himself be a suffragist, the proposal was at the last minute defeated. The Liberal Association simply acknowledged the receipt of the women's resolution and stated that the SBLA did not 'think it desirable to restrict its choice of candidate'.[2] This decision may have been swayed by the public outrage at the suffragette window-smashing raids on the West End in early March. The fact that the Wycombe suffragists' re-launch coincided with this new development in suffragette militancy, does seem to have made their task more difficult.

At the March launch meeting of the Wycombe NUWSS, Miss Dove issued a challenge to those in the audience to give their names as 'adherents to the cause', stating that 'their strength lay in their numbers'.[3] However, a drawing-room meeting at 'Ulverscroft', Godstowe School on 31st May, showed that the members in the Wycombe NUWSS still only numbered 78.[4] This was fewer than the number of members in the Mid-Bucks NUWSS, which stood at over 100 at that time.[5] Unfortunately, there is no consistent record of numbers of members or 'friends' of any of the suffrage societies in Buckinghamshire, so it is difficult to gain an accurate picture of the comparable growth of these suffrage societies. Of course, the Wycombe NUWSS now covered a much smaller geographical area than Mid-Bucks. But given the more populous nature of the High Wycombe area, coupled with the fact they had been campaigning longer, this would suggest the

---

[1] *SBFP*, 1st March 1912.
[2] *SBFP*, 19th April 1912.
[3] *SBFP*, 8th March 1912.
[4] *SBFP*, 7th June 1912.
[5] *BE*, 29th March 1912.

Wycombe suffragists probably felt frustrated by the low level of support, and clearly saw the need for a more energetic campaign with a wider appeal.

The next suffragist meeting in June may have provided the renewed impetus for which the suffragists were hoping.[1] Maude Royden's announcement, to a meeting held at 'Ulverscroft', of a dramatic change in the non-party approach of the NUWSS was also potentially controversial. Royden introduced the recent NUWSS decision to form an electoral alliance with the only party which had publicly announced its support for women's suffrage, the Labour Party. While Miss Royden recognised that they would inevitably lose, 'a certain amount of support', but felt that most of those lost to the movement as a result did not view women's suffrage as the most important of all political reforms. Not only did she feel that the Union had already been 'inspired to new life', but that the new policy would provide renewed enthusiasm to convinced supporters of women's enfranchisement.

Miss Royden went on to tell of the launch of an election fund of £20,000 for NUWSS workers to support Labour candidates in constituencies where the candidates of other parties did not include women's suffrage in their election addresses.

Only one question was forthcoming on this new policy, reflecting either general agreement with this change, or perhaps a certain degree of subdued uncertainty. Despite the apparent enthusiasm of the meeting, it is unclear whether the Wycombe suffragists took up Miss Royden's closing challenge for the launch of a visitation programme for each district, organised by 'working women' who would become 'missionaries' for votes for women. But Miss Dove, in closing the meeting and congratulating the Secretary and host, Mrs Berney, on the growth of the movement locally, certainly attempted to encourage others to take up the challenge of at least visiting a dozen homes each.

The same day Miss Royden also gave a lecture at Godstowe on 'Jeanne d'Arc,' a figure who had come to symbolise the determination and sacrificial courage of the women's movement.[2] Royden restricted herself to a historical study of the French martyr's life, but at the conclusion of her lecture, issued an appeal to sign 'a petition for the liberation of Miss Malecka'. The case of Miss Malecka, a British subject who had been sentenced in Warsaw to four

---

[1] *SBFP*, 7th June 1912.
[2] *SBS*, 6th June 1912.

years in a Siberian prison for her association with Polish socialists, was a celebrated one at the time.[1]

Miss Sterling's visit to Wycombe, a week after the previous meeting at 'Ulverscroft', showed the suffragists keen to project an image of exciting development, after the newly announced policy of an alliance with the Labour Party. This well attended meeting was held in the Red Room of the Town Hall. In the course of the afternoon it emerged that Mrs Longsdon, a teacher and housemistress at Godstowe, had covered the costs for hiring the hall.[2] Her involvement and the emergence of others who were apparently new to the movement helped to reinforce a sense of growth and forward momentum.

Alongside Miss Dove, Mrs Scott and Mrs Berney on the platform were Miss Christie and Miss Daniel. Also on the platform and mentioned for the first time in relation to a local suffragist event, was Mrs Ensor from Sands, who later joined the 1913 pilgrims on their march through the area.

In her opening remarks about the 'vigorous youth' of the local movement, Miss Dove made much of the fact that, having been Secretary of the NUWSS, Miss Sterling was 'at the heart of things'.[3] Beginning her speech, Miss Sterling denied that the women's movement was 'revolutionary.' Instead she asserted that 'however much it might appear to be a vast change, it was not in any way a change in fundamentals.' She ridiculed the popular 'antis' arguments about the threat to home life posed by women gaining the vote and instead anticipated 'better homes'. Miss Sterling similarly derided the 'physical force' argument, calling it 'a sham from top to bottom'.

Miss Sterling concluded her remarks with a rousing challenge:

'She felt that the time had come when their supporters should make a great sacrifice... She thought the reason why they had not got the vote by now was merely because they had not all been working hard enough. The moment they laid the matter clearly and openly before the ordinary person they would get sympathy and support'.[4]

---

[1] *Colonist*, Volume LIV, issue 13422, 21st May 1912, p. 5, online: papers past - May 2012

[2] *SBFP*, 14th June 1912; *Godstowe School: an Informal Story of its Beginnings*, p. 6 and Godstowe archives.

[3] *SBS*, 13th June 1912, p. 2.

[4] *SBFP*, 14th June 1912.

The summer of 1912 demonstrated the extent of Miss Dove's reputation and popularity in the county. Miss Dove spoke at a meeting in Aylesbury on the question of women's employment. She spoke on the subject of 'The National Insurance Act in its relation to Women Workers' at an Aylesbury Vale Oddfellows meeting, 3 Walton Grove.[1] The event was chaired by Dr. Leonard West, who had demonstrated his support for women's suffrage at events in Wendover in 1909 and 1910.

In speaking about the formation of the women's Oddfellows lodge in the district, Dr West estimated from the 1911 census returns that the number of women workers in the county impacted by the new legislation would be nearly 20,000. Ten thousand of these were in domestic service, 2,000 were dressmakers, 1,500 laundry workers, 1,300 school teachers, while 800 were in lacemaking, although not all these would be affected. Other smaller numbers of workers included those in bookbinding and printing and paper manufacturing, as well as grocers, confectioners, charwomen and those in the hotel trade.

The event shows Miss Dove's concern for all young women needing to find rewarding and well-paid employment in a limited and often male-dominated job market. Wycombe suffragists chose to highlight the negative side of this social issue with their exhibition of 'sweated industries' the following year.

By that autumn, the number of NUWSS Wycombe members had reached 100, which indicates significant numerical growth over the summer months, during a period usually devoid of campaigning.[2] A growing confidence among local campaigners was evident in the presence of delegates from High Wycombe at a regional meeting of NUWSS activists in Reading in September, to launch the next session of campaigning.[3] This meeting was addressed by Maude Royden, who was again engaged in persuading this wider audience about the wisdom of the NUWSS support for Labour Party candidates.

Towards the end of 1912, the Wycombe suffragists either dramatically increased the frequency of their meetings, or simply ensured these were more prominently advertised, or both. The local movement in High Wycombe must have received a significant financial boost, as from November 1912 there was a central front page advertisement for suffrage meetings placed in the *Free Press* every month, sometimes more than once a

---

[1] *BAAN*, 15th June 1912, p. 9.
[2] *SBS*, 21st November 1912.
[3] *SBFP*, 4th October 1912.

month. Not only that, the Wycombe NUWSS appears to have taken over the lease of 1 White Hart Street, which had been the club-house of the Worker's Education Association. The annual rent for the WEA club-house was previously recorded as £13.[1] It appears, from an earlier article, that the WEA encountered financial problems in 1911, before being temporarily rescued by funds raised at a New Year Party, organised by Mrs Scott of Godstowe. [2]

Mrs Amy Scott and her family, outside Godstowe School, c.1905. Those from the Gillie family who took part in the women's suffrage battle were Mrs Scott's sisters Helen (seated far right) and Nancie (standing far left), as well as Rev. Robert Gillie (seated far left wearing a straw boater) and one of Mrs Scott's daughter's, Maisie (seated far left). Courtesy of Dorothy Ball

Later the Wycombe NUWSS moved its offices to the Godstowe schoolhouse, 'Ulverscroft', home of the Secretary, Mrs Berney. This change

[1] *SBFP*, 30th April 1909.
[2] *SBFP*, 19th April 1912.

was mentioned in a 1914 advert.[1] Whether this was due to lack of funds for the lease, a lack of support for the programme of lectures there, or some other reason, is unclear.

Developing funding streams must have taken a considerable amount of time away from direct campaigning. However, many of the leading Wycombe suffragists had extensive experience of organising and fundraising. And it is likely that much of the funding for the office and the advertising, for example, was raised from various sales and social events, including whist drives. Mrs Berney was later pleased to report that a sale of work in December 1912 had raised over £20, which she said was being, 'expended on propaganda'.[2]

From November 1912, the Wycombe NUWSS advertised 'At Homes' at their office in White Hart Street, between 3pm and 5pm every Wednesday, with a hearty welcome, a speaker and refreshments.[3] These were very similar to the WEA lectures. One of the first speakers at this type of event, was Mrs Louis Fagan from the Committee of the WTRL. This is one interesting example of co-operation between constitutional suffragists and those prepared to break the law in a more passive way. Mrs Fagan commented that 'They felt more than ever hopeful that tax resistance was the best method of working for the vote when they found that this was the method decided upon by the men of Ulster if the Home Rule Bill should pass'.[4] Several local people signed up to be associates of the WTRL at the end of the meeting, which indicates that while they were sympathetic, none of them were prepared immediately to take the step of resisting paying taxes.

Another of these afternoon events was reported later that month as a lecture on different aspects of the third chapter of J.S. Mill's book, 'The Subjection of Women'.[5] Four discussion starters were addressed by local suffragists: 'A vote is a means of self-protection – ought it be denied to those who most need it?', introduced by Mr W. Bailey; 'Is the political capacity of women equal to that of men?', introduced by Mrs Edith Berney; 'How far is the mental distinction between men and women artificial?', introduced by Miss Reeves; 'Women are morally better than men – How far ought the Sovereign Power i.e. of the people to be conditioned by morality and how

---

[1] *SBFP*, 27th March 1914.
[2] *SBFP*, 31st January 1913.
[3] *SBFP*, 8th November 1912, p. 1.
[4] *SBFP*, 22nd November 1912.
[5] *SBS*, 28th November 1912.

far by sex?',[1] introduced by Mrs Rushby Smith. The office was a prime location for a propaganda campaign in the town.

These smaller-scale, educational events, presented by local speakers, were combined with regular, well-advertised public meetings, usually addressed by a well-known speaker from further afield. Mr Harben of Newland Park, Chalfont St Giles, was regularly called upon and he was the chief speaker at a meeting in the Guildhall on 20th November, 1912. Miss Dove opened the meeting by attempting a balanced response to suffragette militancy. Saying that 'honour may be due to those women for the sacrifices they had inflicted on themselves', she then went on to say that, 'it was not their desire to follow in their steps' and to reiterate her firm belief that it was not right to carry out illegal acts to try to get the law changed. Introducing Mr Harben as a student of Eton and graduate of Magdalene College, Oxford, Miss Dove repeated her appeal for, 'a large increase in the membership of the society'.[2]

This meeting was the first time local reporters mentioned the presence of a group of young women stewards in the NUWSS colours of red, white and green, who helped people to their seats, gave out literature and took up a collection at the end of the evening.

It was at this meeting that Henry Harben revealed that his home, Newland Park, was being used as a country retreat for suffragettes recently released from prison. In response to a barbed question from an 'anti' claiming that the vote was only being demanded by 'a few old maids and young ladies with nothing better to occupy their time', he commented:

'He had a very large acquaintance with people who were "clamouring" for the vote - he lunched that day with five or six who had been in prison, and they were the most charming individuals: one was married and another was her daughter... It was the active-minded and those who worked who were claiming the vote'.[3]

A fellow suffragist and protégé of Henry's C.E.M. Choad, later wrote of his experience of the Harbens' Newland Park home:

'Suffragettes, let out of prison under the 'Cat and Mouse Act', used to go to Newlands (sic.) to recuperate, before returning to prison for a fresh bout of

---

[1] *SBS*, 28th November 1912.
[2] *SBS* and *SBFP*, 21st and 22nd November 1912 respectively.
[3] *SBFP*, 22nd November 1912.

torture. When the county called, as the county still did, it was embarrassed to find haggard-looking young women in dressing gowns and djibbahs reclining on sofas in the Newlands drawing-room and talking about their prison experiences'.[1]

A similarly delightful picture is evoked by the account of a suffrage dance at Newland Park.[2] Originally planned to be held at Ebury Hall, Rickmansworth, the association with the Chorleywood branch of the WSPU meant that the trustees of the hall refused to hire it out for an event supporting women's suffrage. Instead, eighty people enjoyed the music and catering laid on at the Park, with many others having to be turned away. The list of those present reveals numerous names not recognisable from the story of the suffrage campaign in South Buckinghamshire.

The close association between Mr and Mrs Harben and the more militant suffragettes, does not seem to have dissuaded the Wycombe suffragists from employing him regularly as a speaker.

Harben finished his speech at the Guildhall, in November 1912, by moving the proposition, 'That this meeting calls on the House of Commons to include the enfranchisement of women, on broad and democratic lines, in the Franchise and Registration Bill'. This was seconded by the Rev. Rushby Smith, who said he supported women's suffrage for moral and spiritual reasons. The resolution was carried with six dissentients. Several written questions were taken, which Harben responded to in a witty manner. A letter was also read from the new vicar of High Wycombe, Rev. C.P.S. Clarke which also raised a laugh. He wrote, 'I am strongly in favour of giving the vote to working women, but would hesitate to enfranchise idle women, and I should like to disenfranchise idle men'.[3]

The international dimension of the struggle for women's suffrage was again highlighted at the first meeting of the Wycombe NUWSS in 1913. The Secretary of the branch, Mrs Berney, hosted the meeting on 8th January at 'Ulverscroft', Godstowe School, which was presided over by Mrs Constance Davies and addressed by, 'the Russian lady', Mrs Matheson.

Tracing the development of the political history of Russia and the movement for liberation from serfdom, Mrs Matheson declared that the position of women in Russia was generally better than her sisters in the rest of Europe, as Russia had been, 'the first country to recognise the property

---

[1] Choad, C.E.M. - *Under the Fifth Rib: a Belligerent Autobiography*.
[2] *BE*, 30th January 1914.
[3] *SBFP*, 22nd November 1912.

rights of women'.[1] And she believed that women were expected to be educated to the same level as men, including now taking up posts as doctors and lawyers. Mrs Matheson finished by declaring that, despite the women having to fight against the government as in Britain, 'in the very near future, if Russia obtained power through its Duma, there would be no question as to whether the suffrage would be granted to women or not - there was no doubt it would come. (Applause)'.[2]

Wycombe NUWSS advert, *Standard*, 2nd January 1913

Later that January, in the Wycombe Guildhall, Mrs Scott gave a talk illustrated with lantern slides on the subject of 'Women at Work'.[3] Mrs

---

[1] *SBFP*, 22nd November 1912.
[2] Ibid.
[3] *SBFP*, 31st January 1913.

Berney opened proceedings with a short report on local activities, as well as some observations from having attended a recent political meeting in the Town Hall. The previous Friday night women had been treated merely as 'onlookers' and were restricted to seating in the gallery. She promised that the forthcoming Wycombe NUWSS annual meeting in April at the Town Hall would be welcoming to both men and women, would not separate the sexes, and she hoped that they would fill the hall.

Mrs Berney was fresh from having engaged in a lively correspondence in the local papers with Miss Pott, the Secretary of the NLOWS. They exchanged letters over the apparent inability of the anti-suffragists to find a local campaigner to engage in a debate with the Wycombe NUWSS.[1]

During the meeting Mrs Scott confessed to her 'melancholy feeling' due to the recent Parliamentary set-back for the suffragists. This was following Speaker Lowther's ruling that no women's suffrage amendments could be added to the present Franchise Bill. But she said she had been cheered by Mrs Berney's account of local progress. Mrs Scott then spoke about the country's five to six million women workers, mostly unmarried or widowed, who were forced to work for their living. Illustrating her talk with slides, she touched on many industries and the issue of 'sweating', referring to the unequal pay and poor working conditions of many women, which was a hotly-debated topic during a period of growing industrial unrest. Later in the year, High Wycombe itself witnessed a protracted industrial dispute in its largest local employer, the furniture industry. Mrs Scott avoided speaking about local industries, preferring to speak about the celebrated case of the 'pit brow lasses' of Wigan and the north-west. Perhaps the case she mentioned which was most locally relevant was boot-making, where women received 13 shillings, compared to the men who received over 28 shillings for the same work. She commented to applause that, 'If women had the vote, these inequalities would stand a chance of being altered'.[2]

The struggles that women experienced trying to gain equality in higher education were mentioned, as were the difficulties of women doctors. The appearance of Girton College in the picture show highlighted the personal significance to many local suffragists, including Miss Dove, of being able to sit examinations without yet being able to receive the formal recognition of a degree.

Mrs Scott closed her talk with a more forceful resolution than usual, which was seconded by Mr Dairy, who with his wife was involved with the

---

[1] *SBFP*, 31st January 1913.
[2] Ibid.

Workers Education Association.[1] The resolution stated that, 'This meeting desires to place on record its strong indignation at the Government's failure to redeem its pledges, and repeats its demand for a Government measure of women's suffrage'.[2]

This January meeting was swiftly followed by a public meeting on another hot topic at the time, the issue of the 'White Slave Trade' (prostitution). The same month 'The Electroscope Theatre' featured a three day run of a domestic drama called 'A Girl's Adventure' which, according to the advert, dealt with the White Slave Traffic, 'an important matter now attracting so much attention in Parliament'.[3] There was standing room only in the Guildhall for that January meeting. Many of the familiar local suffragists were present, but the meeting was chaired by Mrs F.J.K. Cross of Aston Tirrold Manor, Wallingford, Chairman of the NUWSS Oxon, Berks and Bucks Federation. The main speaker, Miss Alice Abadam delivered an emotive speech about the plight of many innocent girls forced into prostitution due to financial pressures and starvation.

Miss Abadam was originally a member of the WSPU, later joining the WFL split. However, she seems to have become disillusioned with all forms of militancy, becoming a member of the NUWSS and President of the Norwood and District branch in 1913.[4] Alice began her talk that evening by declaring that 'one of the reasons why women wanted franchise was because they had studied the social conditions of the country and found them sadly wanting'.[5] She asserted that such social evils were what brought women out onto public platforms to talk about this shameful 'degradation', and she accused the government of contributing to the problem by underpaying its female workers. Before moving the resolution that enfranchising women would be one of the most effectual means of checking prostitution, she said 'woman was the moral sentinel, but her hands had been bound for too many centuries. (Hear, hear)'.[6] The resolution was carried by an overwhelming majority, as a similar resolution had been passed at a White Slave Traffic meeting in Chesham, the previous year.

Mrs Berney said that nearly £4 had been given at that evening's collection, and went on to report two members had joined the society and

[1] *SBFP*, 2nd May 1913.
[2] *SBFP*, 31st January 1913.
[3] *SBFP*, 21st February 1913.
[4] Crawford - *WSM*, p. 2.
[5] *SBFP*, 7th February 1913.
[6] Ibid.

that 22 people had also signed up as 'Friends of Women's Suffrage', just since the last meeting.

There was an 'At Home' at Speed's Hall, close to the Guildhall, on 12th February. After tea had been taken, the meeting was addressed by Miss Irene Cox, Secretary of the Industrial Law Committee. Introduced by Miss Rochfort of Marlow, Miss Cox spoke of how women were affected by industrial legislation, including a total of 1.8 million female workers in factories, workshops and laundries.

The Wycombe suffragists continued on a similar theme when they proudly advertised their next venture. This was an 'Exhibition of Sweated Industries', between 2pm and 10pm on 19th February in the Town Hall.[1] Such a prolonged and creative event marked a new development for the movement, and indicates the movement's growth in both confidence and numbers.

The event was a collaboration between the Anti-Sweating League, the artistic group of the Women's Suffrage Atelier and the South Bucks NUWSS societies. As well as a display of goods from 'sweated industries', there were placards made by women from many different countries appealing for the vote. A collection of posters and banners were also there. These banners had been displayed by some suffragists on their recent march from Edinburgh to London. Miss M. Oland was in charge of a literature stall and Miss Gwen Butler helped distribute books and pamphlets. Those present were drawn from across South Buckinghamshire, and included the first recorded appearance at a local suffrage event of Colonel and Mrs Angela James, who supported the NUWSS pilgrimage later that year.

A celebrated figure in both the women's trade union movement and the women's suffrage movement, Mrs Ruth Cavendish Bentinck, opened the exhibition at Wycombe's Town Hall.[2] She was a socialist who had joined the WSPU in 1909. Three years later, she left the WSPU and joined the NUWSS. By 1913 she was already amassing a significant library of feminist literature, which went on to form a significant part of the Women's Library. Mrs Cavendish-Bentinck observed that 'Chivalry allowed them 18 Factory Act Inspectors for women and 130 for men. Yet if they took away their railways, mining and shipping, there were far more women employers than men.'[3]

---

[1] *SBFP*, 7th February 1913, p. 1.
[2] Crawford - *WSM*, p. 51; Doughan, David - *DNB*, 2004-13.
[3] *SBFP*, 21st February 1913: this account mistakenly refers to 'Miss Susan Laurence'.

Mrs Susan Lawrence, Labour London County Council Candidate for Poplar, also spoke. Taking issue with those who argued that the answer for sweating was for women to organise themselves into unions, she commented that 'she could see hardly any ray of light upon organisation in respect to home workers'.[1] What was needed in her view was for the introduction of a minimum wage as well as extending and strengthening existing Trade Board legislation. She confessed to having very little sympathy for those who asked for the vote simply as a right. Instead, she argued that, 'what they were out for was to protect, uphold and strengthen the weaker woman.' Mrs Lawrence concluded with an appeal for all to work together not only for the vote itself, but, 'for the vote as a means to an end. (Applause)'. Mrs Scott, in the chair, then invited those present to tour the exhibits.

Following tea, there was a musical interlude before the evening meeting. Miss Doreen Pendlebury sang, Mr Arnold Pendlebury played two violin solos; then Fraulein Elfriede Birkenstock and Miss Mason entertained the visitors with solos, accompanied by Mr W.W. Weaver, Associate of Trinity College, London.

In the evening, Mrs Ada Nield Chew from Rochdale gave a 'forcible address'. Mrs Chew was a socialist from Staffordshire, who became a worker for the Women's Trade Union League in 1900, but later gave up her trade union work to concentrate of campaigning for votes for women.[2] She was a gifted writer and speaker for the women's movement. Between 1911 and 1914 she was a NUWSS organiser based in Rossendale.[3]

Mrs Chew observed that if sweating was defined by the recent suggestion of Mrs Constance Smith, of less than 15 shillings a week, then virtually all women workers, with the exception of those in the cotton industry, could be said to be 'shamefully sweated'. She could only see that women's wages would be raised by women themselves having 'power to bring pressure on the Government. (Applause)'.[4]

Mrs Berney drew the evening to a close by declaring the exhibition a success and appealed for more people to join the local suffrage socieities. The *Standard* also agreed that the event was a 'great success', given the 'good number' of visitors.[5]

---

[1] *SBFP*, 21st February 1913.
[2] Chew, Doris - *The Life and Writings of Ada Nield Chew*.
[3] Crawford - *WSM*, p. 107.
[4] *SBFP*, 21st February 1913.
[5] *SBS*, 20th February 1913.

On 26th February, the local NUWSS and NLOWS entered into a debate, held at the Guildhall. Miss Kate Raleigh spoke in favour of the specific resolution that, 'extending the Parliamentary franchise to women is just, expedient and necessary for representative government'.[1] She included the observation that, 'At present they had one slave for a parent, but they would rather that they would have two free parents'. Miss Frances Low, who had agreed to speak for the NLOWS against the resolution, failed to make an appearance, so Mrs Macdonald came forward. She said that Miss Raleigh's arguments that evening had failed to persuade her. She objected to the usual suffragist arguments that women gaining the vote would mean she would also gain equal pay, and pointed to the example of New Zealand, where even though women had been enfranchised for 20 years, they had seen little change in the wages paid to women, compared to men. At the conclusion of the evening, the resolution was passed by a significant majority. The *Free Press* counted 70 'for' to 27 'against', while the *Standard* had 70 to 24.

Some of the comments from the audience, reported more fully in the *Free Press*, highlight the variety of views represented. Mr Hallasey observed that, 'when women had got the vote they must remember they would not be in heaven. (Laughter)'.[2] Mr S. Brooks, a member of the Wycombe Liberal Club, said that 'the way certain women were acting at the present time was making some of them, who had always believed in votes for women, feel like re-considering...'. Councillor Archibald Jupe asserted that 'sweating' would not be prevented by women gaining the vote. He believed that, 'Politics would not elevate women, who possessed something better than the vote, and that was influence. (Hear, hear)'.[3] Mr A. Smith, probably a local Labour Party supporter, said he stood for adult suffrage. Mrs Scott made a point of expressing regret in relation to any actions of suffrage militancy. Mr W. Stedman voiced his support for women having the vote if they paid rates.

March 1913 saw a significant but apparently short-lived development, when Miss G. Coyle started a series of meetings, appealing directly to those working in the local chair factories. The meetings had to be abandoned, due to popular outrage at the recent suffragette arson attack on Saunderton Station.[4] It seems that the Coyle sisters were together responsible for running the White Hart Street office.[5]

---

[1] *SBS*, 27th February 1913 and *SBFP*, 28th February 1913.
[2] *SBFP*, 21st February 1913.
[3] *SBFP*, 28th February 1913.
[4] *SBFP*, 14th March 1913.
[5] Burgin, p. 50.

Following this attack on a local suffragist, Ronald Rice wrote a letter to the *Free Press*. In it, he praised the local newspaper for its previous impartiality and even favourable coverage on women's suffrage.[1] However, he took issue with a previous 'Gossip' column in the paper by stressing that the 'disorder' was mainly caused by 'children and lads'. He felt that it was 'ridiculous to associate this rowdyism with the state of the public mind on the question of women's suffrage'. The Editor of the *Free Press* briefly responded to this correspondence, arguing that it was, 'folly to shut one's eyes to the fact that the militant outrages are causing widespread hostility to the women's cause'.[2]

The next advertised meeting, organised for 8th April, was another free lecture, although the advert stated that tickets could be purchased from W. H. Smith, in order to reserve seats.[3] This was an illustrated talk on Town Planning, given by Mr Charles C. Reade, Acting Secretary of the Garden Cities and Town Planning Association. The chosen topic reflected that the issue of housing was another important concern for suffragists at this time, alongside prostitution and low wages. Also advertised was a talk at the White Hart Street office, due to be given by Miss K. Coyle on an unspecified topic.

Mr Reade was introduced by Miss Dove, whose experience of witnessing local people living in slum conditions as a result of her work with the Central Aid Society gave her a particular interest in the question of better housing for all. Mr Reade began by arguing somewhat tenuously, that town planning was relevant to women's suffrage, because 'garden cities had to do with... every individual member of the community'.[4] He described London as being 'in a mess', contrasting the housing there with places like Hampstead, Letchworth and Hitchin. Reade also observed that Wycombe had a housing problem and expressed the hope that a way might be found for building affordable homes for the working classes. After his talk, Councillor Archibald Jupe objected to something he thought Miss Dove had said and to Mr Reade's suggestion of workers having a bath in the scullery. Further observations were made about the feasibility and desirability of garden city developments locally.

While the suffragists were keen to appeal to a more varied audience by encouraging debate on wider issues, this meeting demonstrates how easy it

---

[1] *SBFP*, 4th April 1913.
[2] Ibid.
[3] *SBFP*, 28th March 1913, p. 1.
[4] *SBFP*, 1st April 1913.

was for the subject being considered to effectively obscure any consideration of the importance of giving women the vote.

The NUWSS national pilgrimage gave the Wycombe suffragists the unusual opportunity to continue campaigning during the summer. An open-air meeting at Frogmoor on 22nd July to welcome the pilgrims to Wycombe was advertised, as well as a previous Jumble at Godstowe School, to help raise funds and maximise publicity. The Mid-Bucks suffragists used a similar strategy.

An interesting personal story was reported in *Free Press* in September, which would have confirmed all the worst fears of many 'antis'.[1] Miss Florence Chapman of High Wycombe had just come before Birmingham Magistrates, charged with assault by her brother-in-law, Mr Nicholls. He had originally agreed for Florence, known to be a militant suffragette, to visit him in Harborne, in order to look after his consumptive wife. He commented ominously that 'From that moment his home had ceased to be a home'. In court, the defendant described how he had repeatedly asked Miss Chapman to leave, to no avail. He went on to accuse his sister-in-law of having first turned his wife and daughter against him, so they no longer prepared his meals, and then of having attacked him so violently with a walking stick that he had to lock himself in the bedroom. Miss Chapman said she 'had not touched the defendant' but refused to return home because of her duty of care to her sister. The Magistrate's Clerk advised the man that he could 'turn the key on her' if she had not left by the next week.

The regular autumn session for the campaign in Wycombe got underway on 8th October, with a meeting in the Red Room of the Town Hall, addressed by Mrs Helena Swanwick, on the subject of 'Politics and the Child'. Mrs Swanwick was a writer who had previously written for the Manchester Guardian. At the time, she was the editor of the NUWSS newspaper, *The Common Cause*, who went on to be a leading figure in the Women's International League for Peace, during and after the First World War.[2]

In her opening remarks, Mrs Helen Ensor said she felt she 'ought to emphasise that they were in no way connected with any society which advocated militant methods'.[3] Mrs Swanwick, in proposing a resolution which included women in the process of drawing up legislation, began by objecting to the current legal system which denied the mother any rights

---

[1] *SBFP*, 19th September 1913.
[2] Harris, Jose - *DNB*, 2004-10.
[3] *SBS*, 9th October 1913.

over her children. She also predicted that the elementary school system was likely to be overhauled shortly, and said that if it was, 'the thoughtful women of the country... wanted to be in at those changes'.[1] Suggesting that women should become Magistrates and be more involved in the legal system, Mrs Swanwick finished by praising the suffragists who took part in the recent NUWSS pilgrimage, saying that it reflected the positive spirit of the suffrage movement as a whole. The motion was carried unanimously, probably because the inclement weather that evening had dissuaded those not sympathetic to the cause from turning out. Mrs Swanwick may have stayed overnight in the town, as she then went on to take part in a debate in Beaconsfield the following day.

At the end of October, the newspapers carried Miss Dove's notice to electors of the East Central Ward, prior to the next Council elections. Her appeal included the observation that as 'more than two thirds of the population are women and children, I venture to think that the women's point of view is not unimportant on the Municipal Council.'[2] However, her appeal fell on deaf ears, and she came in at the bottom of the poll.

The next advert in the *Free Press* that same week, revealed the twin strategy of the suffrage campaign in Wycombe. Larger meetings addressed by high-profile speakers, were complemented by educational meetings with lesser-known, local speakers which anticipated a smaller audience.[3] On Monday 3rd, Mrs Smith-Masters gave an educational talk at Godstowe School on the subject of children. The next day, Mr Henry Harben and Mr J. Cameron Grant spoke at a meeting in the Guildhall on the subject of 'The Endowment of Motherhood' and 'Women in Industry'.

Mrs Smith-Masters addressed the causes of childhood delinquency and infant mortality. As well as poor diet and the change from a country to a town upbringing, the speaker identified 'picture houses' as being partly responsible for leading children into a life of crime. She finished by observing that, 'In America they maintained that women's work as probation officers was magnificent, and it was to be hoped that this country would soon realise that fact. However, women could not extract ideal results from an administration that was fundamentally wrong therefore they should have a voice in legislative matters as well'.[4]

---

[1] Ibid.
[2] *SBS* 31st October 1913.
[3] *SBFP*, 31st October 1913, p. 1.
[4] *SBS*, 6th November 1913.

Mr Harben introduced Mr Grant the following evening. Mr Grant started by noting his disappointment that the room was full of women rather than men. He described how he was the owner of an industrial works which produced complicated instruments, where the whole department was run by women because they were defter than the men with the machines. He asserted that his employees 'received some of the highest salaries in England for women's handicraft'.[1] But the most notable and amusing exchange of the evening came when a woman from the audience asked, 'Is it the apathy of the country or the inequity of the politicians which was keeping back the vote?' From the audience, Mr Matheson suggested that 'sheer stupidity' was to blame and Mr Grant quipped that the politicians' 'inequity passeth understanding'. Mr Harben then weighed in with the comment that, 'he felt certain that women would have got the vote if the Prime Minister had been anyone else but Mr. Asquith'. He concluded by asserting his belief that women would get the vote, 'in a very short time'.[2]

Harben's comments here about the Prime Minister highlight the fact that earlier that year he had resigned from the South Bucks Liberal Association, of which he was both a member and a Vice-President. In the letter, he protested at the Government's, 'policy of coercion and repression towards the women who are demanding a share in the responsibilities and privileges of citizenship.' He also went on to protest the Home Secretary's announcement that any subscribers to the WSPU could face prosecution. Stating that both he and his wife had supported the WSPU financially, he went on that he did not 'recognise the right of any power... to dictate to us what opinions we should hold, or in what way we should spend our money'.[3]

On 26th November, following a tea at Godstowe School, Mrs Neathes gave a talk on the subject of 'Votes for Mothers', which drew on her experience of living in Canada. The meeting was well supported. The speaker traced the history of 21 years of the women of Canada annually attempting to get legislation on 'feeble-minded' children changed. It had been eventually passed in a mutilated form, but she believed that if women had had the vote, the legislation would have been passed immediately. She also mentioned the much lower infant mortality rate in New Zealand, which she put down to women's enfranchisement there.

---

[1] *SBFP*, 7th November 1913.
[2] *SBS*, 6th November 1913.
[3] From a letter dated 5th May, written from Hotel Belle Rive, Thonon-les-Baines, Haute Savoie, *SBFP*, 16th May 1913.

That same week there were lengthy descriptions of the industrial unrest in the Wycombe furniture factories, with 2,000 union members holding a meeting in the Town Hall, with three firms from the local Employer's Federation themselves threatening some form of direct action if their employees did not return to work. Despite the suffragists' presentations and debates over women's employment, all the discussions revolved around the position of both union and non-union men, with little consideration given to the non-union women workers of the town.

The Wycombe suffragists finished the year with a Christmas Jumble Sale at Godstowe, again seeking to raise funds for further propaganda work.

A new development at the end of 1913 helped to give a fresh boost to the suffrage movement, which had appeared to lose some momentum after the pilgrimage debacle. South Bucks MP, Sir Alfred Cripps, was elevated to the peerage, so this precipitated a by-election in January 1914, which galvanised parties on both sides of the debate.

In the same newspaper issue describing the suffragists' renewed activities, came the news of the selection of the Conservative candidate for South Bucks, Mr W. Baring Du Pre.[1] He had been living at Taplow House, near Maidenhead, but due to his selection was planning to move back to the family seat at Wilton Park, Beaconsfield. Described as a keen sportsman and motorist, he promised to 'study the subject carefully before the General Election', when he was approached by Miss Helen Ward and other suffragists.[2]

The Wycombe NUWSS broke new ground by organising a meeting, chaired by Mr Berney, at the Schools in Hazlemere on 8th January. Miss Wright of St Mark's Home, St Dunstan's and Mrs Earp both spoke, followed by a discussion 'of a most instructive and interesting order'. It was also reported that many people signed 'Friends of Women's Suffrage' cards and bought NUWSS badges. Such new initiatives were actively encouraged by the NUWSS Federation, who provided funding for branches who broke new ground.[3]

The report contributed to both newspapers stated that the canvassers had 'met with much sympathy and encouragement'. A series of open-air meetings were being held at Frogmoor every day at midday and in the evening, which were being addressed by Miss Helen Ward, Mrs Whalley, Miss Ashton Jones, Miss Power and Miss Dora Mason (organiser-in-charge).

---

[1] *SBFP*, 16th January 1914.
[2] *BE*, 30th January 1914.
[3] *Third Annual Report*, NUWSS Oxon, Berks and Bucks Federation, p. 12.

And Mrs Earp and Miss Power spoke to the women workers at Ford's Blotting Paper Mill at Loudwater.

The Liberal candidate for the bye-election was Mr Tonman Mosley, Chair of Buckinghamshire County Council.[1] An Oxford graduate who had trained at the bar, Mosley had controversially left the Conservative Party in 1912 and joined the Liberals over the issue of Irish Home Rule.[2]

Mosley was entertained by the suffragists at the 'Witheridge' home of the prominent local Liberals, Mr and Mrs Davies, on Wednesday 21st January.[3] Several leading suffragists from both the local and national scene were present to add weight to their appeal. Following Mr Dixon Davies' mentioning the Labour Party's official support for women's suffrage, Miss Marshall from the NUWSS London Headquarters added her voice with specific challenges to the candidate. These included the question of whether he would pledge to personally support women's suffrage in his election address and if he would urge his party to make it part of their programme if they were in power. Mrs La Pla, a member with her Congregational Minister husband of the FCLWS, confessed to knowing that Mr Mosley was sympathetic, but urged him not to treat the issue lightly. Finally, Miss Corby Ashby of the Liberal Women's Suffrage Union, also pressed him to include the issue in his election address.

In response, having asserted his belief that the numerous suffrage societies were succeeding in destroying 'the popular cry that women did not want the vote', he went on to say that it was impossible to include votes for women in his electoral address. There were other important matters he also had no choice but to exclude, like temperance, in order to keep his speech, 'within reasonable bounds'.

Mosley had already mentioned his support for women's suffrage in his speech to the meeting of Liberal Party workers, when he was accepted as the Liberal candidate at Wycombe Guildhall on 16th January.[4] However, the suffragists refused to support either Mosley or Du Pre, the latter having turned equanimity into an art-form, with the following statement:

> 'Mr Du Pre expressed himself as feeling some sympathy with the movement, especially as regards the claims of women on the municipal

---

[1] *BE*, 13th March 1914: reporting Mosley's re-election as Chair of BCC.
[2] *BAAN*, 18th May 1912, p. 8 and 25th May 1912.
[3] *SBFP*, 23rd January 1914.
[4] *BE*, 23rd January 1914.

register, but was as yet unable to convince himself that women were not naturally disqualified, by reason of their sex, from the political sphere'.[1]

On behalf of the local suffragists, the overall organiser for the election campaign appointed by the NUWSS, issued an official statement of their position the same week:

'The National Union of Women's Suffrage Societies is supporting neither candidate in the present election. Mr Mosley, although a convinced suffragist, is not supported for two reasons: first, because he declined to put Women's Suffrage in his election address, and secondly, because the Union is precluded by its election policy as laid down in Council (February, 1913), from supporting at by-elections any government candidate, however favourable his personal views, so long as a government measure for women's suffrage is withheld. Mr Du Pre is not supported owing to his neutral attitude on the subject.
(sd.) DORA MASON
(Organiser-in-charge, S. Bucks Election Campaign.)'[2]

This announcement caused some controversy and would have been particularly questioned by some Liberal suffragists. It was indeed challenged publicly at the meeting in Wycombe Town Hall, when a written question for the speakers read: 'If you don't care a rap about either candidate, what shall you do? (Laughter)'.[3] But nothing would deflect the local campaigners from following the approach laid down by the NUWSS, especially as a number of figures from the NUWSS leadership were directly involved.

A front-page advert in the *Free Press* the same day, announced meetings at Wycombe Town Hall, as originally planned, along with other meetings in Slough, Amersham and Burnham. This programme was further extended, and the same advertising space in the next issue of the *Free Press* also trumpeted meetings in Wycombe Marsh, Gerrards Cross, Cores End, Lane End, Beaconsfield and Marlow.[4] The range of local speakers the suffragists could draw on was also notable, including Miss Muriel Matters and The Honourable Mrs Bernard (Angela) James.

The public meeting in the Wycombe Town Hall on 30th January was addressed by Miss Maude Royden and Miss K. D. Courtney who, according

---

[1] *BE*, 30th January 1914.
[2] *BE*, 30th January 1914.
[3] *SBFP*, 6th February 1914.
[4] *SBFP*, 6th February 1914, p. 1.

to a note scribbled on the *Free Press* advert, was a founding member of the NUWSS 'Election Fighting Fund'. In remarking on the position of both candidates, Miss Royden argued that those who claimed to be suffragists but did not see the need for a government measure on the issue, were not taking into account the experience of the women's suffrage movement. She finished by directly appealing to the men present to help the women in their struggle.

Miss Courtney then tackled the common view of the anti-suffragists by asserting that 'There was nothing in true womanliness that a woman would lose by having the vote'. Several questions were asked towards the end of the meeting, including the matter of female MPs. Mrs Courtney simply said that this would be a matter for the electorate in the future. Someone else asked if the NUWSS was proposing to give votes to the wives of working men, to which she replied that theirs was the most logical position, of asking for the same terms as the men.

The meeting was closed by Miss Dove, who was clearly pleased at such a large and attentive audience. She appeared in reflective mood, seemingly looking back on 16 years of persistent campaigning. She congratulated the present committee, Miss Mason and Mrs Berney.

Both suffragists and 'antis' later reflected on successful campaigns. For the suffragists, both indoor and outdoor meetings across the district were well-attended by both men and women, with audiences ranging from 40 people to 350. The sense of excitement felt by whoever contributed the article for the *Free Press* is palpable, in the reporting of 550 people having signed 'Friends of Women's Suffrage' cards in the constituency.[1] The following week, a similar report in the *Free Press* stated that the total had reached 800 signatures.

On the strength of the numbers attending and the sympathetic hearing given, a new branch was immediately launched in Slough. People there had to be turned away from a meeting at the overcrowded Town Hall. New ground was broken with a meeting at Burnham, where 79 people signed cards in support. And a meeting at Chalfont St Giles Schools on the 16th, announced the intention to form a branch there.[2] Mr Henry Harben and Mrs Ayrton Gould spoke. Mrs (Barbara) Gould had joined the WSPU in 1906 and became an organiser by 1909. She was imprisoned in Holloway in 1912 and later fled to France. By 1914, Barbara and her mother, Hertha Ayrton, an eminent physicist, had both left the WSPU to join the United Suffragists.

---

[1] *SBFP*, 13th February 1914.
[2] *BE*, 20th February 1914.

Barbara became the new society's first secretary. She may also have played a part in establishing another branch of the United Suffragists in Amersham, in early 1914.

At the Chalfont St Giles meeting, Miss Aldred, in the chair, read letters of sympathy from the local Rector and Mrs Whittingstall. She proposed a resolution which declared that 'this meeting protests against the treatment of the women in this movement, and demands a government measure for the immediate enfranchisement of women'.

The aims of the NUWSS campaign were summed up in the *Free Press* report: 'to convince many already aroused of the justice of the cause... and to awaken a wide-spread interest among those hitherto untouched by, or outside, this great movement'.[1] However, there was no Labour candidate to contest the seat, which left the suffragists fighting a negative campaign, with no prospect of being able to claim a victory. As it was, the election was won with a reduced majority by Du Pre, the Conservative candidate, who was the least sympathetic of the two men and went on to be included in the most belligerent group of MPs opposing votes for women.

Ultimately, the anti-suffragists won the war of numbers in South Buckinghamshire, initially claiming that over 1,000 people in the South Bucks constituency had signed a petition against women's suffrage.[2] The number was subsequently revised to nearly 1,200 in a later report in the Standard. Canvassing had been organised across the area, as well as open-air meetings held in High Wycombe, Slough, Marlow and elsewhere. The Anti-Suffrage Committee Rooms, in 7 Crendon Street, according to the *Standard*, were presumably hired just for the campaign, and were run by Mrs C. H. Bray, assisted by Miss Allison of Beaconsfield. The report in the *Free Press* made a point of saying that they had support from 'all classes of the community', going on to list married women, widows, spinsters, nurses, teachers, factory hands, domestic servants, ministers of religion, tradesmen, policemen and postmen.' It went on to mention 'One lady from Australia, who was a voter at the last election there, also signed the petition, in company with her husband, a Clerk in Holy Orders'.

The *Standard* reported on the launch of the new branch, at the home of Mrs Gregson Ellis, Claremont House on Amersham Hill. Chesham anti-suffragist, Lady Susan Trueman, introduced Mrs Gladstone Solomon of London who addressed the meeting. The local branch organiser, Mrs Bray,

---

[1] *SBFP*, 13th February 1914.
[2] Ibid.

announced that there were 326 subscribing members of the new society, 243 of those being Wycombe residents.[1]

Meanwhile, it was reported that 'many Wycombe people' took part in the great NUWSS demonstration in the Albert Hall on 14th February.[2] Over 300 trade unions and other men's organisations from across the country were also represented at a meeting addressed by Mrs Fawcett and by Miss Maude Royden. The local suffragists clearly wanted to encourage the growing public support from the trade unions. So, in the same article they announced that they had organised a meeting to address Wycombe workers at the Fountain in Frogmoor at the end of February. Miss Dora Mason, NUWSS organiser for the Oxon, Berks and Bucks Federation, was originally advertised as the speaker for this meeting. Whatever happened, this event does not appear to have been reported, but a later meeting in March, addressed by Mrs Cooper, did receive coverage. This was presumably Mrs Selina Cooper from Lancashire[3]. It was advertised in the *Free Press* two weeks consecutively.

Also advertised was an earlier meeting on 'The religious aspect of the Women's Movement'.[4] For the first time, buses were provided to transport people from the meeting, to three locations in High Wycombe, for a nominal fee.

The Rev. Canon J. Rushby Smith chaired this Town Hall meeting which, had a 'large and representative attendance'.[5] Rushby Smith spoke at length before introducing the two guest speakers, Rev. Claud Hinscliffe, founder of the CLWS and Rev. Robert Gillie, of the FCLWS. Rev. Gillie was eldest brother of Mrs Scott, Godstowe Headmistress. Living in Paddington, Mr Gillie wrote a number of religious books and went on to be appointed Moderator of the Presbyterian Church in England.

Rev. Rushby Smith told the meeting about two men he knew. One, from a church in London, had been 'converted' to the suffragist view after a long period of deliberation and therefore came to support the election of women onto a particular 'board' he belonged to. Another continued to be an 'anti', for the obtuse reason that he felt women would do a better job than men, and therefore the men on the board would be 'swamped' by capable women. Arguing from first principles and from the book of Genesis, that men and women were 'equal in the sight of God', Rushby Smith concluded by

---

[1] *SBS*, 26th February 1914.
[2] *SBFP*, 20th February 1914.
[3] Liddington, Jill - *DNB*, 2004-13.
[4] *SBFP*, 6th March 1914.
[5] *SBFP*, 13th March 1914.

asserting that 'They did not want to carry politics into their religion… but they wanted to carry religion very much into their politics'.[1]

Rev. Hinscliffe took issue with women who did not want the vote. He countered that, 'when a woman wanted the vote she realised the value of her own being'. Imagining that an 'enormous blow' would be struck against prostitution if women won the vote, he argued controversially, that, 'It was to a large extent, the great mass of middle-class women who were keeping back the clock in regard to the women's movement'.

Rev. Gillie began by denying the usual depiction of the women's movement as some kind of 'whirlwind or destructive storm'. Rather, he believed that there was a large number of women who had been 'quickened into vitality of conviction and devotion to service through this movement…'. Asserting the intimate connection between the women's movement and morality, he commented that 'Christianity would never be right until women were as brave as men and men were as pure as women'. Robert's closing observation was, in view of the 'simple, direct and human way' Jesus had treated women, he would work for the success of the women's movement.

Miss Dove and Mrs Scott responded to the speeches. Miss Dove commented that she had 'often felt that their leaders in the Church had been very much behind-hand in putting before them the truths about women'. The unspecified motion was then passed, 'with acclamation'. This event was part of a wider awareness across the county, that churches should respond positively to the women's political struggle. Both established and nonconformist churches were gradually waking up to the reality of the women's movement. At Chesham Bois in 1914, the Amersham Ruri-Deacanal Conference held discussions on the issue of women's enfranchisement, which caused some heated debate.[2] The motion expressing sympathy for the women's struggle was passed by 13 votes to 11. There was also agreement around this time about allowing women to be voted on to Church Councils, a development supported by the Rt. Rev. E. D. Shaw, the Bishop of Buckingham, previously vicar at All Saints, High Wycombe.

However, following this meeting in Wycombe, one anonymous 'Churchman' expressed his disapproval in a letter. He viewed the suffrage movement as 'the artificial product of an effete civilisation' and as, 'antagonistic to religion, contrary to nature, Holy Scriptures and social life'.[3]

---

[1] Ibid.
[2] *BH*, 13th June 1914, p 11.
[3] *SBFP*, 19th March 1914.

A more immediate and positive response was declared at the annual meeting of local rescue workers, which took place the very next day in the Church House, Crown Lane. The annual report announced that 51 local girls had been sent to homes and to service, in order to save them from prostitution. Responding to the report, the vicar of All Saints Parish Church, Rev. C.P.S. Clarke who chaired the meeting, commented: 'They all felt that there was at the bottom of the movement for giving women the vote a tremendous force, because they realised that if they had more power, they could do more towards dealing with the causes of the evil'.[1]

Just over a week later, Mrs Ethel Snowden came to speak to the young people of the Wycombe Free Churches at the Town Hall. President of the Young Helper's League and member of Union Baptist Church, Alderman Daniel Clarke welcomed Mrs Snowden, who spoke on the topic of 'Peeps at Parliament, through a woman's eyes'. Mr Clarke, who had supported women's suffrage meetings in the town in the 1870s, was possibly the longest standing most prominent male suffragist in the area.

---

[1] *SBFP*, 13th March 1914.

Foundation stone of High Wycombe Town Hall, featuring the name of Daniel Clarke, previously long-serving Town Clerk and later Mayor. Photo: Colin Cartwright

Bust of Daniel Clarke, on the Red Room staircase in Wycombe Town Hall. Courtesy of High Wycombe Town Council and the staff of the Swan Theatre

Mrs Snowden drew on her 'sometimes painful experience' of visiting the House since her husband's election as an MP in 1906.[1] Clearly disappointed with the House, that 'not enough attention was given to the more serious questions', she also observed that there were no 'giants' like Disraeli or Gladstone in Parliament. Going on to talk about some of the leading political figures, Mrs Snowden's repertoire extended to an imitation of Mr Austin Chamberlain. Talking of Prime Minister Asquith, she said that she did

---

[1] *SBS* and *SBFP*, 19th and 20th March 1914 respectively.

not view him as 'altogether hopeless', but derived some encouragement from his announcement that, once there was a majority of Liberal MPs in favour of women's suffrage, he would waive his own personal views.

Mrs Snowden concluded with a ringing challenge to her young audience:
'... she asked them not to regard politics as a matter of party, but as a matter of principle; not to look on Parliament as a game, a matter of pitch and toss, but as a great holy enterprise, a duty to their fellow men, and a high and holy expression of their Christian Faith. (Applause)'[1]

A motion of thanks to Mrs Snowden was moved by the Union Baptist Church Minister, Rev. George Rice, and seconded by the Rev. E. Marshall.

The last meeting which seems to have closed activities for the season, was the meeting for Trade Unionists at Frogmoor on 28th March.

Mrs Cooper said she had belonged to a trade union for cotton factory workers for 18 years, and remarked how this level of unionisation among men and women was unique in the country.[2] She said that 10 years previously, due to her background, she had felt that women did not need the vote, but just needed to belong to a union in order to ensure better wages.[3]

Predictably, Mrs Cooper praised the record of the Labour Party in the Commons for consistently supporting women's suffrage. She also praised some of the measures of the current government, including the Wage Board Bill and the National Insurance Act. Encouraging her audience to imagine what 1915 would bring, she said she was confident that next year Parliament would pass a measure introducing votes for women. Few people had foreseen what the summer of 1914 would bring.

One noteworthy achievement for the women at this time was their inclusion in the terms agreed to settle the furniture strike which had beset the local industry in 1913 and 1914. The women responded to the dispute by joining their male colleagues in the furniture workers' trade union, NAFTA. Female membership rose to nearly 200 in a few weeks; an unsurprising development given that the women earned more on strike pay than when they were working.[4] The women of Wycombe were also encouraged by the visits of a number of members of the Women's Trade Union League: Mary

---

[1] *SBS*, 19th March 1914, p. 5.
[2] *SBFP*, 3rd April 1914.
[3] *SBS*, 2nd April 1914.
[4] Burgin, p. 41.

Macarthur, Isabel Sloan and Miss Keen.[1] Miss Sloan in particular linked trade unionism and the women's struggle for the vote.

The dispute was settled in May 1914.[2] The pay settlement established between the workers and their bosses, published after the war, was mostly about safeguarding the men's jobs on a reasonable wage. However, the very inclusion of the women 'outworkers', who mostly worked from home rather than in the factories, was a significant development. Women were also, for the first time, allowed to work as French Polishers, on condition that there were no men available for the work.[3] Mentioned under 'The Women's Section', were the minimum prices given for each cane chair and for the work of 'Matters' and 'Upholstresses'.[4]

At the outbreak of the war in August 1914, the WSPU suspended its militant operations across the country, and threw all its energies instead into supporting the war effort, including campaigning against industrial action. Few of the women's suffrage organisations, including the NUWSS, were initially wholehearted in their support for the war as a significant proportion of their members were either socialists or pacifists. The beginning of hostilities produced a brief period of uncertainty and some soul-searching within suffragist ranks. Writing the annual treasurer's report for the NUWSS Federation shortly after the outbreak of the war, Mrs Berney, commented:

> 'Under the present circumstances, it is to be feared that it will be some time before we can do any direct propaganda work, but we shall, in any case, start our fourth year in a sound financial position'.[5]

However, all the NUWSS branches in the county, and probably the other suffragist societies too, were soon to be prominent in galvanising their members to show themselves to be useful citizens, either by rallying behind the war effort, or by engaging in charity and medical work. Miss Dove herself seems to have remained unconvinced of the wisdom and necessity of turning Wycombe Abbey School into a military hospital.[6] But she and her fellow suffragists were prominently involved in raising money to help

---

[1] *SBS*, 1st and 8th January 1914.
[2] *SBFP*, 8th May 1914.
[3] *SBFP*, 10th October 1919.
[4] Mayes, L.J., - *The History of Chair-making in High Wycombe.*
[5] *Third Annual Report, 1913-14*, p. 12.
[6] *SBFP*, 18th August 1914.

refugees and the unemployed in the town, for example.[1] But at the same time, the NUWSS and other suffrage societies, rather than completely abandoning their original aims, still harboured hopes of electoral reform, and continued in more subtle ways to add weight to the women's claim to full citizenship.

---

[1] *SBFP*, 9th October 1914.

Chapter 9: Burning in Buckinghamshire - Militant Attacks, 1913-14

'I think the only way to stop these outrages would be to have these fiends privately flogged in prison by the officials, before they have time to begin their "hunger strike".'
From a letter written by Mrs Frances Anne Collins, 18 Roberts Avenue, High Wycombe (*SBFP*, 23rd May 1913).

FIRE and destruction was first visited upon Buckinghamshire by the suffragettes in 1913. Ten years after the WSPU had been launched, the people of the county were sent a clear message about the extent of the women's frustration at the government's stalling and broken promises, as well as their anger at the treatment of fellow suffragette prisoners. These attacks on property were at once an expression of rage, a tactic aimed at bringing maximum pressure on the government, and finally a statement of intent. Ever since 1910, the Pankhursts and their followers had issued dire warnings about the consequences of their just demands not being met.

However, it was not until 1912, with the resumption of militant tactics by the WSPU at the end of 1911, that any impact of this was felt in places like Buckinghamshire. Following the window-smashing raids in London's West End in March 1912, the Chief Constable for Buckinghamshire sent a message from the Metropolitan Police to constables in all parts of the county. It alerted the local force to keep a watch out for Christabel Pankhurst.[1] The following month, the police raided the WSPU London headquarters and Christabel fled to Paris.

Also in April, Mrs Pankhurst was released on bail, pending her trial for conspiracy. According to Sylvia's account, she was 'recuperating with friends in the country'.[2] This may have been a rural bolt-hole she is alleged to have secretly secured in the village of Stewkley, north Buckinghamshire.[3]

Christabel's exile in Paris signalled the final escalation in the suffragette struggle. From the summer of 1912, Christabel first began orchestrating a

---

[1] Bucks Constabulary Memoranda Books, 1911-15, 13th March 1912.
[2] Pankhurst, E. Sylvia - *The Suffragette Movement*, p. 383.
[3] Mayne, Kate - *Stewkley, Bucks: A Brief History of the Church and the Village*, pp. 13-14. I am grateful to Stewkley Local History Society for outlining further evidence for this claim.

concerted arson campaign against a variety of targets, mostly empty buildings. But suffragette arson first visited Buckinghamshire the following year.

In March 1913, an arson attack gutted Saunderton Station, located between West Wycombe and Princes Risborough.[1]

As was the case with some of these attacks on properties, Saunderton Station fire could have been a reprisal attack. It may have been a calculated revenge for the nine months prison sentence received by another suffragette arsonist with links to Buckinghamshire: Hugh Franklin. Perhaps it is no coincidence that Franklin was sentenced on 8th March, just two days before the Saunderton Station fire.

The identity of those involved is still unknown, but it is possible that Hugh Franklin's girlfriend, Elsie Duval, was one of them. She was in between prison sentences in March 1913, but in April that year was arrested in Mitcham, Surrey, in possession of inflammable materials, and was implicated, with Phylis Brady, in several other arson attacks. After her arrest in 1913, charges were being prepared in relation to other arson attacks, one of which was supposedly at 'Saunderstead' Station. With the trial taking place in Surrey, this may have been a typing error, with Saunderton in Buckinghamshire being originally intended.

The various newspaper accounts of 10th March are only able to hint at what happened, because the suffragette raiding party left no clues, except the ones they intended to leave, as they ghosted in and out of the Saunderton area. The various newspaper articles are contradictory on several points, but are helpful in re-creating these dramatic events.

The *Free Press* described that Sunday night as 'dark and stormy', commenting that this was an ideal cover for anyone wanting to carry out such an attack secretly.[2] According to all the accounts, the fire was well under way when it was first spotted after one o'clock on the morning of Monday 10th March. Local reports credit Mrs Harman as the one who raised the alarm. Living in a cottage 50 yards from the railway bank, she was woken by what she thought was hail on her roof, but the sound was actually the debris from the fire being carried on the strong wind. Having looked out of her window and seen the blaze, she immediately called on the stationmaster, Mr Kitson, who lived nearby.

From the signal box, Mr Kitson first called the fire brigade in Princes Risborough, then the one in High Wycombe. Running to the scene of the

---

[1] Archer, Jean - *Buckinghamshire Headlines*, pp. 107-117.
[2] *SBFP*, 14th March 1913.

blaze, Mr Kitson was soon joined by Mr A.G. Smith, a railway packer from Bradenham, who had been alerted to the emergency by the barking of his dog. He had then called on the 'ganger', Mr A. Smith and they both rushed to the station. Mr Kitson then alerted the Saunderton Workhouse. The workhouse master, Mr C.D. Preston, and Mr Penner, the porter, attempted to extinguish the flames by means of chemical grenades, but this was unsuccessful. On arrival at the scene, the High Wycombe Volunteer Fire Brigade found the station was already a 'sheet of flame'.[1]

The fire gutted the stationmaster's office, the parcels office, the porters room and both the general and the ladies' waiting rooms. Only the lavatories were saved from more serious damage. The flames were so fierce that they melted the coins in the stationmaster's safe, and the estimated cost of the fire was between £500 and £600.

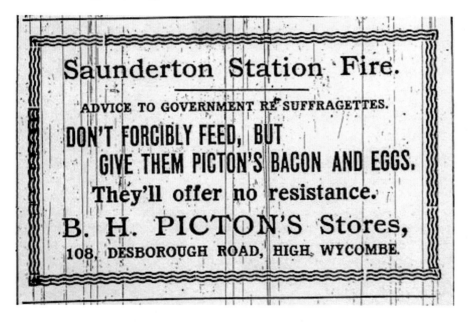

Saunderton Station Fire.

ADVICE TO GOVERNMENT RE' SUFFRAGETTES.

DON'T FORCIBLY FEED, BUT GIVE THEM PICTON'S BACON AND EGGS.

They'll offer no resistance.

B. H. PICTON'S Stores,

108, DESBOROUGH ROAD, HIGH, WYCOMBE.

One response to the Saunderton Station fire. *Free Press*, **March 1913**

It was only with the dawn that the cause of the fire came to light. Two placards were discovered one pinned on the railings of the station fence, and the other on the railway tracks. They read: 'Votes for Women' and 'Burning

---

[1] *SBS*, 13th March 1913.

to get the Vote'. Only the *Herald* questioned the authenticity of these notices.1 However, the same account saw fit to print a rumour that had been circulating about the sighting around midnight, near the station, of a 'large and fast looking car containing three ladies, heavily veiled, and a chauffeur in a dark livery...'.

The Chief Constable of Buckinghamshire, Major Otway Mayne, was soon on the scene with several other police officers, incluuding Superintendent Trevener from High Wycombe and two plain clothes detectives from the Great Central Railway. They failed to find any further clues. However, they concluded that the suffragette arsonists had used a car to arrive at the station and gained access to the station by squeezing through a gap between the railings and the adjoining hedge. There were reports of sightings of suspicious women in the area, both that night and also in the days prior to the outrage. The High Wycombe fire crew reported having seen a woman on her way to the fire, 'in the Bradenham Road'. The *Free Press* reporter also repeated a story that:

> '...two young women who were comparative strangers, had called on one or two occasions and partaken of tea at a house not far from the scene of the fire. They had paid for their meals and went away without giving their names or mentioning anything as to their mission in the district'.2

There was one immediate result of this particular incident, which according to the article in *The Times*, had caused 'much indignation' in the area.3 A planned series of open-air meetings organised by the local Wycombe NUWSS had to be abandoned. In the opinion of the local speaker, this was a direct result of the Saunderton fire.4 The meetings were being held during the afternoon tea break for the workers of two chair factories in Denmark Street: Birches and Howlands. They attracted between 300 and 400 people. The first meeting on 6th March passed off with only some good natured 'chaff'. This was, it seems, the first such meeting at which Miss G. Coyle spoke publicly about votes for women. The following day some orange peel and banana skins were thrown at the speaker. The meeting on Friday 14th however, ended in uproar, despite Miss Coyle being accompanied by other local suffragists.

---

1 *BH*, 15th March 1913.
2 *SBFP*, 14th March 1913.
3 *Times*, 11th March 1913, p. 8, online archive.
4 *SBFP*, 14th March 1913.

Having invited questions, Miss Coyle was assailed with comments about the Saunderton fire. One woman in the crowd shouted, 'Set 'em alight!'. Coyle's insistence that she was no suffragette was either lost on the crowd or simply not heard amidst the noise. The observation she made, perhaps subsequently, was that 'People were apt to confuse non-militants with militant Suffragettes'. This brave woman was twice knocked off her chair and had to seek sanctuary in Aldridge's shop on the corner of Temple Street. Chief Constable Sparling appeared just when the factory whistles sounded and the crowd quickly dispersed.

Not surprisingly, the Wycombe NUWSS branch had already felt it necessary to distance themselves from the militant actions of the WSPU and sent a letter reminding people that the NUWSS had issued public protests about self-defeating 'political violence' at its national annual general meetings in 1908, 1909, 1911 and 1912. This seems to have been the first letter specifically on this subject, written by a local Bucks branch, as opposed to the publication of previous letters about militancy, from NUWSS Head Office.[1]

Whoever was responsible for the Saunderton incident, perhaps also carried out a similar attack the same night, on Croxley Green Station, a few miles away in Hertfordshire. This was a similarly remote station, also recently erected. The fire here was reported to have been first sighted around 2am. A police officer apparently reported having seen two well-dressed women in the area, half an hour previously, who were walking rapidly towards Rickmansworth.[2] This shows that, as there had been no prior attacks in the area, the local police were not particularly alert to the possibility of such militant suffragette activity. Subsequent incidents demonstrate that they soon became much more vigilant. Indeed, the Chief Constable for the county sent a message from the Metropolitan Police to policemen in all the districts, asking them to keep a watch out for Christabel Pankhurst.[3]

The next arson attack in the county, which occurred only two months later, resulted in the wrongful arrest of two un-named local women thought to be 'dastardly suffragettes' by a Beaconsfield policeman. They were suspected of trying to burn down the village church of Penn, just outside High Wycombe. There is one clue as to why the church was perhaps chosen as a target. It contained family monuments of the Curzon family and Lord Curzon was one of the most prominent opponents of women's suffrage.

---

[1] *SBFP*, 14th March 1913. Letter from Mrs Berney dated 12th March.
[2] *BE*, March 14th 1913.
[3] Bucks Constabulary Memoranda Books, 1911-15, 13th March 1912.

And it is possible that Miss Mary Gawthorpe had initially scouted the area when she stayed in Penn in October 1912, from where she issued a national appeal for a Christmas hunger strike that year.[1] When she was interviewed by the *Daily Mail* on Penn Common, Miss Gawthorpe admitted that so far only one fellow suffragette, Mrs Florence Hodgson of Chelmsford, had offered to join her in the hunger strike. So that day she issued a wide appeal, mentioning 'well-known suffragist head mistresses', which was probably a challenged to Miss Dove, Mrs Scott and Miss Christie.

The following year, on the afternoon of Wednesday 14th May, two women came to Penn. One was a well-known and respectable woman from High Wycombe, wanting to view the historic church with a visiting friend. During their tour of the 13th Century church, the women were 'dismayed' to see flames coming from the organ. They immediately informed the vicar, Rev. Kirby, who telephoned the Wycombe Fire Brigade and frantically rang the church bell to call for help. The villagers managed to put out the fire with buckets of water before the fire brigade arrived, without the fire spreading to other parts of the church.

The vicar then discovered a newspaper cutting had been placed inside the lectern Bible, which showed a report of the recent catastrophic arson attack on Farringdon Hall, Dundee. The article was headed: 'Suffragette Incendiarism', and 'The Suffragette Cause: Incendiarism for Votes'.

Having left the scene, the two women then came across Constable Young at Tylers Green Common and told him to proceed to the church. They were in for another surprise. In the words of this Wycombe woman, the Constable 'coolly walked us back to the Church and detained us'. The women were not released for five hours, despite the remonstrations of several local people, including Dr Leslie Reynolds and Sir Philip Rose, of 'Rayners', Penn, who were both willing to stand bail for the accused. The reporter commented that 'The ladies were provided with tea in the church vestry, and were made as comfortable as possible.' Inspector Dibben of Beaconsfield and Superintendent Bunker of Chesham also attended the interviews being held about this crime. Eventually, at 10pm, these two women, along with another who was found to have had 'legitimate business in the village', were released without charge. [2]

Mrs Frances Anne Collins' letter in the newspapers the following week, demonstrates both the strength of local outrage at such an attack and also the extent to which public opinion was becoming extremely polarised. While

---

[1] *SBS*, 10th October 1912.
[2] *SBFP*, 16th May 1913.

she called for the suffragette prisoner 'fiends' to be flogged, others were writing letters of protest against the government 'policy of coercion and oppression'. Appearing on the same page which featured the news of the arson attempt at Penn Church was Henry Harben's letter of resignation from the South Bucks Liberal Association.[1]

The previous year Mr Harben had withdrawn as Liberal Party candidate for Devon, in protest at the Government's treatment of imprisoned suffragettes.[2] This time, Harben had been prompted to put pen to paper by the Liberal Government's decision, announced by Home Secretary McKenna to the Commons, that anyone contributing to WSPU funds could be liable for prosecution. The owner of Newland Park, near Chalfont St Giles since 1903, admitted in the letter that his wife was a member of the WSPU and that he too had contributed to WSPU funds. He wrote of the 'outrage of forcible feeding' and continued, '... that those who sympathise with (the suffragettes) should find elementary freedom of speech denied to them by a Government professing Liberal opinions is another question, as to which there should, in my view, be no room for argument at all'.[3]

Despite the more widespread alienation of people from the suffragette cause, nothing deflected the most dedicated from carrying out the orders of the WSPU leadership. These attacks continued, the battle of wills escalating in the next incidents. May 1913 seems to have been a particular hotspot for militant activity in Buckinghamshire. This may have been due to the imminent arrest of Mrs Pankhurst, whose licence had expired earlier that month. She was eventually re-arrested on 26th May, at a house near Woking.

Two incidents, surrounding both the church and the railway station, occurred in Aylesbury in mid-May. The police were at this stage on high alert. It seems that a suspected suffragette had been spotted by the police, since her arrival in Aylesbury, probably a few days before the Penn fire. It is difficult to reconstruct the exact sequence of events, but not hard, from the perspective of history, to see the comic aspect of the situation.

On Saturday 10th May, a 'young lady of good appearance and address', visited the church and asked to be shown round by the Verger, Mr J.J. Jenns. He let her ascend the bell tower alone, only to be told by the breathless Vicar that the woman was a suspected suffragette. The reaction of Mr Jenns can be imagined, partly from the *Advertiser* article which talked of a suffragette being

---

[1] *BE*, 16th May 1913.

[2] *Times*, 6th July 1912, p. 8, online archive.

[3] *BE*, 16th May 1913.

reported to be, 'in possession of St Mary's Church tower'.[1] The Verger politely asked the lady to leave, who went on her way in a leisurely fashion, apparently unaware of the suspicions of the church staff. This was all just moments before the arrival of Chief Inspector Pitson, who was prevented from making a significant arrest. As a dedicated policeman, who had been awarded the King's Police Medal in February that year, missing out on arresting a possible suffragette arsonist must have been particularly galling.[2]

St Mary's Aylesbury may have been targeted because the vicar was a known anti-suffragist. Also a fire at this church would have been visible for many miles across the Vale of Aylesbury.

While the *Herald* omitted to cover this incident, it reported on the intended closure of St Mary's Church and tower outside of service times. However, this article went on to report a bomb scare at Aylesbury Station that week. Someone had left a suspicious package under a waiting room seat on the morning of Thursday 15th. A porter had discovered the device, which was making an ominous ticking sound. Placing it in a bucket of water, he delivered the package to the police, who discovered to their relief, that it was only a dummy. It was described as 'a weight and a clockwork apparatus'.[3]

Both local newspapers seem to have put this down to 'the work of a practical joker'. However, it is quite possible that it may have been planted by the suspected suffragette, given that she had left the town that morning. Significantly, the *Herald* commented that several mansions in Buckinghamshire were now being guarded day and night as a result of this hoax. Furthermore, the Aylesbury Station bomb hoax was included in a review of suffragette outrages which the Home Secretary, Reginald McKenna, later listed in a report to the House of Commons.[4]

Church authorities across the county were obviously concerned about these latest developments, in view of the vulnerability of many rural churches. In May 1913, Mrs Humphry Ward was alarmed by the rumour of a sighting of 'two mysterious women... prowling the churchyard' one night. This gave her the idea for her novel featuring a suffragette protagonist, *Delia Blanchflower*.[5] But, the following year, when the Chief Constable heard of a

[1] *BAAN*, 17th May 1913.

[2] From the service records of the Buckinghamshire Constabulary, compiled by Michael Shaw.

[3] *BH*, 17th May 1913, p. 10.

[4] *The Morning Post*, 13th July 1914, online archive - June 2012

[5] Sutherland, John - *Mrs Humphry Ward: Eminent Victorian, Pre-eminent Edwardian*, p. 330.

constable regularly patrolling Wotton Church in response to the sighting of a suspected suffragette, his memo stated bluntly that he could not 'spare constables', and called the church wardens of Buckinghamshire to, 'make their own arrangements'.[1]

A less sensational attack occurred soon after the Aylesbury bomb scare, on Sunday 18th May 1913, near High Wycombe. A maple tree was set alight in Sand Pits and a notice was left on the tree which read 'Votes for Women'. The reporter of this incident, under the pen name of 'Casual', was unable to take the incident seriously. Having questioned the punctuation and called the issue a complex and massive problem, the writer concludes his piece with this tongue-in-cheek reflection:

> 'There is, of course, the imputed suggestion that the tree was fired by suffragettes, and that idea carries us back ages and ages to the early morning of the world when another tree figured in a certain important episode. Every atom... of chivalry that remains in these degenerate days stands up and demands the rejection of the idea! Could it be possible that for the undoing of man-kind this work was done by the modern daughters of Eve? The mere thought makes one tr-remble.'[2]

Despite this example of poking fun, suffragettes were now not so much seen as simply the objects of ridicule they had once been. In the eyes of many, they were now figures deserving of hatred and also represented a genuine threat to property, which inspired fear and disgust. It seemed a short step from being ridiculed, to being loathed. It is equally true that these women were also viewed by others, as an example of courage and self-sacrifice. A Birmingham suffragette, Maud Kate Smith, who travelled alone to London in order to carry out her militant action, later described her feelings that day: 'It was very frightening because you had to do all these strange things alone, and there was always the awful dread that you'd mess it up, you see, suppose it wasn't a really good protest when you'd done it, and you were always alone'.[3]

The example of Miss Emily Wilding Davison, who died at the 1913 Derby trying to stop the King's horse, was held up by some as 'heroic' in the pages of local newspapers. Someone who signed themselves T. Roscoe,

---

[1] Bucks Constabulary Memoranda Books, 1910-15, 20th June, 1914.

[2] *SBS*, 22nd May 1913.

[3] Harrison, Brian - *The Act of Militancy: Violence and the Suffragettes, 1904-1914*, from, *The Peaceable Kingdom*, pp. 80-122, p. 80-122.

wrote a letter in which he commented: 'I know there are many who can only see madness in her action... But if she has made people think about the cause which she felt was worthy of her death, then perhaps she has not died in vain'.[1]

Another suffragette assault in Buckinghamshire came later that summer. This may have been a response to the violence the non-militant pilgrims received at the hands of the mob in High Wycombe at the end of July. On Wednesday 13th August, an empty house in Sands, just outside Wycombe, came close to being consumed by flames. This incident was near to the home of Mrs Ensor, who welcomed the pilgrims to West Wycombe, but it seems unlikely that Mrs Ensor herself was involved.

The property had been visited by a number of people in the weeks prior to the plot being uncovered. Early that morning, the neighbour's gardener, Mr Bishop, was prompted to investigate the scene when a strong smell of burning paraffin reached him. In the cupboard under the stairs he was confronted with an arsenal of equipment used by the suffragette arsonist. These included four hot water bottles, some full, and some recently emptied of paraffin. There was white surgical wadding, pieces of woodcut and some green satin lining, all of which had been soaked in paraffin, as well as some resin and some rush handbags.

A candle had been used to start the fire, but the fire had failed to take hold. This was perhaps due to lack of oxygen in the cupboard, or it may be possible that Mr Bishop had disturbed the arsonist. Care had been taken to try to hide the fire from the neighbours in its early stages, by the arsonist placing a pitch plaster over the scullery window. An issue of the *Suffragette* newspaper bearing the date of 1st August had been left in the grounds of the house.

Investigations by the police concluded that whoever had tried to set the property alight had gained entrance through the scullery window, previously left open for a workman at the property. They also deduced that, given the quantity of equipment used, there must have been more than one person involved. There were no sightings of anyone in the area that night or early morning and the investigation once again failed to provide any leads for the police.

It was nearly a year before there was another case of suffragettes 'burning to get the vote', early in June 1914. This apparent decrease in the rate of attacks may have been due to fewer women being available and

---

[1] *SBFP*, 13th June 1913.

willing to use such extreme tactics. There was also a heightened public vigilance. The county police Superintendents had been warned by memo, dated 2nd June, to encourage those on the beat to be particularly vigilant on night patrol, around 'unprotected places like churches, railway stations, pavilions and boathouses'.[1] This did not prevent the next outrage, which caused damage estimated at £1,500 to both the house and numerous items of antique furniture.

A large house called, 'Park View', near to the school and overlooking the Common at Tylers Green, outside High Wycombe was set ablaze on Saturday 6th June.[2] The property was owned by Mrs Brooks, widow of a 'well-known agriculturalist' from Knotty Green, and she was seeking to sell or let the premises. Two women, between 30 and 40 years of age, had called to view the property on 4th June. They left without leaving any personal details, but not before one of them had asked, 'Does no-one at all sleep here?'[3] Suffragettes always tried to ensure there was no risk to life from their actions.

The fire was first spotted shortly after 2.30am, by the schoolmaster, Mr Long and a neighbour, Mr Pratt. By then the fire was already 'assuming alarming proportions', so the High Wycombe Fire Brigade was called almost immediately. Their manual engine, drawn by four horses, was soon on its way and they began trying to control the fire with water from the nearby pond. Captain Miles, who arrived on his bicycle, observed that the floorboards of the house seemed to be 'saturated by some substance which fed the flames'.

Afterwards, a milk bottle full of petrol was found in the grounds. It was wrapped in black cotton wool and the June issue of the CLWS newspaper. It may be possible to conclude from this that the arsonist was a churchwoman belonging to this League. But it is equally possible that by June 1914 it was difficult to obtain issues of the WSPU's *Suffragette* newspaper, due to repeated police raids on the WSPU offices where the paper had been produced.

This last arson attack may well have been the final suffragette outrage in the county, before the war brought an end to such raids. Very soon after the outbreak of the war, Mrs Pankhurst declared an end to hostilities as she felt a greater enemy needed to be defeated.

There may well have been other cases of arson or other forms of militant attacks in the county. Rumours certainly did circulate around some

---

[1] Bucks Constabulary Memoranda Books, 1910-1915.

[2] *SBFP*, 12th June 1914.

[3] *BH*, 13th June 1914, p. 3.

unexplained fires, like the one at 'The Copners' in Holmer Green, which occurred early in January 1914.[1] However, there seems to be little evidence that this particular fire was suffragette arson. Such events certainly made for some exciting gossip in the quiet villages of Buckinghamshire. It is also true that it sometimes served the interests of the anti-suffragists to exaggerate the reach of the suffragettes. There were cases of suffragettes being accused of incidents not caused by them.

One unusual example of militant activity in the county, which has yet to be corroborated, was a raid on a Beaconsfield golf course. Two ladies were apparently discovered digging up the greens there. Ted Rolph alleged that they were both subjected to being tarred and feathered as a result.[2]

Mapping the attacks which occurred in Buckinghamshire would seem to point towards two particular hot-spots, either side of High Wycombe. One in the vicinity of West Wycombe, the other centred around Penn. This might suggest the local involvement of either two suffragette activists or perhaps just the one group centred in High Wycombe itself. This might implicate a previous suffragette prisoner like Muriel Matters, living as she did near Penn. However, as someone who had already been imprisoned, it is likely she would have been high on the list of police suspects. Any further conviction would have meant a lengthy prison sentence for Muriel. And there is no evidence she was ever involved in serious law-breaking like arson.

Taking an overview of all these militant actions, coupled with an awareness of the WSPU approach, it is possible to conclude that most of them were carried out by small teams of women from outside the county. The opportunities of good railway connections between London and Buckinghamshire, coupled with the growth of motor car use, were maximised by the suffragette teams, who were willing to travel widely to carry out such attacks, partly to throw the police off the scent.

One key suffragette arsonist, Lillian Lenton, commented that, when she wasn't in prison, she managed to burn down two buildings every week. Travelling round the country in small secretive groups like this, meant these suffragettes could create the greatest impact. There may have been a limited amount of help from local sympathisers. Certainly, some of those who took part in the Aylesbury prison protest in April 1912, were reported to have stayed overnight in the town, which might indicate the presence of active, local suffragette supporters.[3]

---

[1] *SBFP*, 14th January 1914.
[2] Pearce, Olive - *Wycombe Rebel*, p. 62.
[3] *BH*, 20th April 1912.

Someone who may have played a minor role is Mrs Emily Ada Ingrams. Mrs Ingrams was born in the district of Penshurst, North-east Kent, in 1886. She became a member of the ILP. This is probably how she came to know the Pankhursts, through Emmeline Pankhurst's late husband, Richard, who was also a native of that area of Kent and a passionate socialist. Mrs Ingrams' obituary in the *Herald* certainly mentions that she was, 'an active member of the suffragette movement and a close friend of the Pankhurst family'.[1] Having married at Sevenoaks in 1912, Emily Ingrams and her husband moved to Buckinghamshire, and in 1913 were running 'The Vine' public house in West End, Weston Turville, just outside Aylesbury. Her personal links to the Pankhursts, coupled with her radical politics and relative obscurity, possibly made her a good local contact at this stage of the suffragette campaign.[2]

A more prominent member of the WSPU who had lived previously at Weston Turville was Evelyn Sharp. Her knowledge of the county, combined with her close involvement in the operations of the WSPU, potentially make Evelyn a likely figure for some kind of role in either surveying possible targets or being involved in the arson attacks themselves. However, without further firm evidence this remains only conjecture.

As the WSPU leadership viewed their campaign as a clandestine military operation, they tended not to share information with anyone outside their immediate circles. It is unlikely that there were many people in Buckinghamshire the WSPU leadership felt sure they could trust. The most militant suffragettes certainly succeeded in keeping both the local and the Metropolitan police in the dark. Very few cases were solved nationally, except for those where the attackers were caught in the act, like Hugh Franklin and Elsie Duval, for example. And no-one was convicted for any of the militant actions in Buckinghamshire, except for the case of the more blatant action of window-smashing in Aylesbury in 1912.

Suffragette arsonists, both women and men, were fiercely devoted to the Pankhursts, and were not about to betray close circles of friends who had sacrificed much for the sake of their sacred cause. However, the suffragettes ultimately found themselves chained, not just to railings, but also to a politics of despair and impotent fury. All that their extreme actions achieved was effectively a more hostile public, a more defiant House of Commons, and a political deadlock, which was only relieved by the greater national emergency of the war.

---

[1] *BH*, 7th March 1985, p. 26, obit.
[2] I am indebted to Wendy Greenway for this information.

Chapter 10: The 1913 NUWSS National Pilgrimage

'For all of us, pilgrims of yesterday, today and tomorrow, there is only one enemy - the spirit of cruelty and injustice; only one aim - the renewal of justice and peace... We claim kinship with Wilberforce, with Lord Shaftesbury, with Mrs Butler and Elizabeth Fry'.
- *Common Cause*, 18th July 1913, p. 247.

THE year 1913 presented a significant crisis for the whole votes for women campaign. With the unexpected ruling against the female suffrage amendment by the Commons Speaker in January 1913, there seemed little realistic prospect of further immediate legislation to re-introduce the issue. The militants in the WSPU seemed increasingly likely to abandon any attempt to work within the parliamentary process, which had failed to deliver much progress. Divisions had already been exposed within the WSPU, between those who supported extending militant campaigns of window-smashing, bombings and arson, and those who did not want to further alienate public opinion. Those in the wider movement who continued to favour constitutional means, increasingly felt both that further legitimate political pressure should be brought upon the government, and that they should distance themselves from the more extreme methods of the militants.

Open-air processions, along the lines of the public displays held in London from 1907, had been largely abandoned by the NUWSS, due to the popular animosity which suffragette demonstrations had more commonly come to provoke. However, the particular idea for a national Pilgrimage to support women's suffrage was first suggested by Mrs Katherine Harley on 18th April 1913, at a NUWSS sub-committee meeting. It appears, however, that others may have made a similar suggestion around this time. Mrs Harley, sister of Charlotte Despard and General Sir John French, and a member of the Windsor and Eton CLWS, probably derived the idea from a much smaller pilgrimage, from Edinburgh to London the previous year.[1] Despite its small numbers, the event managed to gain publicity and to capture the imagination of the public. Thousands of signatures were collected en route.

Enthusiasm for a new, similar venture was high. Plans were very quickly agreed for what was intended to be a grand public spectacle encompassing

---

[1] Crawford - *WSM*, p. 549ff.

the whole country. Organising such an event in so short a time would suggest the wide extent and depth of the NUWSS movement throughout the country, and also how well-drilled most of its various Federations and branches had become in furthering the cause of 'votes for women'. Afterwards, some estimates put the total number of the pilgrims who walked all or most of the route at around 10,000, although it is difficult to see how this could have been calculated accurately.[1] A Spanish newspaper subsequently reported that a total of 50,000 pilgrims had converged on the capital, adding that as well as travelling on foot or by the usual transport, 'some came... in boats... others by swimming, some in a balloon and two in an aeroplane!'[2]

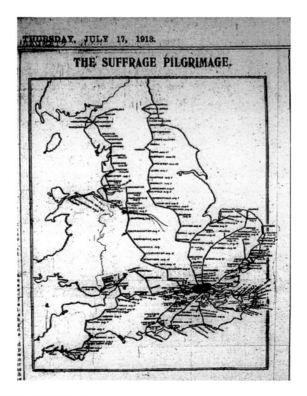

Map of the 1913 NUWSS Pilgrimage, *Standard*, 17th July, 1913

[1] *BE*, 15th August 1913.
[2] *BE*, 22nd August 1913.

Participants were encouraged to wear the traditional garb of pilgrims, with cockle shells on their hats, coupled with sashes in the colours of the NUWSS: red, green and white. Banners made by the branches from different towns and regions were proudly held high. Many of the banners made especially for the occasion bore the phrase 'non-militant'. This phrase was prominently included on the banner which headed the 'Watling Street' pilgrims', as they marched through Buckinghamshire.

Starting on 18th June from the furthest-flung places like Carlisle, Newcastle and Lands End, the marchers began to converge on London from all over England and Wales. Pilgrims travelled to London, mostly on foot, in some cases on bicycles or horses, while some had the luxury of travelling by caravan. They converged on the capital along six main routes.

From Carlisle, along the Watling Street route, participants were joined further south by parties from Manchester and Criccieth. From Lands End, groups from south Wales met them in Bristol, who then later combined with a group from Gloucester, Cheltenham, Cirencester and Swindon at Marlborough. The southern marchers, starting at Bournemouth, Salisbury and Southampton met up at Guildford and were joined by a group from Brighton and other coastal resorts. The Kentish pilgrims, from northern and southern coasts there, converged on Tonbridge. East Anglian pilgrims, who began their march at Yarmouth and Cromer only combined within London itself. The northern band traced a line from Newcastle-upon-Tyne through centres in Yorkshire, Derbyshire, Nottinghamshire and Lincolnshire, before combining with a group from Hunstanton and Kings Lynn.

It is interesting to speculate why this exact route through Buckinghamshire was chosen and why they were called 'the Watling Street pilgrims'. The reference to Watling Street was to the established walkway dating back to ancient Britain, subsequently used by Christian pilgrims from the north who wanted to visit Canterbury. The route largely follows the arterial roads of the A5 to London, passing through the pilgrimage centre of St Albans. So from the Midlands the suffragist pilgrims took a route west of the real Watling Street. This was to enable them to include Oxford.

The route from there to London had to take in Buckinghamshire and Wycombe was an obvious centre to include. Aylesbury was not visited. This may have been because of the disturbances in the market square the previous year, or perhaps because the town council there continued to maintain its ban on public suffragist meetings. The NUWSS organisers themselves may have felt there was not a strong enough local suffragist campaign there, and that visiting Aylesbury would associate them too closely with the militant demonstration the previous year.

How important it was to differentiate themselves from the extreme actions of the WSPU militants is demonstrated by Mrs Berney's letter reproduced in the *Standard*, the week before the women arrived in the county. She wrote, 'I so often hear it implied and asserted that our local Women's Suffrage Society is connected with the Militant Societies... I can only advise those who may still hold to this view to come to the meeting at the Fountain at 8pm on Tuesday, 22nd to hear what our speakers have to say.'[1]

At the same time, the NUWSS wanted to demonstrate that there was widespread public support for women's suffrage. So visiting centres where there was well-established core support and public sympathy was vital. They were hoping to decisively contradict the view of some politicians that a referendum on the issue would demonstrate that only a relatively small minority of wealthy women supported the principle of female enfranchisement. The NUWSS wanted to re-create a sense of a spiritual crusade, in keeping with campaigns led by prominent Christian figures during the Victorian era. Mrs Fawcett and her fellow leaders wanted to reclaim the moral high ground in the debate which had become bogged down by party political differences.

The pilgrimage took advantage of the recently renewed swell of public outrage against women being forced into prostitution. Parliament had passed legislation in 1912 which failed to satisfy most campaigners. Both constitutional and militant suffrage campaigns took advantage of the moral outcry and many meetings across the country were arranged by suffrage societies, like the ones in Chesham in June 1912 and High Wycombe in February 1913.

Combining with local suffragists and sympathisers along the route, the Watling Street pilgrims approached Buckinghamshire from the direction of Oxford and Thame. On Tuesday 22nd July, covering as they planned an average of between 10 and 16 miles each day, they travelled to Princes Risborough and on to West Wycombe. Stopping overnight in High Wycombe, the pilgrims then included a visit to the historic village of Penn, before going on to Beaconsfield, where they stayed the night. Marching then through Gerrards Cross and Denham, the travelling suffragists left Buckinghamshire en route to Uxbridge, on Thursday 24th July. In most

---

[1] *SBS*, 17th July 1913.

places, the majority of the pilgrims were accommodated by local suffragists. However, sometimes this proved impossible and they had to pay for lodgings, with one lady recording having to spend as much as £6 before she reached Buckinghamshire.[1]

Among the initially small party of pilgrims from the early days was Mrs Katherine Harley, the overall organiser of the pilgrimage. Lady Rochdale from Carlisle joined the marchers for much of the route. Both Miss Deakin and Mrs Duffield apparently walked all the way from Keswick. Twenty seven representatives from the Manchester Federation joined further south, along with Miss Margaret Ashton, the first woman councillor on Manchester City Council, who came in her car.[2] From Miss Margory Lees' diary of the pilgrimage, it is clear that eight came from Oldham, including herself: Mrs Fletcher, who was an Oldham Poor Law Guardian, Mrs Bridge, who was Secretary of the NUWSS Oldham branch, along with Mrs Tuke, Mrs Siddall, Miss Annie Dixon, Miss Milly Field and Miss Eda Sharples.[3] Those from Oldham employed two caravans, pulled by horses named Noah and Ham.

Others who joined included: Miss E. Murgatroyd, a weaver from Nelson in Lancashire and Miss Langton who was also from Lancashire. These two may have been part of a group which the *Standard* referred to: 'There were also present a number of factory girls from the North, who were taking their annual holiday spending it on the road in this way'.[4] There was also Miss Mason, Miss Penton, Mrs and Miss Tees, Mrs Tiffin and Margaret Greg, some of whom may have come from Liverpool and Warrington. Miss Watson, Chief Organiser of the NUWSS Midlands Federation, joined the march in the Potteries. There was even international representation, in the form of Miss Scatter from Winsconsin and Miss Slater from California. Margory Lees also mentions another Californian, Miss Park, who joined the marchers later. Previously that same month Miss Park had spoken at The International Womens' Suffrage Congress in Budapest, where 3,000 delegates attended from 26 countries. Finally, there was the American reporter from *The Daily News*, Miss Vera Chute Collum, who accompanied the pilgrims on her horse from Banbury.

One of those who started in the north-west and marched through Buckinghamshire was Mrs Jane Mason from Bolton. Mrs Mason joined the

---

[1] Crawford - *WSM*, p. 551.

[2] Mohr, Peter D. - *DNB*, 2004-11.

[3] Lees, Margory - *Adventures of the Ark and the Sandwich*: Transcript of Margory's account of the Pilgrimage.

[4] *SBS*, 24th July 1913.

pilgrim band in Stockport on Saturday 5th July. Then in her 50s, she was given pride of place at the head of a party belonging to the Bolton Women's Suffrage Society. Mrs Mason was a Poor Law Guardian, mother of 10 children and keen canvasser on behalf of the Women's Liberal Association.[1] Travelling some of the way by bicycle, she was accompanied part of the way by Miss Bridson (Secretary of the Branch) and Miss Winstanley (Treasurer) and all of the way by Miss Pemberton. Mrs Mason, interviewed by the *Bolton Evening News* before she set out, was reported to have said that 'she was confident that the journey would be both healthful and interesting'.[2] The paper described the first stage of this part of the journey:

> 'The Bolton Society sent about thirty of these (in spite of its being the last day of the holidays), most of whom, headed by their banners, walked the seven miles to Stockport. The road, for the most part, runs through a densely populated district, and it was lined nearly everywhere with spectators. Most of these were sympathetic...'.[3]

Sympathy and curiosity were the most common reactions the pilgrims seemed to have received. Several of those who recorded their experiences, including Miss Margory Lees from Oldham, remarked on the level of support from the churches. Church of England vicars and Free Church ministers up and down the land preached sermons on the cause of women's emancipation, provided hospitality and held special church services for the pilgrims. A local newspaper similarly commented: 'The clergy throughout have shown sympathy through their sermons and addresses'.[4]

However, from the experiences of the Watling Street pilgrims, they encountered some form of disruption to the majority of their meetings from Macclesfield onwards. In particular centres there were groups of people who were determined to voice their opposition, to cause discomfort for the suffragists and to prevent them receiving a hearing in one way or another. Just before entering Buckinghamshire on 21st July, the Watling Street pilgrims encountered a significant level of hostility in Thame. In one incident a shopkeeper refused to sell some potatoes to Mrs Fletcher, saying that he

---

[1] I am indebted to Mrs Mason's great grand-daughter, Linda Price-Cousins, for much of this information.

[2] *BEN*, 5th July 1913.

[3] *BEN*, 7th July 1913.

[4] *MBA*, 26th July 1913.

would, 'prefer to see her starve first'.[1] A report in the *Herald* stated that an attempt to hold an evening meeting in the market square here was broken up in confusion. Lady Rochdale and Mrs Harley were drowned out by the crowd. The reporter concluded that it was 'only after an hour's pandemonium that the town assumed its normal quietude'.[2]

Miss Lees also reported that when the caravans stopped for the night at the recreation ground in Thame, a group of 150 people came along in the dark, making 'a fine old row with horns, hooting and booing'. A few policemen were present to restrain their spoiling tactics, beyond cutting some tent ropes and scattering some of the food for the horses. They left after about 20 minutes, crying out, 'Good night, you Suffragettes!' This indicates that here, as elsewhere, those bent on disrupting the pilgrimage refused to distinguish between militant and constitutional campaigners for votes for women. Alternatively, they may have simply been unaware of the distinction.

On the next morning of 22nd July, after another 'rowdy' public meeting in Thame market place, addressed by Mrs Fletcher, the party moved off towards Princes Risborough. Here they received a more friendly reception. One eye-witness described their arrival amidst a curious crowd:

> 'The pilgrims arrived in various ways, some on foot, some in motor cars, others on bicycles. A halt was made in the Market Square, where a short meeting was held, addressed by three ladies, whose speeches certainly left some impression on their hearers. After the meeting a number of the pilgrims commenced distributing literature amongst the audience, while others solicited signatures upon cards, showing who were their friends...'[3]

The *Herald* account describes the procession being quite 'imposing', including three 'well-appointed caravans', as well as 'motor cars, bicycles and other conveyances'.[4] The reporter mentions long bannerettes being distributed which bore the names: Aylesbury, Chesham, Chesham Bois, Stoke Mandeville, Wendover, Kingshill, Ballinger and Hampden.

---

[1] Lees, Margory - *Adventures of the Ark and the Sandwich*: under 'Remarks')

[2] *BH*, 26th July 1913.

[3] *SBFP*, 25th July 1913.

[4] *BH*, 26th July 1913.

Pilgrims and local supporters gathered outside West Wycombe School. From High Wycombe Library

Members of the NUWSS affiliated Mid-Bucks Suffrage Society met the procession at Princes Risborough.[1] The party lunched at the George and Dragon Hotel and were photographed before marching off in the direction of West Wycombe. In a retrospective report, the *Examiner* stated that 18 representatives of the Mid-Bucks Society had joined the march for some of the route.[2] Mrs Pilley, who lived at a large house called 'Sonamarg' in Little Kingshill, which featured a 'commodious motor house' used for a suffragist meeting earlier in the month, put her motor at the disposal of the pilgrims.[3] Her car was adorned with the Aylesbury and Chesham banners. The *Herald*

---

[1] *BH* and *SBFP* accounts. A combined list mentions, along with the Courtauld sisters and Mrs Pilley, Miss Wright from Ballinger, Miss Hawkins from Little Hampden, Miss Lyon from Prestwood and Miss P Leach, with Mr J. and Mrs F. Briars from Aylesbury.
[2] BE, 15th August 1913.
[3] *BH*, 19th July 1913.

suggested that Catherine and Sydney Courtauld were planning to complete the pilgrimage together, and it is quite likely that they accompanied Mrs Pilley in her car. As the 1913-14 Mid-Bucks annual report suggests that three local suffragists walked to the rally in Hyde Park, it may be that Mrs Pilley left her automobile garaged in Wycombe.[1]

The Courtaulds' local celebrity status was certainly enhanced by the fact that the two sisters were among the biggest benefactors of the pilgrimage, each of them apparently donating £300 to the fund, which made up nearly 20% of the initial contributions. These figures were revealed in the *Anti-Suffrage Review* in an attempt to ridicule the suffragists' claim that the pilgrimage demonstrated widespread support within the general population.[2]

According to the *Herald*, an estimated 70 pilgrims were in the party at this stage. Surprisingly, no mention is made in any of the accounts of the fact that the route took the pilgrims past the scene of the first and arguably most notorious case of suffragette arson in the county. Just a few months previously, on March 10th, suffragettes firebombed the deserted station at Saunderton during the early hours. The outrage sparked by this unprecedented act may have had something to do with the hostility the marchers were to encounter further along their route.

From Princes Risborough, Miss Margory Lees and Mrs Fletcher had been sent on in a motor to address a meeting in West Wycombe at 4pm that Tuesday. There they were met by Helen Ensor and her husband and other Wycombe suffragists.[3]

Mrs Ensor (nee Fisher) was brought up in the Manchester area. Here she married the socialist writer, Robert Ensor, before moving to London. In 1910, with a growing family, they moved to 'The Beacon', in Sands, between High Wycombe and West Wycombe. The Ensors' location, coupled with the fact that they probably knew some of the marchers from Manchester, made them an ideal choice to welcome the pilgrims. It is likely the Ensors had got to know some of the local suffragists through her oldest daughter Diana, who had probably started attending Godstowe School the previous year.[4]

Colonel Bernard James and his wife, the Honourable Angela James, were also reported to have joined the women pilgrims at West Wycombe. Mrs James (nee Kay-Shuttleworth) was an early member of the Women's Co-

---

[1] *SBFP*, 12th June 1914.
[2] *ASR*, August 1913, pp. 171-2.
[3] *SBFP*, 25th July 1913.
[4] 1881, 1901 and 1911 England and Wales Census; Brock, Michael - *DNB*, 2004-12: Sir Robert Ensor. I am indebted to Richard Ensor for much of this information.

operative Guild and joined the NUWSS soon after its launch in 1897.[1] Grand-daughter of an MP, who was a pioneer of elementary education in Gladstone's government, Angela became a school governor of three East End schools at the age of 18 and joined the Labour Party.[2] Her husband, Bernard, who went on to be promoted to a Colonel, shared her progressive views. He resigned from the army in 1910, after being ordered to suppress rioting dock workers in Liverpool. They moved to Fingest Grove in Lane End, not far from West Wycombe in 1912. Just the previous year, Angela had tried to convince her sisters and her governess to support votes for women, by inviting them to a women's suffrage meeting in Folkestone. So Mr and Mrs James would have felt at home amongst the Wycombe suffragists and the NUWSS marchers.

Also there to greet the pilgrims at West Wycombe were: Mrs Edith Berney and Miss Eliza Parker from Godstowe School, Mrs Ethel Fleck (Dr William Fleck's young wife), Dr Eva Meredith, Mrs Constance Davies and Mrs Matheson from Beaconsfield, and Miss Scott (presumably Miss Anna Maria Scott of Wycombe Abbey School), along with Miss North and Miss M. Oland. The *Standard* adds Miss Reeve and Miss Plumridge to this list.

Mrs Ensor addressed those who had gathered about the justice of their cause, after which Miss Lees described the last two weeks on the road. Mrs Fletcher then spoke about how the Good Book talks of Adam having a 'help-meet', which she took to mean 'to walk side by side'. She denied the often mentioned argument that giving women the vote would mean that they would neglect their 'household duties'. She finished her speech by pointing out that 'they were law-abiding, and had nothing whatever to do with the militant suffragettes. They demanded the vote for women on the same terms as it was granted to men.[3]

Miss Lees said that it was because the local schoolmaster, Mr George Holland, was sympathetic to the cause, that Mrs Fletcher was able to address a crowd, including the schoolchildren, on the green outside the West Wycombe Elementary School. A photograph was taken there before the whole party moved off to enjoy tea in West Wycombe itself. The banners identified from the photo read: 'Justice is ever the best policy', 'In Freedom's Name' and 'Be just and fear not'. A fourth banner is unclear, but this may have been the banner of the High Wycombe branch, which bore the Godstowe School motto, *Finem Respice* (Look to the goal).

---

[1] Denton, Penny - *A Remarkable Woman*, p. 8.

[2] *SBFP*, 29th December 1967, obit.

[3] *SBFP*, 25th July 1913.

The day's recruits were then marched off to the Black Boy, where a tea was laid on by Mr and Mrs Probets, assisted by the Misses Green from London. The original marchers were entertained by Mr E. Harman at the British School, near the West Wycombe Caves.

Later at 6.30pm, gathered under the village clock, a 'forcible address' was given by Miss Watson, who was listened to attentively by the crowd. They were joined by other local suffragists.[1] Mustering for the march in the George and Dragon yard, with a roll call at 6.50 pm, the pilgrims fell in behind the Wycombe Town Band, led by Mr Harris in the absence of Mr Sears. There was a minor controversy over the matter of why the Sons of Temperance Band had not been employed in this fashion, as had been previously agreed.[2] Apparently this was simply due to the Temperance band being more expensive.

To the tune of the pilgrim's marching song, the suffrage campaigners left West Wycombe in the direction of High Wycombe. Immediately after the band the Watling Street banner was proudly displayed and behind this walked Lady Rochdale, in her pilgrim cockade hat and NUWSS sash in red, white and green. Other locally-produced banners appeared at this point. They read: 'Law Abiding', 'We have nothing to fear from Freedom', 'Without representation there is no freedom to progress', 'No taxation without representation'.

At this point, news reached the ears of the suffragists from a 'trustworthy source' that there had been an exceptional demand in High Wycombe for tomatoes and stale eggs that day. The report was to prove accurate.

The previous evening an anti-suffrage meeting had been held at Frogmoor. It was clear that some of the locals were in no mood to welcome the pilgrims, whether they were law-abiding or not. One account of the meeting describes how Mr Lofting, a speaker from NLOWS, repeated the common argument that women were 'not capable of full citizenship for the simple reason that they were not available for purposes of national and imperial defence'.[3] The reporter referred to their being a 'fair attendance' which later assumed, 'large dimensions'. Echoing the anxieties of many people at the time, Mr Lofting finished his address by stating that anything

---

[1] *SBFP*, 25th July 1913. Those listed here include Mrs May Scott of Godstowe, Miss S. Steevens who was a local temperance campaigner, Councillor T. Sutton and Mr Chipps, the carpenter.

[2] *SBFP*, 25th July 1913: 'The Suffrage Pilgrims' March'.

[3] *SBS*, 24th July 1913.

diverting the attention of women from home and care of children would 'inflict the worst possible injury on the highest welfare of the nation'. The closing resolution against votes for women, proposed by the second speaker, Mrs Stocks of Reading, was passed with 16 votes against.

The pilgrims had clearly been warned about the likelihood of disturbances. So, as the caravans were drawn by horses, these were sent on ahead to the planned overnight pitch, in the grounds of Godstowe School. With the crowds growing more numerous and the way ahead narrowing, Mrs Harley and Miss Lees, alongside a dozen other pilgrims, set the pace ahead of the band. Miss Lees remarked pointedly that 'the policemen did not go in front to keep the way clear as they had done in other places'.[1] This description differs from the account in the *Standard*, which praised the 'herculean' efforts of the police in clearing the way for the pilgrims. Along the straight road between West Wycombe and High Wycombe the atmosphere changed. Miss Lees commented, 'I never saw so many evil faces gathered together'.[2]

The procession was met by Miss Dove, Miss Harley, Mr Crawford and Mr Berney, at the end of Westbourne Street. There had been a platform erected at the fountain in Oxford Street from which to address the expected crowds. However, the crowd was estimated at 10,000 strong and was packed in, 'almost to suffocation point'. According to the *Standard* reporter, the pilgrims were 'hailed as house and property burners... the rough element of the crowd assuming that if the women were in favour of their enfranchisement, they must be disciples of Mrs Pankhurst and her host'.[3] In the same article, Miss Collum reported that various male members of the local ILP took a stand against the rush on both sides of the pilgrim procession. She herself was able briefly to drive her horse between the crowd and the pilgrims, until the mare became frightened by someone blowing a trumpet.

Miss Dove and the other speakers succeeded in reaching and ascending the platform (a lorry provided by Messrs' Baines), but were drowned out by the jeering crowd. Councillor Turnbull tried to appeal to the crowd for a fair hearing. But none of the speakers could be heard, including Miss Mason, NUWSS Chief Organiser for the Oxfordshire, Berkshire and Buckinghamshire Federation. The crowd let fly with rotten eggs and tomatoes, as well as bags of flour and sawdust saturated in oil. There was a

---

[1] Lees, Margory - *Adventures of the Ark and the Sandwich.*
[2] Ibid.
[3] *SBS*, 24th July 1913.

concerted surge forward, as those intent on mischief tried to surround the lorry and overturn it.

The police, under the command of Chief Constable Sparling, immediately sent for their nearby reinforcements. Sparling, who was due to retire from the police in three week's time after 39 years service, may have been taken by surprise at ·the size of the crowds and the violence of the protests. He had 21 officers under his command, in a town with a reputation for disturbances surrounding elections times. The most recent elections in 1910 witnessed mobs rampaging through the streets of the town and the police had then responded by having the Riot Act read.

The banner of Godstowe School. The Wycombe suffragists adopted this motto and carried a banner bearing 'Finem Respice' into High Wycombe, as part of the women's suffrage pilgrimage. Courtesy of Godstowe School. Photo: Colin Cartwright

In common with these previous disturbances, despite the displays of animosity towards the suffragists, none of the pilgrims seem to have been seriously hurt. The police themselves received minor injuries. P.C. Smith was tripped and injured his leg in the crush. He was conveyed to Mr Pearson's restaurant, but was shortly able to return to helping his colleagues. P.C. King was also 'considerably bruised'.[1] Mr Berney and Mr Chipps, in front of the lorry, trying to defend it from the onslaught of the crowd had a particularly rough time, but emerged unscathed. Banners were seized and torn to shreds. It is doubtful whether many, if any, of the banners escaped the hands of those desperate to deny the suffragists any publicity.

The attempt to hold a meeting was abandoned and the pilgrims left the square as best they could by various routes, many of them pursued by angry mobs. Some managed to get away in taxi-cabs. Miss Dove escaped via Temple End, having to seek refuge at Mr Nash's house. Miss Lees managed to slip away with Miss Collum, who, following the lead of a friendly man in the crowd, stabled her horse and escaped up the hill to Godstowe School. Other women were not so fortunate and were pursued along Priory Road, Hughenden Road and Priory Avenue. Along Castle Street, the pilgrims found it difficult to shake off their pursuers. Headmistress of Godstowe, Mrs Scott, who had one arm in a sling from a cycling accident, was 'subjected to rough treatment' at the hands of the mob.[2] The Misses Highfield of Easton Street came to her assistance and prevented a more serious assault.

One small party of pilgrims fared better. Dr Fleck escorted Mrs Harley and Mr Crawford to his house in the High Street (number 39, Tudor House). From the steps of his front door the Doctor reminded the pursuing crowd that these were law-abiding citizens, as he hoped were the residents of Wycombe. His words seemed to calm those present and Mrs Harley and Mr Crawford took the opportunity of addressing the crowd. Mrs Harley spoke, she estimated later, for around 15 minutes. She was reported, by the *Free Press*, to re-iterate that they were absolutely opposed to violent methods. She went on to say that, 'the pilgrimage had been organised throughout the country in order that they might tell the people why women wanted the vote, and what kind of work they were prepared to do when they obtained the franchise.' With pointed irony which won some applause, Mrs Harley finished by asserting that '... in this campaign (the women were) simply

---

[1] *SBS*, 24th July 1913.
[2] *SBFP*, 25th July 1913.

appealing to the men's sense of justice and they felt certain of success, they hoped in the near future.'[1]

Some of the rioters attempted to rush the offices of Messrs Baines for having provided a lorry for the marcher's platform, but they were prevented by the police. The next target chosen was the premises of Davenport-Vernon's shop and garage, where the pilgrims' motor had been parked. Some of the pilgrims had been forced to take refuge here. Windows were broken by stones hurled by the mob. The police caught up with the rioters and mounted a charge which succeeded in clearing Corporation Street. After an estimated two hours of disturbances, the town was reported to have returned to a normal Tuesday night scene by 11 o'clock that night.

Some of the pilgrims were outspoken in response to these events. Speaking to a reporter from the *Standard*, one Lancashire woman commented 'In Lancashire they had respect for women, but in Wycombe that quality seemed to be entirely absent'. Other women apparently, 'looked at the matter with the delightful philosophy of youth, and saw nothing to grumble at'.[2] In an undated letter, sent from 'Kelsale' in Wycombe's Priory Road, the Lancashire weaver, Miss Murgatroyd, made no mention of the trouble there, preferring instead to tell Mrs Cooper about their time in Oxford.[3] However, a number of the pilgrims sent a letter to the *Free Press*, which expressed their thanks, first to 'those brave, kindly and fair-minded men for so nobly - and at personal risk of injuries - for preventing the unruly element from rushing our platform...'. The letter finishes by also thanking the police for, 'their efforts to control the crowd.'[4]

In his memoirs of this period in Wycombe's history, Ted Rolph makes the claim that those who caused trouble for the suffragists had been paid to disrupt these events.[5] It is impossible to know whether this was in fact true. What is obvious is that in various places, Wycombe included, the anti-suffrage movement mobilised to organise prior counter-demonstrations. Some people clearly felt that the suffragette attacks on property justified, even demanded, a violent response. And flooding the streets for organised 'rushes' and breaking windows, for example, both seem to be clear cases of

---

[1] Ibid.

[2] *SBS*, 24th July 1913.

[3] Letter of Miss Murgatroyd to Mrs Selina Cooper, sent from High Wycombe, July 1913.

[4] *SBFP*, 25th July 1913. The letter was signed by J.F. Dove, Katherine M. Harley, Violet O. Slater, Beatrice Rochdale, M.C. Scott, Edith Berney and Dora Mason.

[5] Pearce, Olive - *Wycombe Rebel*, p. 43.

aping WSPU tactics. Perhaps such actions were a sign of a deeper, more primitive hostility to women and the women's movement within the general population, which had little to do with the often tortuous rationalisation of the 'gentlemanly' anti-suffragists.

Some of the pilgrims clearly felt that the violence against them had been orchestrated. One eyewitness commented that, in Thame for example, 'a signal was seen to be passed round the crowd for the rowdyism to begin'.[1] Although they stopped short of accusing the NLOWS itself, there was a strong sense among marchers and supporters that the hooliganism was worst in places where there had been anti-suffrage meetings before the arrival of the pilgrims. In response, the September *Anti-Suffrage Review* stated that, 'this League... has no intention of playing into the Suffragists' hands by helping them to obtain spurious sympathy as the victims of unseemly behaviour'.[2]

The morning after the Wycombe disturbances, the pilgrims and their supporters filled the Parish Church for morning worship at 10 o'clock, led by the Vicar, Rev. C.P.S. Clarke and the Rev. G. Hyde Gosselin. The hymn, 'O God our help in ages past' was sung; an appropriate choice for the 'stormy blast' the pilgrims had just weathered, as well as the hopes they held for the outcome of their pilgrimage. Meetings were held near Dr L.W. Reynolds house, 'The Priory'. Miss Helen Ward, Chief Organiser of the NUWSS London Federation, who lived in Beaconsfield at Bull Farm Cottage, Park Lane, spoke to a 200 strong crowd there, while Miss Watson addressed another audience in Corporation Street.

It seems the pilgrims resumed their travels in good spirits. Viewed with friendly interest by a large crowd, the marchers lined up in the High Street and made their way along Crendon Street. They were accompanied to the Borough Boundary via Amersham hill, by Miss Dove, Mrs Fleck, Mrs Scott, Mrs Berney and Miss Gillie (one of Mrs Scott's sisters). Lady Rochdale was prominent in the procession. Leaving Wycombe, the pilgrims again encountered a mixed response. One elderly gentleman loudly told the women in the procession to 'go home and wash their dirty clothes'. Some women watching made other uncomplimentary remarks. Having passed Terriers, where Dr Priestley made a financial contribution to the NUWSS, Commander and Mrs Gubbins then invited the pilgrims for refreshments at Carlton Lodge. Those also offering support included Mrs Burnett Brown, Miss Reynolds of Totteridge House and Mrs Priestley.

---

[1] *Common Cause*, 15th August 1913, p. 328.
[2] *ASR*, September 1913, p. 8.

The three policemen accompanying the march, Sergeant Haynes and Constables Gutteridge and Chambers handed the party over to Sergeant West and Constables Young and Hill on reaching Penn Road, Hazelmere. Their services were soon called upon again, when the pilgrims reached Penn itself at 1 o'clock. A meeting was held at the Common, Tylers Green, where several women addressed an attentive crowd.[1] A few rotten eggs were thrown from an adjoining yard, but they flew wide of the mark.

Introduced by Mrs Constance Davies, Miss Helen Ward gave another 'forcible address', in which she mentioned the contribution which women were already making to society through Education Committees and Boards of Guardians. Miss Watson also spoke. There being no questions from the audience, Mrs Davies put a resolution to the meeting in favour of giving women the vote. This was carried overwhelmingly, with only three and a half (including a child) opposed to the resolution.

Lunch was enjoyed by the pilgrims 'al fresco'. Then the party moved off to Mr and Mrs Davies' home, Witheridge, where they were entertained to tea. They did not set off for Beaconsfield until 6.50pm, when names were called. On the two mile march to the next town, the pilgrim's spirits were raised by marching songs, including one set to the tune of 'John Brown's body', a clear echo of the historic anti-slavery campaign. The words of this song were written by Theodora Mills, entitled, 'Rise up Women!' The first line of this song must have seemed very appropriate to the marchers: 'Rise up women, for the fight is hard and long.' The overall theme song chosen by the Watling Street Committee was the 'Song of the Suffrage Pilgrims', set to the tune of the 'Song of the Western Men', which Henry Daw Ellis had been inspired to write for the pilgrims.[2]

Before the pilgrims arrived, a crowd had already gathered in Beaconsfield Broadway for an anti-suffrage meeting. They passed their own resolution amidst cheers and greeted the pilgrims' arrival in Beaconsfield with loud booing. At least one rotten egg was thrown in the direction of the pilgrims and Miss Collum received a direct hit. Undeterred, the marchers continued to their agreed halt, the Old Rectory. From there they returned to the village green for their meeting, which was estimated to involve an overall audience of 6-700.[3]

---

[1] *SBFP*, 25th July 1913. Local people who were mentioned included: Mrs E.E.N. Bartlett, Dr Wynne, Mr R.F. Hayman and Mr Stanley M.A. Galpin.

[2] Crawford - *WSM*, pp. 644-5.

[3] *SBFP*, 25th July 1913. Those present included, Mr and Mrs Dixon Davies, Mrs A.S. Commeline, Mrs J. Bailey Gibson, Mr J. Hatch and Mr J. Russell-Seller.

A railway lorry, provided by the Wycombe branch of the National Union of Railwaymen, served as a platform. Miss Ward addressed the crowd. The novelist, G.K. Chesterton, was present with an anti-suffrage friend to try to ensure the women received a fair hearing. The *Middlesex and Bucks Advertiser* reported an amusing exchange between this local celebrity and a member of the pilgrims, described as 'police woman' on the march, who somehow mistook him for a foreigner. In response, Mr Chesterton, 'assured her that the ballot was all a silly tradition, and gave her to understand that he considered women ruled the roost already'. [1] The writer of the *Common Cause* article claimed she heard him say, 'Their cause is just'.[2]

During her often interrupted address, Miss Ward sought to challenge the contention of the anti-suffrage speaker, Mrs Stocks from Reading, who at a meeting in Beaconsfield the previous day had apparently raised the spectre of women in Parliament. Miss Ward asserted that this would not automatically follow from women being given the vote. This provoked some uproar. Eventually, a resolution was proposed in favour of women getting the vote, which was carried by a considerable majority. Then, continuing to be hounded by a section of the crowd, some of the suffragists headed for the station, being occasionally pelted with sods of grass and rotten eggs.

The pilgrims spent the night either in Beaconsfield, or those in caravans at their pitch at Witheridge. During the night the *Common Cause* correspondent had her windows smashed by 'the milk boy and another', and some eggs and 'something that smoked' were thrown indoors.

Thursday 24th, according to Margory Lees, was a 'lovely day'. Most of the pilgrims headed for Gerrards Cross, although some, including Miss Lees, did a detour to visit Jordans Meeting House. The reporter from the *Middlesex and Bucks Advertiser*, describing the pilgrims' arrival at Gerrards Cross Common, captures the scene and the organisation vividly:

'The contingent was timed at Gerrards Cross at midday on Thursday and when the "Advertiser" man arrived at 11.45, he found an advance guard already on the green in front of the Bull Hotel. There was somewhat of a military air about the scene. A large motor lorry stood by packed with luggage like a baggage wagon, and under the trees sat a circle of women holding a Council of War, but really as we were informed, having a committee meeting. Private moter cars and pony traps had brought in numbers of sympathisers from the surrounding countryside and numerous

---

[1] *MBA*, 26th July 1913.
[2] *Common Cause*, 1st August 1913, p. 291.

bicycles were temporarily riderless, while their owners - the scouts, collectors and literature distributors, rested in the shade, partook of light refreshments, or indited local picture postcard to distant friends. Quite punctual to time, the pilgrims came slowly up the hill, dusty of foot and bronzed of complexion with the warmth of the day. They were led by two large holiday caravans, and a prominent figure was the young lady on horseback, the "Daily News" correspondent. In the meantime, the Gerrards Cross and district members of the National Union had assembled at the railway bridge in Station Road, and a very good muster made as, headed by their banner, they proceeded slowly across the Common, and met the pilgrims on the way. After uniting they wended their way back to the football pitch, in front of The Packhorse for a meeting, still headed by the banner. This was a beautiful bit of work, carried out by the Artist's Suffrage League, from a design by Miss Ramsden. With the words, "'Gerrards Cross" along the top, and representations of three typical red-tiled Gerrards Cross houses underneath, the design and colouring both typified both the cause and the place. After Miss Eskrigge had announced the local arrangements, Lady Rochdale made a short speech, urging that the vote would enable women to take a deeper interest in the country, a stronger patriotism would be felt, and their minds enlarged by the exercise of political privileges. She said that those who knew the streets and alleys of the great cities, realized the need for stronger protection of women and children, and that something more should be done to perfect present day conditions. Miss Helen Deakin, who has come with the pilgrimage from Carlisle, also spoke very ably. She urged that politics concerned the whole human family, not men only, but women and children as well.'[1]

The *Common Cause* records, 'many "Friends" were enrolled at Gerrards Cross, as they had been at Tylers Green previously. Following the meeting, the pilgrims were entertained in the Assembly Rooms to refreshments by the local members.'[2]

In the early afternoon the procession moved off towards Denham, where a smaller meeting was held, followed by tea at The Plough. Here they were met by Councillor Hutchings, Chairman of Uxbridge Urban District Council, who marched into town at the head of the procession alongside Lady Rochdale. Two meetings were held at opposite ends of George Street square. Lady Rochdale, Miss Watson, Councillor Hutchings and Miss Gladys

---

[1] *MBA*, 26th July 1913.
[2] Ibid. Amongst others present were Miss Ethel Stevenson and Miss Ramsden, President and Vice-President of the Gerrards Cross NUWSS branch respectively, and Miss Dowson and Miss Roscoe.

Rinder spoke from one platform, while Mrs Katherine Harley, Mr J.G. Kennedy and Miss Dora Mason from the other.

Finally leaving Buckinghamshire, on the first sunny day since Banbury, the pilgrims continued to create quite an impression on those who turned out to see them. Miss Collum herself described the scene: 'With banners flying and pennants streaming and the whole long line gay with the red, white and green, marched gaily into the town. The smart cyclist corps brought up the rear, and all the pilgrims kept their line with military precision and marched in step to the sound of their own pilgrim songs.'[1]

This was the impression they wanted to create in every town. The warm welcome in Gerrards Cross and Uxbridge must have helped to make up for the reception they had received in Wycombe and Beaconsfield. The Watling Street pilgrims were certainly deserving of the judgement of one reporter, who according to Margory Lees pronounced, 'You are a plucky lot'.[2]

The marchers own reflections on reactions of the people along the way are briefly recorded by the reporter for the *Free Press*:

'(the marchers)... tell us that through the whole north of England they met with practically universal sympathy; and only after they reached the Potteries did they get meetings occasionally disturbed by bands of hooligans. The interest roused in country places was very great, and the understanding and sympathy of the London people most marked'.[3]

Uxbridge provided the penultimate overnight stop for the pilgrimage. The following morning, Friday 25th July, proved to be another sunny day, perfect for the culmination of the pilgrimage. The route across the outskirts of London took the swelling ranks of the suffragists through Ealing Common to Acton, through Shepherds Bush, past Notting Hill Gate and into Bayswater. Various meetings were held along the way which met with largely sympathetic hearings. That evening the pilgrims were welcomed to a service at the Ethical Church on Queens Road. Following a celebratory dinner, the Oldham pilgrims then rewarded themselves with the comforts of the Waverley Hotel in Bloomsbury, next door to the church where Emily Wilding Davison's funeral had taken place several weeks earlier.

On Saturday 26th July each part of the pilgrimage had been assigned various assembly points from which to converge on Hyde Park. The Watling Street pilgrims, whose numbers had swelled to around 400 at this point,

---

[1] *MBA*, 2nd August 1913.
[2] Lees, Margory - *Adventures of the Ark and the Sandwich*: 'Remarks'.
[3] *SBFP*, 15th August 1913.

gathered at Elgin Avenue, Maida Vale. Miss Lees comments that, 'It was a fine sight to see the processions coming in from different sides.' This was a well-worn route, previously taken by many of the earlier suffrage marches of 1907-1910. The correspondent of the *Middlesex and Bucks Advertiser*, reporting on these dramatic scenes, wrote this:

> 'The four processions entered the Park practically simultaneously, the Watling Street contingent entering via Victoria Gate, and headed by several suffragists on horseback. One banner was very prophetic in its phrase, "The old order changeth". Inside the Park the nineteen platforms, from which about eighty spoke to the immense crowd, were ranged in a huge circle round the site of the Reformers' Tree.'[1]

The Watling Street pilgrims were to gather around platform number five. They were addressed by Miss Maude Royden (Chair) and by Miss Mason, NUWSS Organiser. Mr F.J.K. Cross, Mrs Haverfield and Mrs Robert Uniacke also spoke. The *Advertiser* reporter concludes: 'The demonstrations commenced at five o'clock, and lasted one hour only, at the close of which, to the sound of a bugle, the resolution was put... and carried with few dissentients amid tremendous cheering'.[2] Miss Lees records that afterwards, she and her party repaired to Alan's Tea Rooms in Oxford Street, which was managed by suffragette sympathiser, Miss Marguerite Alan Liddle, sister of WSPU organiser, Helen Gordon Liddle.[3]

The day after, 1,000 pilgrims attended a service of thanksgiving at St Paul's Cathedral. The organisers of the pilgrimage used the groundswell created as an opportunity to ask to see the Prime Minister. Finally, on 8th August, Downing Street welcomed a deputation for women's suffrage, the first to be received by Asquith since the militants had re-started their attacks in November 1911.

The pilgrimage also succeeded in raising £8,000 for NUWSS campaign funds. Over half a million leaflets were distributed and over 39,000 'Friends of Women's Suffrage' had been enlisted up and down the country. The whole extended spectacle succeeded in raising awareness of the extent of support for votes for women and the strength in depth of the non-militant

---

[1] *MBA*, 2nd August 1913.

[2] Ibid.

[3] Crawford, Elizabeth - 'Suffrage Stories: Suffragettes and Tea-rooms: Alan's Tea-rooms', from *The Woman and her Sphere* blog - September 2012.

suffragists. However, by the end of 1913, the suffragists were no nearer securing any effective legislation to enfranchise women.

That August there was an attempt to burn down a house on the outskirts of High Wycombe, perhaps as a reprisal for the treatment of the suffragist pilgrims. In November, a retrospective meeting was held in the Wycombe Guildhall, where the key speakers were Mrs Harley, Mrs Margaret Ashton and Miss Dora Mason.[1] Mrs Harley blamed the events of 22nd July on 'outsiders coming in and rousing the hooligan element' and also on the 'inadequacy of the police arrangements'.[2]

She went on to comment on the positive response of the general public and said that 'for the first time they had fair play in the Press'. Mrs Ashton spoke about 'Political powers, their use and abuse' and proposed a resolution which was seconded by NUWSS organiser Miss Dora Mason. The resolution called upon the government to 'redeem its pledges by introducing a Government Bill to enfranchise women. (Applause)'.[3]

It is, however, Mrs Harley's more general observations on the pilgrimage which neatly summarise what the NUWSS leadership felt the event had achieved: 'She thought it was a revelation to the country generally to realise that it was the quiet stay-at-homes, the wives and the mothers who really felt the enormous need for the vote (Hear, hear). The pilgrimage represented all classes of women, women of all ages, and all sorts of women, and all felt the necessity of enfranchisement (Applause).'[4]

It is difficult to measure the impact of this unique march on the county, and to judge how important a part it played in the campaign overall. It certainly revealed the continuing latent and often irrational opposition to 'votes for women'. However, the pilgrims also attracted a huge amount of largely sympathetic press coverage. More significantly, many people for the first time took the opportunity of publicly associating themselves with the cause. A significant new development was the public support offered to the suffragists by several local Trade Union branches in the county. In describing the end of the pilgrimage, the *Examiner* drew attention to the national support of 25,000 trade unionists, represented at six platforms at the Hyde Park demonstration.[5]

---

[1] *SBFP*, 21st November 1913.
[2] *SBS*, 20th November 1913.
[3] *SBFP*, 21st November 1912.
[4] Ibid.
[5] *BE*, August 15th 1913.

This extended national demonstration did not lead to any immediate political breakthrough. This was partly due to the growing resistance within both government and the general population to increasingly extreme suffragette methods. However, the NUWSS Pilgrimage may have marked the beginning of a sea-change in thinking about the general justice of the women's claim in the year before the outbreak of the war. Moreover, for many individual suffragists and for the county of Buckinghamshire itself, the 1913 NUWSS Pilgrimage, despite its difficult moments, marked the high point of many years of women campaigning for the vote.

Conclusion: The Outbreak of War and Winning the Vote

'Women have undoubtedly won the right to a voice in the government of the country, if only by the splendid spirit they have shown during the war. ... if any (women) ... are prepared to come forward fearlessly and confess their age - with a minimum of 35 or even 30 - what man could say them nay?'.
- From a letter by Lieutenant-Colonel Hobart, written from the front line and read at a meeting of the South Bucks Liberal Association at High Wycombe Guildhall. *SBFP*, 2nd March 1917.

AT the outbreak of the war, local women's suffrage groups were quickly and, for the most part, quietly included in wider groups within Buckinghamshire. A groundswell of people who could not themselves fight, agreed to devote themselves to the war effort in different ways. Many suffragists in Buckinghamshire gave time to nursing and different forms of community service and charitable work, including helping Belgian refugees.

The way that old antipathies were forgotten and both suffragists and 'antis' rallied round the flag was demonstrated in a number of ways throughout the war within the county. Under the new leadership of Sydney Renee Courtauld, the Mid-Bucks suffragists, although clearly not in unanimous agreement, wrote a letter in September 1914 offering their services for the war's recruitment campaign (see Appendix 11) Then, in Chesham, following a comic charity football match to raise money for Belgian refugees, between the 'Top Hats' and the 'Bonnets' (men in drag), Mrs Agnes Harben was mentioned as having agreed to kick off another charity match in Amersham, between Chesham Town and the Amersham Adult School.[1]

Similarly, in October 1914, for example, the Wycombe Women's Suffrage Society reported a successful fundraising 'Badge Day', which raised over £130 for the Belgian Relief Fund.[2]

Later in the war, writing as President of the Bucks County Nursing Association, Lady de Rothschild quoted approvingly from a similar letter in

---

[1] *BE*, 2nd October 1914.
[2] *SBFP*, 9th October 1914.

The Times, written by Welsh suffragette, Lady Rhondda.[1] And a meeting at Wycombe Abbey School on women's employment was attended by suffragists like Miss Dove and Miss Whitelaw, and was also supported by the prominent anti-suffragist, G.K. Chesterton.[2] The continuing drive for female employment was evident in an advert in the *Herald* around this time. Under the heading, 'Your work could help win the war', Putman's Southern Works in Aylesbury were offering work and training for women carpenters, woodworkers, machinists and hand sewers.[3]

It is ironic that women anti-suffragists, who were similarly if not more imbued with patriotic fervour than their suffragist sisters, unwittingly contributed to the national feeling that women deserved the vote due to their service in the war effort. For example, the anti-suffragist, Miss Gladys Pott, was appointed Travelling Inspector of the Food Production Department. In November 1917, Miss Pott gave a talk to the Women's War Agricultural Committee in Buckingham.[4] Having helped to form the Women's Land Army, Gladys was busy encouraging the formation of local Women's Institutes, to provide welfare for the 181 'Land Girls' working in isolated villages in the county.[5]

For all the outward show of national unity, many suffragists still harboured hopes of a change of heart coinciding with the lessening of an atmosphere of national crisis. Most of those who campaigned so passionately for the right to vote before the war, did not readily forget, during the war, the years of struggle for freedom and equality. Many felt the fighting spirit of the women's suffrage movement had only been temporarily suspended and could be easily revived on occasion if necessary. This was certainly the case for the Headmistress of Wycombe High School, Miss Mary Christie, who donned her suffrage colours before attending a meeting in 1916, to make a case for giving war-time bonuses for women teachers. A chance encounter on Amersham Hill with Miss Christie was vividly recalled by one of her pupils, who saw her 'striding down the hill dressed in suffragette colours on her way to a meeting.'[6]

---

[1] *SBFP*, 3rd August 1917.

[2] *SBFP*, 16th November 1917.

[3] *BH*, 1st December 1917, p. 4.

[4] *BAAN*, 24th November 1917, p. 1.

[5] Pugh, Martin - *DNB*, 2004-13.

[6] From the personal reminiscences of Joan Greening, used with permission of Timothy Clarke. I am indebted to Jackie Kay of the High Wycombe Society for this information.

In February 1917, the NUWSS contributed an article on the national scene, ostensibly based around the theme of 'Women's National Service'. However, while the article started by mentioning the large number of women working in munitions factories, and the proposed government scheme for women to temporarily take on men's jobs to free more men for the front, it finished by highlighting the low wages of women teachers and also the positive benefits of women's suffrage in New Zealand.[1]

Later that year, there was a meeting of the Workers' Educational Association, reminiscent of pre-war suffrage campaigning.[2] Meeting at 'Gahvan' on Amersham Hill, the home of the Mathesons, Miss Susan Lawrence of the London County Council spoke about 'Women's work during the war and after'. Miss Lawrence was able to predict, with great accuracy, the problems women workers would face at the end of the war, including unemployment and lower wages. As a Labour member of LCC, she later went on to become one of the Labour Party's first female MPs. At the Wycombe meeting, Lawrence suggested 'an extension of the system of Trade Boards, the building up of the Factory Acts... which would have the effect of safeguarding the women workers of the country, and securing for them the remuneration to which they were entitled'.[3] While there was no mention of women's suffrage, the concern for women's pay and conditions echoed much of the later suffrage campaigning in Wycombe.

The abandonment of the militant campaign by the WSPU at the outset of the war, the war service of many thousands of women, combined with the quiet diplomacy of the leaders of the constitutional suffragists, helped to create the right climate for the coalition government to extend voting rights to women, as well as the opportunity for women to stand for Parliament.

On the national stage, the change in Prime Minister, from Asquith to Lloyd George, probably helped to enable the passing of this once bitterly contested reform. One of the greatest obstacles to giving women the vote was Prime Minister Asquith himself. At the 1912 tax protest in Wendover, Miss Mabel Smith of the NLOWS had quoted Asquith's opinion that 'the granting to women's suffrage would be a disastrous thing for the nation, and if that was the general opinion of the country, it would not be justice, but injustice to give it'.[4]

---

[1] *SBFP*, 2nd February 1917.
[2] *SBFP*, 3rd August 1917.
[3] Ibid.
[4] *ASR*, May 1912, p. 103.

Once Asquith was no longer Prime Minister and no longer the subject of such suffragette animosity, he was able to respond in a more statesmanlike manner. Opening the parliamentary debate on the Speaker's report on the proposed electoral changes, on March 28th 1917, he urged that the recommendations, including a qualified women's suffrage, should be accepted in full.

A whole swathe of women across Buckinghamshire must have rejoiced at this news. However, there was one further, ironic, twist to this story. After many years fighting to gain the vote, especially in most of Buckinghamshire, the December 1918 General Election must have come as a huge anti-climax. As both the candidates for Mid-Bucks and South Bucks, Rothschild and Du Pre respectively, were accepted as standing for the post-war coalition government, there was no contest. The large numbers of suffragists and the small minority of suffragettes in central and southern Buckinghamshire were still not able to exercise their right to vote. There were national events to mark this historic breakthrough, like the celebration at the Albert Hall on 13th March, 1918.[1] But, given the fact that no women were able to vote in two of the three Buckinghamshire constituencies that year, it is no wonder there was little or no mention of this historic development in the newspapers.

The women of Wycombe continued the struggle for political representation after the 1918 election. It is notable that it was largely the next generation of teachers and headmistresses who took up the challenge. The Women Citizen's Association was formed in March 1919. Those on the committee included the familiar figures of Miss Whitelaw of Wycombe Abbey School, Mrs Turner of Godstowe (formerly Mrs May Scott) and Miss Wheeler. Some were slightly less familiar, although they also played a limited role in the local campaign for female enfranchisement: Miss Wright of Dunstan's Home and Miss Steevens, temperance campaigner and member of the Co-operative Society. The planned programme for this new group was, 'the formation of a National Service Corps, and discussions on Housing, Education, Moral Laws and National Unity'.[2]

There were a number of women present at the launch of the new WCA, who did not feature in the women's suffrage campaign locally, including Miss Blanche Brew, who had recently been appointed as Headmistress of Wycombe High School. Miss Brew presided over a subsequent meeting of the WCA, when two of their number were nominated to stand for election

---

[1] *Albert Hall programme* - John Johnson Collection.
[2] *SBFP*, 17th March 1919, p. 2.

to the Town Council. Mrs Longsdon, a teacher and housemistress for the boy's boarding house at Godstowe School, was nominated to stand for West Central Ward, with a special emphasis on Housing and Education.

Mrs Watkins, of 'Ridgmount', Rectory Avenue, was invited to stand for the East Central Ward. Her acceptance speech most clearly resonated with earlier suffragist campaigning when she stated '...the best work could only be done by a sympathetic co-operation between men and women... The Women's Citizens' Association was non-party and non-political.'[1] Both women however came bottom of the polls for West and East Central Ward.[2] In what were described as 'surprising results', the Labour Party won several new seats in this local election and two recently demobilised servicemen both came close to topping the polls.

It is fitting to close this story of the struggle for vote in Buckinghamshire, with a glimpse into the life of someone from the next generation of women, who was closely associated with the Wycombe suffragists. Maisie Scott was the oldest of May Scott's daughters, who grew at Godstowe School, surrounded by suffragist talk and paraphernalia. On 5th February 1920, she wrote a letter to her fiancé, out of her desperation to become both a municipal and a national voter.[3]

> 'Also, I secured a piece of information I've been after for some time: how I can get a local government vote; the mere fact of me marrying you makes it impossible for me to get a lodger's vote - I shall get a vote, not on my merits, but because I'm the wife of a ratepayer when I'm 30 - but till then, the only thing for you to do is to make over White Lodge to me and you become my tenant. I shall get a vote as a householder, and you as a lodger (wives are not lodgers, specially provided, but apparently husbands may be!). But seriously, I should like you to give me a sufficiently legal grant to convince the Registrar, for I should be desolated not to be able to vote till I'm 30...'

There was one local development which would have gladdened the heart of Miss Dove and her fellow campaigners, before the voting qualifications were equalised for men and women in 1928. South Buckinghamshire returned its first woman MP in the 1923 election. Lady Vera Terrington defeated the sitting Conservative MP and determined anti-suffragist, William Baring Du Pre, at the second attempt. This defeat, viewed together with

---

[1] *SBFP*, 10th October 1919.

[2] *SBFP*, 7th November 1919, p. 2.

[3] I am indebted to Dorothy Ball, family historian, for this and other details.

Major Lionel de Rothschild's earlier comments about him accepting women's suffrage because he did not want to appear out of touch with popular opinion, indicates the degree of change brought about by the women's suffrage movement. Despite the small female electorate at this stage, it seems that it was increasingly difficult to be elected to Parliament for those who openly voiced their opposition to equal opportunities for women.

So it was exactly 70 years after the Buckinghamshire MP, Benjamin Disraeli, spoke in the House of Commons in favour of 'votes for women', that some women finally gained voting rights. The women and men of Buckinghamshire had played their part in exposing this unbalanced semi-democracy, and in ultimately establishing equal voting rights for all British citizens. Perhaps their story is all the more remarkable given the degree of apathy and the high levels of opposition they encountered during their long march towards freedom.

Women gaining the vote was a historic breakthrough; a huge sign of progress towards gender equality. This had been won by the courage and sheer bloody-mindedness of a minority of women and an even smaller minority of men. The story of the women's suffrage movement in Buckinghamshire testifies to the hard work and also the discouragements which must have been part of this struggle. It is impossible to underestimate the enormous effort that it took to begin to change public opinion. But it is not hard to imagine the great pride which must have been experienced by those women's suffrage campaigners who were first able to register their political opinions in national elections and also within the historic chambers of 'the mother of Parliaments'.

'... who can lift the veil of the future. But the universe is alive in every way and we also, although we may wear different raiments in future pilgrimages, we shall know and remember'.
- From a letter of Mary Gawthorpe to Teresa Billington-Greig, 5 August, 1956.

HERE is a small selection of photographs of memorials in Buckinghamshire (and Hertfordshire) to some of the individuals featured in *Burning to get the Vote*. Most of these are in addition to the sites which can be visited by following the heritage trails published in the booklet produced by myself and Andrew Clark in 2012: *Walking with Buckinghamshire Suffragettes*. Copies of the booklet are available from Buckinghamshire libraries and museums, as well as being available online: www.chilternsaonb.org/walks-rides-leaflets.html, or: www.chesham.gov.uk/Walks/Chesham_Walks.aspx.

The grave of Mrs Humphry Ward, St John the Baptist churchyard, Aldbury. Photo: Colin Cartwright

The grave of Sylvia Pankhurst, Addis Ababa. Courtesy of Neil Rees

The grave of Louisa Matilda Page, Chesham graveyard. Photo: Colin Cartwright

The grave of Annie Brooksbank, Chesham graveyard. Photo: Colin Cartwright

The grave of Countess Alice Kearney, St John the Baptist churchyard, Little Missenden. Photo: Colin Cartwright

The grave of Mrs Alice Pilley, St John the Baptist churchyard, Little Missenden. Photo: Colin Cartwright

I encourage you: go on your own pilgrimage and be inspired by these women and men, who did so much to remind us of the importance of gender equality and the value of being a citizen of a democratic country.

Colin Cartwright

Appendices

Appendix 1

(Letter written by Miss Anne Knight, Quaker anti-slavery campaigner and early campaigner for women's suffrage. Undated, but probably June/July 1852, the year after Miss Knight had helped to establish the first British women's suffrage organisation, the Sheffield Female Political Association).

Honoured fellow country Men and Women, the enlightened inhabitants of Aylesbury, Beaconsfield, Marlow, Slough and Wycombe

Our revered friend Dr Lee, whose election for the good of his constituents and the cause of humanity at large, we ardently hope to see achieved (or obtained) by the aid of your efforts and the Blessing of kind Providence: the contemporaries and the sisters of that illustrious band whose names you have heard in your midst; the excellent of the earth; the Herschelles, the Somervilles, the Lovelace(,) the Moores, the Elizabeth Frys, the Barbaulds, the Stricklands, the Martineaus and of the hundreds who might be named who could make good use of their votes"; some of the <u>unnamed</u> would dearly invite you to come forward in obtaining <u>for us all</u>, the right which is inherent in every human being; the Right of choosing the person who is in the councils of the nation to enact the laws which brother are sister are alike compelled to endure, the taxes which all are equally compelled to pay; this Birthright which should be enjoyed by every adult human being unstained by crime and we rejoice in the hope that by the combined energies of the just and good of our day the frightful injustices will soon be heaved from our Country and the World, of refusing a sister's vote and sending her just demand: we rejoice most thankfully to learn of your noble banner, with this inscription, worthy to be written in letters of Gold, Dr Lee and Women's Rights. This first noble standard true claimant for immortality, we hope will be the propitious signal, the peace battle-word of rallying to the counties, the nations around; that flag after flag will be hoisted in every town, on every mountain top, till the enfranchised millions shout the anthem of Liberty to the downtrodden, to the prisoners, the black and the white slave in every land – 'til the universe shall resound with the anthems of the free. Yes noble men and women of Buckinghamshire! Unite your voices of those of your sisters of Sheffield, of London, of Pennsylvania Ohio, of Paris, of Dresden, and the struggling unnamed in all countries who are under the yoke and panting to be free! Yes dear friends, undo the heavy burdens and bid the oppresses go free"; Dismiss from your politics the grievous vice of sex and say "liberty for all the enchained; franchise for all the tax payers; talk not of education to precede Right we have no right to parly with human right; it is too sacred thing this we said for the black slave and now we say, the white slave is as moral as the black to make good use of their unfettered limbs to walk at large in the upright dignity of Humanity(.) Let your cry then be, "no more Laocoons!"(*) Untwist the wreathing serpent from the poor agonising body politic and a blessing on the head of noble Dr Lee and his upholders!

We remain in Christian love your friends

Anne Knight	Lucretia Mott
Edith Holmes	Sarah Pugh
Louisa King	J Elizabeth Jones
Lucy Stone	Elizabeth L Stanton
Hannah Tracy	Agnes Renton
Frances V Gage	Margaret Arrour (?)
L Holmes	Abiah Higginbottom
Harriet W Torrey	Mary Ann Warren
Elizabeth Wilson	Caroline Stanton

(*Laocoon - figure from Greek mythology, strangled to death by sea serpents)

(Reproduced by kind permission of the Centre for Bucks Studies, Aylesbury. Document reference: D 15/10/5)

Appendix 2

Wycombe Abbey School,
Bucks

d. Nov 29, 1906

Dear Madam,

I am writing for Mrs Reid in answer to yours of Nov. 26th.

We are still much interested in Women's Suffrage here, but though I made several efforts last summer, I have not been able to secure a Secretary outside of the School Staff, and therefore the work is hanging fire, as we simply have no time to push it ourselves. Possibly Mrs Beecher Carter whom you mention might be the right person. I have consulted Mrs Lehmann at Bourne End on the subject, and have asked Mrs Carter to be so good as to come and see me next month.

Yours truly
J.F. Dove

WOMEN REPRESENTATION ON THE TOWN COUNCIL

To the Editor of the SOUTH BUCKS STANDARD

Sir,

This important change made by the Legislature, comes somewhat as a surprise to most of us, and like all changes, we are at first inclined to be prejudiced against it - at least, I gather that to be the feeling with many of the burgesses. The suffragette agitation has in this way done harm to the true cause of "women's rights".

We must however, discriminate between the justice of a principle and the conduct of some of its advocates.

No-one can deny that in the present day women have interests that need special representation by their own sex, whether in the factory, the school, or in business life, and assuming that qualified candidates are forthcoming, their public services should be welcomed by all parties.

It was my privilege to sit for a time on our Education Committee with a representative of the women teachers (*), and her presence convinced me of the great value of such an element on that body – indeed, I felt that there should have been more than one.

And so in the present case, as the Town Council have the Education Acts, the Factory Acts, and the Food and Drugs Acts to administer, and many other affecting the health and interests of thousands of women, I trust that Wycombe will honour itself by returning the first woman burgess to the Council of this ancient Borough, and that in the future, each ward will select and return one woman representative.

This would be only an eighth of the total number, so there would be no immediate danger of a revolution.

Yours faithfully,
CHARLES W. RAFFETY.

High Wycombe.

October 28th, 1907

(*This may have been Mrs Caroline Franklin, who was appointed to the Bucks Education Committee in 1902).

WOMEN AND THE GENERAL ELECTION

To the Editor of - the "SOUTH BUCKS FREE PRESS."

Dear Sir

There is one vital issue for the electors at this crisis, which, whatever their view thereon may be, must be of keen and lively interest to every .... man and woman amongst us. Yet this issue, strange to say, finds no place in the election address of either of our local candidates. I refer, of course, to the burning question of Women's Suffrage. It is just here where a true and self-respecting press steps in to counteract the limitations of our party system. The leaders of both parties have alike specifically declared that this is no party question, hence the silence of their respected followers, yet in the constituencies the question has to be faced. Here in Marlow, Sir Alfred Cripps, questioned at the Town Hall, declared himself an uncompromising opponent, with the bewildering reservation however, that if our franchise were based upon a property qualification, he would extend it to women, a pious opinion which helps us not at all, though it may explain his further declaration against any extension of male suffrage. The answer of the Liberal candidate is not yet to hand, the shape which the question has assumed at the hands of the outgoing Government places an (.......) duty upon all lovers of justice in our midst to see to it that with the new Parliament a new and better policy may be inaugurated. Repression and coercion can no longer stifle the expanding aspirations of English women than they have ever done in the past in the case of English men. It is not by teaching their sons to run away from the enemy's guns that English mothers have borne their share in making the greatness of England. How can (.....) expect them to the false to their own teachings now ? -

   We remain, dear Sir, yours sincerely

W.A. MACDONALD, HELEN MEREDITH MACDONALD.

Mundy Dean, Marlow,   Jan. 2nd 1910

Chat by "Suffragette" (edited)

This week I have so many things to speak to you about that I scarcely know where or how to commence.

I must tell you that there is another great treat in store, for on Saturday, July 9th (that is the provisional date) the women of Great Britain are giving another peaceful demonstration, upon a much more gigantic scale than the last. It will consist not only of our league and others who took part in our last, but the Women's National and all other Constitutional Societies will join us. I am also given to understand that the Women's Liberal Federation will also take part. It will be a most beautiful pageant, so I trust every woman will make an effort and join the ranks of the public spirited on Saturday, July 9th. It is not you - the individual - who will be seen on that day. Come out, for you will be lost among the thousands that stand as corporate womanhood. You will even forget yourself. You will not feel your isolated heart, but the heart of a great world movement beating in your pulses

... Now for the monster demonstration. There is one word and one word only for it, it was "magnificent". It was absolutely an unqualified success in numbers. In organisation, in enthusiasm and beauty it surpassed expectations. I had the pleasure of being a banner bearer in the Irish contingent. I am proud to say I am an Irishwoman by birth and to the backbone. Our little band numbered about a hundred. Most of the ladies had travelled all night from London and Belfast. Among them were the Hon. Miss Massey, Mis Duffy (daughter of Sir Charles Duffy), the Misses O'Connell (granddaughter of the liberator), Mrs Sheehey Skeffington, M.A., Miss Carson, P.L.I., Miss Sheely, B.A., Miss Shannon, B.A., Dr Elizabeth Bell.

Long before the hour of starting the streets were full of people and the hour allowed for forming up was none too long. Banners had to be arranged and flowers distributed. It is difficult to estimate the number of those in the procession: 10,000 is the figure used in the press accounts, but in view of the fact that it stretched from the Albert Hall to St James Palace it is likely the total is greater than this amount.

Our General, Mrs Drummond, was in supreme command. Miss Vera Holme and the Hon. Mrs Haverfield acted as aide de camps. The three ladies were mounted on splendid horses. Miss Charlotte Marsh, who suffered forcible feeding for three months, bore our colours, and our ladies Drum and Fife band won universal admiration. The prisoners' pageant, all in white, 617 strong, carrying their silver wands, symbolised the terms of imprisonment. It was a glittering pageant.

The air was filled with the music of 40 bands; 700 banners, all colours, sizes and designs, floated above the steadily marching women. Some of the mottoes were as follows:- "From Prison to Citizenship"; "It's dogged that does it"; "Where there's a will there's a way"; "Go on Pestering"; "Fair play, Fair pay for all who serve the State"; "Equal reward for equal merit"; "Hear it old Europe, we have sworn the death of slavery";

"Carve your way to glory or perish in the fight"; "28 years served in prison for liberty"; 'Rebellion to tyrants is obedience to God"; Hitch your waggon to a Star"; "What's good for John is good for Jean"; "Unity is strength"; "Dare to be Free"; 'Woe to Wobblers"; "Play up and play the game"; "Preston lasses mean to have the vote" etc., but the two liked the most were "Individuality" and "Deeds not Words".

I noticed the crowd had marked preferences, some contingents receiving much more attention than others. The women Gymnasts, the Nurses, and the Lady Doctors, Artists and undergraduates especially. The Irish contingent had a splendid reception the entire route. I don't know why it is quite, but the English always seem to have a warm corner in their heart for their poor unfortunate neighbour.

We had the usual chaff to contend with such as "Mark time, ladies"; "There's nothing like Home Rule"; "Good old Ireland, never say die"; "Well I'm blowed, if they aint brought their cabbages" (this referred to our garlands); "Where's the taters, Bridget?" "And there won't be no trees in Ampstead tomorrow"; an aged veteran was frequently greeted with "I'm surprised at you mother"; a bus driver shouted "Oh, give them the vote but don't stop the traffic"; a foreign gentleman interrogated me with "It is no goot. Vat you do it for? Can't you get a husband?"; a cabby shouts "Bravo Suffragettes, I'm just beginning to like you"; and another cabby says "It makes me all funny in my inside." One man dismally remarks "Only corned beef for the old man's dinner tomorrow", but he is unheeded. We were not reminded once to go home and mind the baby that does not exist, or to do the washing we are supposed to be incessantly at from early Monday morning until Saturday night. Once a voice called out as the prisoners hove in sight "Anyone want to see the governor?" and "Aint they got grit? Not half!"

The crowd was very orderly and apparently interested and sympathetic. As we enter the Albert Hall, the most conspicuous feature is our great banner "God befriend us, our cause is just." There is not a vacant seat in the building; it is crowded to excess and we are nearly all attired in white; it is indeed a most eager, enthusiastic audience. After Mrs Pankhurst, Lord Lytton and others had spoken the money began to flow in, cheques, coins, banknotes, wholesale, until a grand total of £5,217 is reached. Amidst much laughter a cowardly sympathiser, it is announced, has given 3 s. (?)

Annie Kenney, our last speaker, came to London five years ago in a mill band, with £2 in her pocket wherewith to begin the conversion of London for Votes for Women. She beautifully summed up the great procession as the outward sign of an inward spirit. I must confess that night I returned home, oh! so tired, but very happy.

We have but one word in our thoughts to-day and that is victory. If the Government should thwart or postpone that victory now, "God help them in the times that are coming!"

To be continued.

(From the *Examiner*, 1st July 1910. This was the last column, published anonymously, by 'Chesham's suffragette' - probably written by Mrs Emily Charlotte McMahon Brandon)

JUNE 17th, 1911

SENT BY A. MARCHER.

Speech Day is the event which most of the readers of the "Gazette" connect with the historic date, June 17th, 1911. But another event – of even wider import than Wycombe Abbey Speech Day – occupied the thoughts of the visitors from far and near who filled the Capital of our Empire on that memorable day; for on June 17th, 1911, the Coronation festivities were opened by a mammoth demonstration, organized by that portion of His Majesty's subjects which is unrepresented in the British Parliament.

The procession of women who marched through the streets of the Metropolis, to sow their demand for the vote is without parallel in the history of London pageantry. Its length alone can justify its importance. Seven miles of women, marching five abreast – what a spectacle to greet the eyes of any astonished stranger who happened to reach London on the Saturday before the Coronation. The procession, however, did not consist simply of seven miles of women in ordinary workaday dress, but of a gorgeous and artistic display. It was headed by the leaders of the modern Suffrage Movement, dressed respectively in purple, green and white; then followed the Prisoners' Pageant, representing the seven hundred imprisonments suffered by those who are striving to win recognition of the political status of the women in this country; then came a great historical pageant, illustrating the great part of which women have played in the history of these isles in the past, and finishing with representatives of the countries in which women do vote. After this came and endless stream of banners and emblems, signifying the aims and objects of the workers in the great cause.

Mile after mile the societies of women streamed by. Every branch of women's work put forth its claim for recognition. The doctors were there in their brilliant silk robes, the university women in their more sober academic dress, while the musicians, the actresses, the writers, the gymnasts, the gardeners and the artists, all marched behind the banner of their callings. The women who had no special profession, whose work consists in fulfilling their domestic duties, were represented in the various branches of the Suffrage

Societies. The Freedom League marched behind their flags of gold, white and green, while the red, white and green of the National Union of Women's Suffrage Societies was very prominent throughout the procession. The sweated workers from East London and elsewhere, the toilers in the potteries and factories of the North, whose lot calls most of all for some means of political protection, were not absent from the great gathering.

In places the regular procession was broken by symbolical pageantry such as the Great Empire Car, on which were represented all the different countries of the British Empire, and the pageant of Queens, from Queen Bertha to Queen Victoria, which called forth universal admiration.

Those who were themselves taking part in the demonstration could form no conception of the beauty of the entire spectacle, as they "were there to be seen", and had to contribute to the harmony of the whole by obeying orders and remaining in their appointed places. But the sacrifice of the pleasure of seeing the procession was small in comparison with the joy of taking part in it. In a few years, when women have won the vote, it will seem incredible that they should have had to fight for it for so long, just as it now seems incredible that it was only in the last century that men were pulling down the railings round Hyde Park, and mobbing Archbishops in order to obtain their enfranchisement; but if these great demonstrations have to be, it is good to take part in them; and the thrill which passes through the marcher as the band strikes u p, and she shoulders her banner, and realises that she is following in the wake of some of the greatest women of her day, and aiding, if ever so slightly, the progress of humanity, is a feeling which is never to be forgotten.

The crowds who watched the demonstration seemed also to realise its great significance. The whole of the route, from the Embankment to Kensington, was lined with spectators, and from start to finish hardly a disparaging remark was heard. Humourous incidents occurred, it is needless to say, for was there ever a London crowd devoid of humour. The most comical, though at the same time pathetic, sight was noticed at Knightsbridge, where a sorrowful row of sandwich men displayed placards (some of them upside down) announcing that "women do not want the vote;" this, in the face of seven miles of women marching through London to show that they do not want the vote, was a touch of irony which served to give spice to the proceedings.

The procession came to a fitting close at the great meetings which were afterwards held in Kensington. All that available halls in this part of London were secured; the National Union occupied the Portman Rooms, the

Freedom League the Town Hall, while the Albert and Exeter Halls were filled by the Women's Social and Political Union. In the Albert Hall, crowded from floor to ceiling with enthusiastic demonstrators, who had reached their journeys end in time for the meeting, it was hard to believe the words of the Chairman when she said that the end of the procession was only then leaving the Embankment.

The keynote of the meetings was one of triumph. In numbers, in artistic effect, in organization, the Demonstration had been an unqualified success. In the face of this further proof of the capabilities of women for public service, and in consideration of the deep justice of their claim, and the urgent need for speedy satisfaction, it seemed that before June, 1912, women must have obtained their political liberty.'

(*Wycombe Abbey Gazette*, IV (11) November, 1911, p.185-7).
Reproduced by kind permission of Wycombe Abbey School.

ANTI-SUFFRAGE TACTICS

To the Editor of the Bucks Advertiser and Aylesbury News

Dear Sir,

As one present at the Tax Resistance Sale on 16th, Mrs Kineton Parkes, Secretary of the Women's Tax Resistance League, as is usual, explained the objects of the League and invited questions from the large gathering present.

At question time, however, instead of the electors of the town being allowed the opportunity, and anti-suffrage speaker, brought down from London, advanced to the rostrum and, on the pretext of allowing the other side to be heard, made a considerable speech on anti-suffragism.

This is the first time in the history of the sales held all over the country by Women's Tax Resistance League, that members of the Anti-Suffrage League, without any of the trouble and expense of getting up a meeting, have made use in this way of a powerful local influence to forward anti-suffrage propaganda in the room paid for by a tax resister.

... Suffragists at all their meetings welcome the presence of anti-suffragists and questions from them, and on this occasion, if notice had been given them, would willingly have arranged a debate in a hall hired for the purpose, but they strongly protest against having a Tax Resistance sale, at resisters cost, exploited by the Anti-Suffrage League in this manner.

MAUD R.R. MACKENZIE

Lyceum Club, Picadilly
17 April 1912

THE MILITANT SUFFRAGISTS

To the Editor of the Bucks Herald.

Sir,

Conversation with friends has led me to believe that many people are deterred from giving voice to opinions which they hold on the question of Women's Suffrage owing to their dislike of what they consider the reasonless violence of many of the advanced women Suffragists. It is my aim merely to overcome this prejudice, so that such people as I have in mind, even if opposed to the enfranchisement of women, may be able to listen to the arguments of the Suffragists without they annoyance which they at present feel.

On what, then do the Militant Suffragists base their very eccentric policy? The answer is the experience of the last fifty years. Ever since 1860 resolutions and bills have been introduced into Parliament almost annually in favour of votes for women. But no bill has ever been carried through all its stages, although since 1886, and even in the present year, there has always been a Suffragist majority in the House of Commons. The reason is not far to seek. In both the great parties there has always been a large number of men opposed to Women's Suffrage, and one cannot in fairness expect an enthusiastic Liberal, for instance, to risk a split in the Cabinet on this question if that would mean the failure of Home Rule, Disestablishment and all the other policies in which Liberals believe. Similarly, if the Conservatives came into power Mr Bonar Law, though a Suffragist, could not be expected to drive Mr Austen Chamberlain, or Lord Curzon, from his Cabinet on this issue. This year too, the action of the Irish members - Suffragist almost to a man - in not voting for the Conciliation Bill because it's passage would mean a week's less time for Home Rule, is typical of the consideration paid even by Suffragist members to "the Cause' when other questions which concern men's votes are at stake.

Women, then have been left to look after themselves by the House, and so also by the men voters. At the last election two candidates were run on the Women Suffrage ticket, both against Liberals and Conservatives, and one scored 35 votes and the other 22. But no sane person would argue there were only 35 male supporters in the Camlachie Division of Glasgow, or only 22 in East St. Pancras. The truth is that few voters like to throw away a vote - given them to use on many issues - on one issue particularly when one of the candidates who asked for their votes on other questions was quite satisfactory on the suffrage question. It has taken fifty years of defeated candidates and shelved bills to make the Suffragists realise the truth of the words of the present War Minister, Lord Haldane, to Mrs Jacob Bright in the eighties: "You will never get the vote unless you make yourselves sufficiently objectionable". The peaceful persuasion of the non-militants was fruitful in converts, but not in political advantage: the Suffragists therefore, had no alternative but to follow Lord Haldane's advice and make themselves objectionable.

Their course of action everyone knows; the Women's Social and Political Union (the Pankhurst, Pethwick-Lawrence organisation) founded in 1903, began its passive career of chaining itself to railings, etc, in 1905; in 1908 it went a step further and took to a policy of damage, firing pillar-boxes, breaking windows etc, which has continued with intervals of relaxation, which give the lie to ministers who say that they would give the vote if it was peacably demanded. It must be remembered that the Suffragists quite realise that the law must punish them and protect the Canadian Pacific windows, or Mr. Asquith's top hat. They never show the slightest animosity when sentenced, though in some cases they may consider their sentences harsh. How different was the action of the men in a like predicament in 1832, when peers to opposed the passage of the Reform Bill could not leave their houses for fear of assault, when men were hung for murders committed during the riots, when the palace of the Bishop and the Mansion House at Bristol were burnt down; in the agitation for the second Reform Bill in 1868 the railings of Hyde Park were torn up and destroyed, and general confusion prevailed. The most violent "Militant" is a lamb compared to what men were in a like predicament.

By the militant policy the Suffragists have in five years made their demands far more felt than ever the non-militants succeeded in accomplishing through all the preceding half century. All the suffrage societies have received an enormous impulse. During the year 1909, which was especially marked by militant agitation, the National Union of Women's Suffrage Societies, the largest non-militant Association, was enlarged from 21,000 members to 30,000 and other societies have grown in like manner.

Of course a few supporters have fallen away; there were men and women whose convictions were so feeble that they could not stand the test when it came in the shape of window breaking and other methods which offended their feelings. No true Suffragist is driven from his convictions by these things; he may regret them, but he is still in favour of votes for women, whether or not a thousand windows are broken. As the cartoon in a recent issue of "Votes for Women" depicted it, the supporters who have lapsed are like the rotten apples which are shaken off the tree to allow of more room for the good fruit. The rotten apples bear the names of Sir William Byles, Mr Philip Foster, and other who forsook their fundamental principles on a question of detail. A year or two ago a great dignitary of the Church was moved to send his resignation from the Vice-Presidency of one of the non-militant Societies because of the militant action. The Secretary of the Society wrote back asking him to re-consider his decision, and expressing the hope that he would not leave the Church of England because he did not approve of all the methods employed by the ministers of other denominations in furthering the work of Christianity.

If those arguments do not convince the reader that the militant methods are the right and proper methods, yet he must not let his disapproval of one branch prejudice in his eyes the great cause after which all, militant and non-militant, are striving. When King Victor Emanuel was fighting for the unification of Italy, his right hand man was the Republican, Mazzini, who buried his republicanism for the time, as he realised that King Victor was the only man capable of uniting his country into a great nation. The militant Suffragists fill the place which in the religious world is filled by the Salvation Army. They touch hearts which less ostentatious methods could not touch, and open up fields which would otherwise have been left fallow. No one can deny that they have added enormously to the general knowledge of the cause, as entertained by the man in the street.

I am, Sir, yours faithfully,
JUVENIS

(This undated letter appeared in the *Herald*, 27th April 1912)

VOTES FOR WOMEN

To the Editor of the Bucks Advertiser and Aylesbury News,

Dear Sir,

It is a matter of serious consequence that the Town Council of Aylesbury has refused to allow the Women's Social and Political Union the use of the Town Hall for a suffrage meeting. We understand their refusal only applies to the present, and we are undertaking a house-to-house canvass, to enable the inhabitants of Aylesbury to express, by signing the petition, thei wish that the Council should reconsider their decision, and allow a meeting at an early date. We have ascertained that there is a decided expression of condemnation amongst the townspeople against the disgraceful proceedings on Saturday, April 13th, which resulted in the breaking up of a suffrage meeting, organised by the Women's Tax Resistance League, by a band of unruly youths. We are arousing by petition a largely expressed wish from the right-thinking people of Aylesbury that free speech, which is always a little liable to be curtailed on contentious matters in Aylesbury, should be allowed to everyone, and that the Women's Social and Political Union should be allowed a fair hearing. If there are differences of opinion regarding the women's suffrage question, or the methods employed to effect that reform so long overdue, that is no reason why we should not be allowed a fair hearing as well as everyone else, and in the matter of refusal of free speech, Aylesbury stands alone. It would seem that Aylesbury is afraid of raising the uneducated element that condemns a cause before it has heard it - an element which should not be allowed to dominate the educated majority on one single occasion, to the exclusion of justice.

Yours faithfully,
Helen Gordon Liddle, Hon. Organiser, WSPU
Aylesbury

(This undated letter appeared in the *Advertiser*, 4th May 1912)

WOMEN'S SUFFRAGE

TO THE EDITOR OF THE BUCKS HERALD

DEAR SIR

May I reply to a few points raised by "A Suffragist" in criticism of a speech I made at Great Missenden?

1) It is true that it would take Suffragists centuries (at their present rate of progress) to convert a majority of women to suffragism. (ie. to get them to join a Suffrage Society). But there will always be the danger that a Women's Suffrage Bill might be passed against the will of the majority - if that majority is apathetic. Hence the splendid work done by the Anti-Suffrage League.

2) I urged women to take part in municipal work, because most of us can bring practical knowledge to bear on questions dealing with education, the care of pauper children, infant mortality, moral questions, sanitation, milk supplies etc; whereas when it comes to the army or navy, Colonies, diplomacy, commerce, shipping etc., we women would lack practical experience.

3) I judge of the sort of legislation Suffragists would go in for (if they ever get the vote) from their speeches and writings. I disapprove of a great deal of it, and would use my vote to oppose that trend of legislation.

4) I am proud to say that I have no "sisterly feeling" for women who burn widows' houses and homes in which women are sleeping.

5) We are still a Democracy, in spite of the fact that women have not the Imperial vote; because the majority of women wish that commerce and Imperial defence should remain in the hands of men. Therefore the will of the majority is law.

6) The writer says that "women would be absolutely invaluable to the State", and the more womanly we are, the more invaluable we become.

Yours truly,

GLADYS GLADSTONE SOLOMON

Consuelo, Hampstead Way, Hendon, N.W.
Feb. 10, 1914.

SUFFRAGISTS OFFER HELP TO RECRUITING

(To the Editor of the "Bucks Examiner")

Sir,

Some of the members of the Mid-Bucks Women's Suffrage Society are anxious to have an opportunity in helping in the work of getting up recruiting meetings; and I write this in the hope that it may come to the notice of those promoting such meetings, to whom I offer the services of our members. In the case of a meeting being arranged for any village, we believe we could be of use, in going beforehand and helping to canvas for the meeting, visiting the cottages and explaining the importance of issues at stake in this war. This work would especially give opportunities of getting at the women, who are not so likely to attend a meeting and often do not understand the need of the country, and therefore in some cases influence their young men against enlisting.

Of course this work would have no connection whatever with suffrage work, but as all our suffrage work is for the present suspended, our society is anxious to use its organisation for the common good. And I may point out that our members have especial experience in this sort of work of canvassing for meetings.

I can also offer a limited number of free copies of a striking colour hand-painted poster, designed for recruiting meetings, and would be glad to send a specimen on application.

Yours faithfully,
(Miss) S. R. COURTAULD
Hon. Sec. Mid-Bucks Women's Suffrage Soc.
Bocken, Great Missenden.
September 15th, 1914

Primary Sources:

Aylesbury Prison Remission Warrants (CBS, HMP-A/11/1 and D-X 1150/7/3-4)

Aylesbury Prison Records (PRO, HO 144/1205/221999)

Aylesbury Urban District Council Minute Books, 1911-13 (CBS, MB 3/1/ 9)

Bucks Constabulary Memoranda Books, Aug 1910-Apr 1915 (CBS, BC/1/5)

Dove, Frances - Letter to Miss Palliser, 29th November, 1906, (TWL)

Elsie Duval and Hugh Franklin Collection, c.1911-1915 (TWL)

Gawthorpe, Mary - Letter to Teresa Billington-Greig, 5th August, 1956 (Suffragette Collections, The Museum of London)

Albert Hall celebration programme, 13th March 1918 (John Johnson Collection, Bodleian Library)

Knight, Anne - Letter to ...'the enlightened inhabitants of Aylesbury, Beaconsfield, Marlow, Slough and Wycombe', 1852 (CBS, D 15/10/5)

Lees, Margory - '*Adventures of the Ark and the Sandwich*': Transcript of Margory's account of the NUWSS Pilgrimage, 1913 (Lancashire Record Office, DDX 1137/3/116)

Miss Murgatroyd, Miss Tiffin - Letter sent to Selina Cooper, undated but c. July 1913 (Papers of Selina Cooper, Lancashire Record Office, DDX 1137/3 116)

Records of the Association of Post Office Women Clerks (TWL)

Suffragette Collections (Museum of London)

Third Annual Report, 1913-14 - NUWSS Oxon, Berks and Bucks Federation, (TWL)

Wilks, Elizabeth - Letter to Nelly Taylor (Taylor Letter Collection, TWL)

WTRL Committee Minute Book, 1909-13 (TWL)

Online Census Records consulted:

1881 England and Wales Census
1891 England and Wales Census
1901 England and Wales Census
1911 England and Wales Census

Newspapers and local publications, with abbreviations where used:

Anti-Suffrage Review (ASR)
Bucks Advertiser and Aylesbury News (BAAN)
Bucks Examiner (BE)
Bolton Evening News (BEN)
Bucks Herald (BH)
Free Church Suffrage Times
Kelly's Buckinghamshire Directory (Kelly's)
Middlesex and Bucks Advertiser (MBA)
South Bucks Free Press (SBFP)
South Bucks Standard (SBS)
Common Cause
Times (online archive)
The Vote
Uxbridge Gazette
Votes for Women (VW)
Wycombe Abbey Gazette

Secondary Sources:

Archer, Jean - *Buckinghamshire Headlines*, Countryside Books, 1992

Basker, Mrs Russell A. - *Godstowe, The First 100 Years, An Informal History*, Gresham Books, nd.

Beale, D., Dove, J. and Soulsby, L. *Work and Play in Girl's Schools*, Longmans, 1898.

Bennett, Daphne - *Emily Davies and the Liberation of Women, 1830-1921*, Andre Deutsch, 1990

Bentley, Michael and Stevenson, John (eds.) – *The Act of Militancy: Violence and the Suffragettes, 1904-1914*, Oxford University Press, 1982

Bowerman, Elsie - *Stands There a School: Memories of Jane Frances Dove, D.B.E, Founder of Wycombe Abbey School*, Dolphin Press, nd.

Burgin, Marion - *The Women's Suffrage Movement in High Wycombe and some Neighbouring Towns, 1907-1914*, Review Article, 1994 (High Wycombe Library)

Caroline Franklin, 1863-1935: Tributes to her Memory, 1936 (Bucks County Library)

Cartwright, Colin and Clark, Andrew - *Walking with Buckinghamshire Suffragettes*, Millipedia, 2012

Choad, C.E.M. - *Under the Fifth Rib: a Belligerent Autobiography*, London, 1932

Cockroft, V. Irene - *New Dawn Women*, Watts Gallery, 2005

Cockroft, Irene and Croft, Susan - *Art, Theatre and Women's Suffrage*, Aurora Metro Press, 2010

Cook, Pat – *HMYOI Aylesbury*, May 1997

Cox, Margaret - *The Manor House, Weston Turville*, Weston Turville Historical Society

Crawford, Elizabeth - *Campaigning for the Vote: Kate Parry Frye's Suffrage Diary*, Francis Boutle, 2013

Crawford, Elizabeth - *The Women's Suffrage Movement: A Reference Guide, 1866-1928*, Routledge, 2001

Crawford, Elizabeth - *The Women's Suffrage Movement in Britain and Ireland: a Regional Survey*, Routledge, 2006

Crawford, Elizabeth - 'Suffrage Stories: Suffragettes and Tea-rooms: Alan's Tea-rooms', from *The Woman and her Sphere* blog, September 2012

Denton, Penny - *A Very Remarkable Woman*, 1994, privately published (Bucks County Library)

Dictionary of National Biography, Oxford University Press

Fletcher, Keith - *Chesham People: Personalities and Achievers, Volume 1*, 2013, privately published (Chesham Library)

Fletcher, Keith – *The Chesham Co-operators: a Brief History*, 2004, privately published (Chesham Library)

Flint, Lorna - *Wycombe Abbey School, 1896-1986, a Partial History*, 1989, privately published

Godstowe School: An informal story of the beginnings, Godstowe archives, nd

Hamilton, Cicely - *Life Errant*, London, 1935

Harrison, Brian - *Separate Spheres: The Opposition to Women's Suffrage in Britain*, London, 1978

Jalland, Pat - *Women, Marriage and Politics, 1860-1914*, Clarendon Press, 1986

John, Angela V. - *Evelyn Sharp: Rebel Woman, 1869-1955*, Manchester University Press, 2009

Kean, Hilda - *Deeds not Words: the Lives of Suffragette Teachers*, Pluto Press, 1990

Kidd-Hewett, David - *Buckinghamshire Heroes*, Countryside Books, 2005

Koss, Stephen - *Asquith*, Penguin, 1976

Liddington, Jill - *Rebel Girls: their Fight for the Vote*, Virago, 2006

Liddington, Jill and Crawford, Elizabeth - *Women do not count, neither shall they be counted: suffrage, citizenship and the battle for the 1911 Census*: History Workshop journal Spring 2011

Mayes, LJ.,*The History of Chairmaking in High Wycombe*, London, 1960

Mayne, Kate - *Stewkley, Bucks: A Brief History of the Church and the Village*, Rush and Warwick Ltd, 1997

McGuffin, J - *Internment*, 1973, chapter 6 (www.irishresistancebooks.com - July 2012)

Memories of High Wycombe, True North Books, 1999

Metcalfe, A.E. - *Woman's Effort: A Chronicle of British Women's Fifty Years' Struggle for Citizenship (1865-1914)*, Oxford, 1917 (TWL)

Mulvihill, Margaret - *Charlotte Despard: A Biography*, Pandora Press, 1989

Nicolson, Juliet - *The Perfect Summer: Dancing into Shadow in 1911*, John Murray, 2006

Pankhurst, Emmeline - *My Own Story*, Virago, 1979

Pankhurst, E. Sylvia - *The Suffragette Movement: An Intimate Account of Persons and Ideals*, Virago, 1984

Pearce, Olive - *Wycombe Rebel: The True Story of Ted Rolph, 1892-1972*, 1982 (High Wycombe Library)

Penn Village Voice magazine

Perrin, Robert - *No Fear, No Favour, Free Press*, 1986

Purvis, June and Holton, Sandra Stanley (eds.) - *Votes for Women*, Routledge, 2000

Raleigh, K. - *15 Objections to Woman Suffrage, by Lord Curzon - Answered by K.R.*, 1913? (John Johnson Collection, Bodleian Library)

Snowden, Ethel – *The Woman Socialist*, London 1907 (TWL)

Snowden, Ethel - *The Feminist Movement*, London 1913 (TWL)

Spearing, Elizabeth (ed.) - *Medieval Writings on Female Spirituality*, Penguin, 2002

Strachey, Ray - *The Cause: A Short History of the Women's Movement in Great Britain*, Virago, 1988

Sutcliffe, Rachel (ed.) - *Wycombe High School: The First 100 Years, 1901-2001*, Wycombe High School Guild, 2001.

Sutherland, John - *Mrs Humphry Ward: Eminent Victorian, Pre-eminent Edwardian*, Oxford, 1990

Tickner, Lisa - *The Spectacle of Women: Imagery of the Suffrage Campaign, 1907-14*, Chatto and Windus, 1987

Walker, Michael - hayes peoples history: *Pinner Prisoners – Suffragetes* (sic.) – July 2012

Walker, Sam - *Mature Times*, January 2012

Ward, Mrs Humphry - *England's Effort: Six Letters to an American Friend*, London, 1916

Ward, Mrs Humphry – *A Writer's Recollections*, London 1918

Why Muriel Matters - centenary booklet, Muriel Matters Society, 2010

Wikipedia